CENTRE FOR EDUCATIONAL RESEARCH AND INNOVATION

PARENTS

AS

PARTNERS

IN

SCHOOLING

ORGANISATION FOR ECONOMIC CO-OPERATION AND DEVELOPMENT

ORGANISATION FOR ECONOMIC CO-OPERATION AND DEVELOPMENT

Pursuant to Article 1 of the Convention signed in Paris on 14th December 1960, and which came into force on 30th September 1961, the Organisation for Economic Co-operation and Development (OECD) shall promote policies designed:

- to achieve the highest sustainable economic growth and employment and a rising standard of living in Member countries, while maintaining financial stability, and thus to contribute to the development of the world economy;
- to contribute to sound economic expansion in Member as well as non-member countries in the process of economic development; and
- to contribute to the expansion of world trade on a multilateral, non-discriminatory basis in accordance with international obligations.

The original Member countries of the OECD are Austria, Belgium, Canada, Denmark, France, Germany, Greece, Iceland, Ireland, Italy, Luxembourg, the Netherlands, Norway, Portugal, Spain, Sweden, Switzerland, Turkey, the United Kingdom and the United States. The following countries became Members subsequently through accession at the dates indicated hereafter: Japan (28th April 1964), Finland (28th January 1969), Australia (7th June 1971), New Zealand (29th May 1973), Mexico (18th May 1994), the Czech Republic (21st December 1995), Hungary (7th May 1996), Poland (22nd November 1996) and the Republic of Korea (12th December 1996). The Commission of the European Communities takes part in the work of the OECD (Article 13 of the OECD Convention).

The Centre for Educational Research and Innovation was created in June 1968 by the Council of the Organisation for Economic Co-operation and Development and all Member countries of the OECD are participants.

The main objectives of the Centre are as follows:

- *to promote and support the development of research activities in education and undertake such research activities where appropriate;*
- *to promote and support pilot experiments with a view to introducing and testing innovations in the educational system;*
- *to promote the development of co-operation between Member countries in the field of educational research and innovation.*

The Centre functions within the Organisation for Economic Co-operation and Development in accordance with the decisions of the Council of the Organisation, under the authority of the Secretary-General. It is supervised by a Governing Board composed of one national expert in its field of competence from each of the countries participating in its programme of work.

FOREWORD

Parents in many OECD countries want to become more involved in their children's schooling and understand the educational process more fully. Governments, too, are beginning to recognise that high standards of achievement depend, to a certain extent, on parental support. More and more are introducing policies which encourage parents, families and the community in general to be more involved in the education offered by their local schools.

These shifts in policy are partly in response to research findings which suggest that parental involvement is associated with high achievement in school, partly due to pressure from parents themselves, and partly because many governments are currently aiming to decentralise their administrations, and make schools more accountable at the local level to those who use them.

The nine countries in this report demonstrate many different forms of parental involvement, including: political activity at the national level, sometimes on policy-making committees; representation on school governing bodies; helping teachers in the classroom; and supporting their children's learning at home. Some of the most interesting developments relate to policies which help parents in areas of socio-economic disadvantage to support their children more effectively. School-based initiatives aimed at involving such families can genuinely reduce social and educational inequality, and encourage lifelong learning, as well as raising the levels of achievement of the children. One of the key findings of this study is that real partnership between parents and schools depends on mutual respect between the partners. This means that each needs to recognise what the other is bringing to their collaboration. For example, parents and teachers can both benefit from joint training sessions. Building partnerships in this way takes time and commitment, but can transform the atmosphere and effectiveness of a school.

In 1993, the OECD's Centre for Educational Research and Innovation initiated a new kind of study under the heading: "What Works in Innovation". The objective is to publish self-contained, empirically-based studies which offer a focused, policy-oriented assessment of developments in an area of emerging importance where significant innovation is taking place. Already published in this series are:

School: A Matter of Choice (1994), *Schools under Scrutiny* (1995), and *Mapping the Future: Young People and Career Guidance* (1996). *Parents as Partners in Schooling* which is the fourth in the series, examines the relationships between families and schools in nine OECD countries (Canada, Denmark, England and Wales, France, Germany, Ireland, Japan, Spain and the United States). The intention, as with earlier studies in the series, has not been to produce a technical report, nor a comprehensive review of relevant research, but to identify key issues in the current state of co-operation between families and schools, briefly to examine how they are being addressed in the participating countries and to offer policy recommendations as to how innovations might be built on, and practice improved. The report was prepared by Dr. Caroline St. John-Brooks and Ms. Kathleen Kelley-Lainé of the OECD Secretariat, with the assistance of Mr. John Townshend, who acted as consultant. It was made possible by the financial assistance, through voluntary contributions, of the Atlantic Provinces Education Foundation (Canada), the Ministry of Education (Denmark), the Department of Education and Employment (England and Wales) and the Japanese Ministry of Education (Monbusho). The report is published on the responsibility of the Secretary-General of the OECD.

TABLE OF CONTENTS

Part I
THEMATIC DISCUSSION

Part II
COUNTRY SUMMARIES

ACKNOWLEDGEMENTS

The analysis which follows is based on background reports prepared by experts from the nine participating countries, on visits to the countries which were carried out by the OECD Secretariat or the consultant to the study, and on previous OECD reports and other research literature. The experts were: Dr. Douglas Willms of the University of New Brunswick (Canada); Mrs. Kirsten Hanskov of the Ministry of Education in Copenhagen (Denmark); Dr. John Bastiani, Independent Education Consultant (England and Wales); Mrs. Roselyn Bonneau-Waltzer, Direction de Lycée/Collège, Paris, France; Dr. Hartmurt Köhler, Stuttgart University, Urback, Germany; Mrs. Deirdre Stuart of the National Centre for Educational Research Centre, Dublin, Ireland; Professor Yoshiaki Nakano, Sophia University, Chiba-ken, Japan; Mr. Enrique Roca, Madrid, Spain; Professor Don Davies of the Institute for Responsive Education, Boston, United States.

EXECUTIVE SUMMARY

This report looks at the co-operation between families and schools in nine OECD Member countries: Canada, Denmark, England and Wales, France, Germany, Ireland, Japan, Spain, and the United States. The intention is not to categorise or exhaustively analyse each country's policies and practices, but to examine the various approaches of the participating countries with the aim of broadly identifying their strengths and weaknesses. A particular objective is to draw out examples of good practice and innovation which might be of use to policy-makers in other countries.

The importance of building partnerships in education is becoming more widely recognised, as a wider range of young people have to be educated to a higher standard than ever before. Parents and families in many OECD countries want to be able to support their children's learning more effectively at home, to work in partnership with the teachers, and to have more choice in selecting schools. At the same time, many countries are currently adopting policies to involve families and, more specifically, parents, increasingly closely in the education of their children. This is partly because parental involvement is associated with higher achievement in school, partly because governments are generally decentralising their administrations and want to make schools more accountable to their clients, and partly due to pressure from parents themselves.

Overall, the report focuses on the strategies employed in different countries to encourage co-operation between the family, the school and the community. A key aim is to help the schools to become more effective, and to raise the level of achievement of school students, by mobilising the energy of parents – enabling them to support their children's learning more effectively, and work in partnership with the school.

Part I is divided into four chapters; it places these developments in their socio-economic context, and discusses different types of parental and community involvement, drawing on evidence from the participating countries, and from OECD and other research. It aims to clarify the many roles which parents play – and which governments wish to encourage – using two main categories of parent participation: collective involvement and individual involvement.

Part II consists of nine sections which summarise the policies, structures and practices with regard to co-operation between families and schools in the nine countries. Each country summary includes case studies, detailing innovative schemes, projects or approaches – in different settings – which involve parents, students, families and communities more closely in the education process. These case studies are designed to be illustrative, but they cannot necessarily be treated as examples from which generalisations can be made.

PART I: THEMATIC DISCUSSION

Chapter 1 discusses parents' legal rights and duties in relation to their children's education, and the socio-economic context within which interest in partnerships between parents and schools is growing. It explores the wide range of reasons for developing strategies to involve parents, and analyses their relationship to other aspects of government policy.

Chapter 2 focuses on the collective involvement of parents in policy making (the main difference between collective and individual involvement being that collective involvement can take place at any level of the system, whereas individual involvement tends to be at school, classroom or one-to-one level). This chapter covers: parental representation on policy-making or advisory bodies – at national or local government level; school governance; parents' associations and class councils; co-operation between school and the local community; and parental influence on the curriculum.

Chapter 3 looks at individual involvement. There are many kinds of individual parental participation, but most fall into two categories: involvement with the whole school or class, and the involvement of a parent with or on behalf of his or her own child. The types of involvement dealt with in this chapter include: direct parental involvement in the curriculum, its delivery and the life of the school; communication between school and home (including updates on children's progress, the use of two-way homework notebooks and journals, newsletters and home visits); and psycho-social support – which may take the form of parental education of various kinds, and also includes support at moments of family crisis, and intensive co-operation and joint planning with the parents of children with special educational needs.

Chapter 4 discusses the nature of partnership and its relation to the idea of "parent power" – and concludes that parents' rights to participate fully in their children's education, or to influence policy-making at different levels, vary a great deal across OECD countries. The nine participating countries have different methods of involving families and communities in the work of the schools, and there are many examples of successful partnerships – but it is rare for good practice to be replicated elsewhere or disseminated throughout the system. One of the most interesting findings relates to the relatively untapped potential of parental education in assisting parents from disadvantaged socio-economic backgrounds to support their children's learning more effectively. Improving their understanding of the educational process not only enables them to become more involved with the school, but can give them the confidence to continue with further education. In this way, school-based initiatives to involve parents can help to reduce exclusion and improve equity, and to encourage lifelong learning.

As a conclusion to Part I, there are four key messages for governments which want to maximise the positive effects of involving parents in schools:

- *Publicising and disseminating examples of successful practice is a crucial step.* In those countries which have committed themselves to increasing parental involvement, there is now an impressive range of successful one-off projects or experiments (see the case studies in Part II). We now have a good idea of "what works".

- *Methods of replicating successful strategies should be developed, so that parents, students and teachers across the country – and in other countries too – can benefit from them.* Too often, the lessons learned from successful innovations are not adequately disseminated or built into the system as a whole; much time and effort is wasted by committed parents and teachers in re-inventing the wheel.

- *Genuine partnership entails mutual respect among the different partners, and a recognition of what each can bring to the collaboration.* Much successful parental involvement comes down to individual teachers and parents learning how to negotiate, to handle differences of opinion and to understand the importance of each other's role – without losing confidence in their own. A clearly understood legal framework setting out rights and responsibilities would be helpful; and training – which need not be extensive – is necessary if successful partnerships are to be built. The most fruitful approaches often involve teachers and parents training together.

- *In order to make best use of the energy and resources of parents, the parental agenda needs to be identified clearly.* Making assumptions about the needs or desires of parents or the wider community may lead to speedier policy formation – but can backfire when the consequences of the policy are working through. Such an agenda would need to involve consultation with a wide range of community groups and agencies, and tap into a broad cross-section of views and experience of different groups of parents. It should not be assumed that parents will always want what the government of the day thinks best.

A fuller version of the overall policy implications can be found at the end of Part I.

PART II: COUNTRY SUMMARIES

Both policy and practice in the nine participating countries are very variable – both between and within countries. In almost every country studied, strong parental involvement at one level is accompanied by complete lack of representation at another. At the same time, innovative schools with highly successful participatory programmes can be found virtually next door to schools in which the level of parental involvement barely reaches the legal minimum (where there is one).

Each of the nine country summaries which make up Part II of the report is structured in the same way, based on Chapters 2 and 3 of Part I. This is designed to enable readers to make comparisons between different countries as easily as possible.

Part I

THEMATIC DISCUSSION

PARENTAL INVOLVEMENT: THE NEW SOLUTION?

INTRODUCTION

The relationship between families and schools in OECD Member countries is subtle, complex and ever-changing. Both are intimately involved in the education of children – but which aspects they are responsible for, and the terms in which that responsibility is conceptualised, vary over time in different countries, and in relation to shifting economic and political climates.

Parents and the family are, of course, children's first educators in all countries. They are responsible for their early socialisation, and for laying down a mental and emotional framework which can be built on by school and community when they move out into the world. Both family and school normally exist within a local community, and the education and socialisation of most young people take place within this threefold context.

As formal education (and the qualifications it offers) becomes ever more important, its methods more diverse, and its purposes more complex, there is a more widespread recognition among policy-makers in many countries that family, school and community each have a role to play in the intellectual, emotional and social development of young people. This recognition goes with other changes which have taken place over the last decade: a general movement towards decentralisation and local autonomy, along with the realisation that in the future most people will need to keep on learning throughout their lives. These shifts are resulting in many countries in a wish – sometimes expressed by parents, and sometimes by policy-makers – for schools to develop a more outward-looking stance, and for their walls to become, as it were, more permeable. The broad aim is that families, schools and the local community should work together in a partnership which is better understood and planned, and therefore more fruitful than in the past – but there are very wide variations in policy and practice among the nine countries in this study.

WHO ARE THE PARENTS?

Most OECD countries are currently adopting policies to involve families[1] and, more specifically, parents, increasingly closely in the education of their children. Of course there are many different ways in which parents and families can become involved: fund-raising for the school or attending school events are the most common. But the new meaning of "parental involvement" is more complex, representing (in ideal terms) a close working partnership between parents and teachers, which enables both to bring their unique insights and experience to the joint task of educating children. It stresses in particular the fact that parents and teachers can learn from each other (Morgan *et al.*, 1992).

But although they are often spoken of as if they all had the same needs and demands, parents are not, of course, a homogeneous mass. Most schools have parents' councils, parent-teacher associations, parent advisory groups, and various types of parent-based fund-raising bodies. But the active, committed parents who join and run these organisations are unlikely to be typical of the parents as a whole – or to represent their views. They may have different levels of education, and ethnic origin; they come from different social classes and have different value systems. They may relate very differently to their children, to teachers, and to schools.

Governments should not assume that all parents want the same thing – or that they all will want what the policy-makers currently deem desirable. In particular, some parents may only be interested in the well-being of their own children, and perhaps be in favour of various forms of segregation; others may not approve of materialistic, competitive or instrumental approaches to education. Fundamentalist religious groups have a significant influence on parental opinion in some countries. Some parents may have doubts concerning the possibility of their children being educated "up" out of the local community; if they belong to an ethnic minority, they may not want to become a homogeneous part of the country's mainstream culture. Far from demanding their rights to participate, some will believe that education is the school's job, and that the teachers should get on with it.

One characteristic which parents share, to be sure, is that virtually all of them want the best for their individual children, but they may not agree on what "the best" is – and their views will probably change as their children grow. Indeed, parenthood in itself is a learning process, and different parents may be at different stages in their own understanding of their role.

What's more, the commitment of individual parents to their own children does not mean that their views would necessarily lead to a fair and effective education system, meeting the needs of all. For example, groups of parents often have conflicting interests, and the demands of some parents may impinge on the rights of others. This is particularly clear with regard to various forms of selective, streamed or segregated schooling. Most parents of children with special educational needs, for example, would like to have them educated in mainstream schools along with their peers. Yet the parents of other children may prefer children with disabilities to be educated separately. Similarly, working class parents often (though not necessarily) want their children to mix with middle class children in middle class schools; middle class parents may not feel the same way. A classic paradox in some countries is that many parents of girls prefer their daughters to be educated in girls' schools; but boys are considered to do best in mixed schools. It would be virtually impossible to construct a coherent education system on the basis of exactly what parents say they want at any given time in their children's development.

Yet, in spite of these and other possible difficulties inherent in the idea of "parent power", the idea of the "parent" has, over the last decade or so, become a powerful ideological construct in many countries. Governments employ it for a number of different reasons – generally on the assumption that the views of the ideal parent would coincide with whatever the politicians want to achieve. Some countries are now flirting with the idea of the parent as a "consumer" with a "choice" of schools[2] – as a way of levering up standards by making parents more demanding and schools more self-critical. While this can be a successful way of raising levels of performance in particular schools, there is a danger in using parental influence as a proxy for sound government policies. In some countries, parent power is promoted politically as a way of reducing the power of the teachers and local education authorities; in others, parents can be used for or against the influence of the churches or fundamentalist religious groups.

Parental participation is also increasing as the result of a push from the parents themselves. The number of parents involved in parents' associations of various kinds is growing in many countries, and the European Parents' Association (EPA) celebrated its tenth anniversary in 1995. Education is rising up the political agenda in OECD countries, mainly because of anxieties with regard to economic performance and social cohesion – but also because parents are increasingly seen as an important political constituency.

Increased parental activism may also result from rising expectations – or from frustration or dissatisfaction: parents may be critical of the teaching their child is receiving; perhaps they would like the school to be more open and co-operative; others would like more choice in selecting of schools. Parents may also desire a closer partnership with the school for more positive reasons and because they want to play their part in their local community. They hope both to support the school (for example, by fund-raising, supervising children on school trips, assisting with sporting activities, or helping teachers in the classroom) and to receive support from it (maybe advice on how to help their child to learn, or a better understanding of the problems of adolescence, or more information on the curriculum).

PARENTS' RIGHTS AND DUTIES IN EDUCATION

Plans and policies which encourage parents and schools to form closer partnerships – whether they originate from policy-makers, schools or the parents themselves – involve conceptualising more clearly the roles of the different parties, and the give and take involved. For example, the Charter of the European Parents' Association (1992) identifies nine different pairings of rights and duties for parents, including:

- Parents have the *right* to recognition of their primacy as educators of their children.
- Parents have the *duty* to raise their children in a responsible way and not neglect them.
- Parents have the *right* to full access to the formal education system for their children on the basis of their needs, merits and talents.
- Parents have the *duty* to commit themselves as partners in education to the school of their children.
- Parents have the *right* of access to all information at educational institutions which concerns their children.
- Parents have the *duty* to give to their children's schools all the information relevant for the attainment of the educational goals on which they work together.
- Parents have the *right* to make a choice for the education which is closest to their convictions and to the values they hold dear in raising their children.
- Parents have the *duty* to make well-informed and conscientious choices about the education their children should receive.
- Parents have the *right* to exert influence on the policy which their children's school implements.
- Parents have a *duty* to be personally committed to their children's school as a vital part of the local community.
- Parents and their associations have the *right* to be consulted actively about the policy of the public authorities in education at all levels.
- Parents have the *duty* to maintain democratic representative organisations at all levels to represent themselves and their interests.

One parental duty identified by the EPA is not accompanied by a corresponding right: "Parents have the duty to help each other to improve their skills as prime educators and partners in the home-school relationship".

Epstein (1992, 1995) also emphasises that obligations go in both directions – from the school to the parents, and vice versa. Parents have both rights and responsibilities as do schools; this is becoming more clearly recognised in many countries. Epstein suggests a useful typology for conceptualising school-family co-operation. She identifies six categories of involvement:

- *Type 1: Family obligations and support for children's school learning.* Families have basic duties to fulfil in relation to safeguarding their children's health and safety, developing their social skills, and raising them in a manner which enables them to make full use of their educational opportunities. Schools have a part to play in helping families meet these obligations.

- *Type 2: Communication between home and school.* Schools have obligations to inform parents about the life and work of the school and their children's progress, and to establish the conditions for good two-way communication.

- *Type 3: Family involvement at school.* Parents, carers and other members of the family help teachers in the classroom, on school trips and in other ways, and come to the school for social activities and to support concerts, plays, sports days and other events.

- *Type 4: Parental involvement in children's school learning at home.* Parents and other family members help their children by supervising homework, partic-ipating in students' research efforts (finding relevant books, videos or other materials for them) and sharing numerous informal educational activ-ities. Schools have a crucial role to play in enabling families to grasp the importance of this process, and in offering information and even adult education to raise parents' own levels of skill and understanding.

- *Type 5: Participation of parents in decision-making, governance and advocacy.* Parents may be represented on school governing bodies, advisory councils and policy boards, and on other associations and committees. They also may be active in educational pressure groups within the community.

- *Type 6: Partnerships between parents, schools, businesses and other community organisations.* Many different institutions, agencies, cultural and sporting associations and other groups within the community have a part to play in rearing and educating children. Work experience programmes in local busi-nesses, health care, integrated support services to families, breakfast clubs and after-school care are all examples of such partnerships.

A fresh recognition that obligations cut both ways can be seen in the current enthusiasm – notably in England and Wales – for the idea of written home-school contracts or agreements. This policy cannot be pushed too far, since there would be no way of enforcing the parent's side of such a contract; and it could not be seriously suggested that the state would refuse to educate a child because of the shortcomings of his or her parents. Indeed, there is a risk of attempting to enforce a fixed model of good parenting which, apart from possibly being mistaken, would be politically unacceptable in most countries.

A project set up by the RSA (Royal Society for the Encouragement of Arts, Manufactures and Commerce) to look at this idea in the United Kingdom context concluded that negotiating this type of agreement with the parents was, in the end, more important than the agreement itself – because such discussions improve relationships with the parents, help to clarify what they expect from the school, and emphasise that the school cannot do all the work. By stating in advance the expectations which the school has of the parent, a partnership based on mutual obligations is established – and parents are alerted to aspects of their child's preparation for school of which they may be unaware. At the same time, such a "contract" emphasises that the child has an entitlement to certain services from the school.

THE BACKGROUND TO CURRENT POLICIES

Change in the family

There are many reasons for the fresh interest in co-operation between school and family – which policy-makers, teachers and parents in most OECD Member countries are beginning to show in varying degrees. One of the most important is the change in the nature of the family. In most countries, there is now a much wider variety of family units than in the past. Individuals and couples today have much more freedom to choose their own lifestyles, which may include single parenthood or living communally. In many countries, more and more children are living with step-parents, or with a single parent, either because a previous marriage or relationship has broken down, or through the choice of the mother.

These developments are not necessarily negative; children can be raised and educated very successfully in a variety of family circumstances. But such changes necessitate a rethinking of the respective roles of family and school – especially when families are disadvantaged in other ways. "The emergence of 'reconstructed' or 'patchwork' families, with children from previous marriages, creates complex situations, the handling of which requires adequate financial resources and particular psychological and emotional skills. It is clear that, when parents do not have sufficient material and financial resources to allow the necessary adjustments (visits, suitable accommodation in each home), the children are affected by situations which are insecure and which are unable to provide them with the stability and regularity they require" (OECD, 1995d).

Economic stress

Many of these social changes have increased the amount of stress on the family. Single parent families in particular are often under pressure – either because the parent (usually a mother) is young and poorly educated, or because the family unit has suffered the emotional trauma of breaking up. They are also likely to have financial problems. In the United States, for example, one in three families headed by lone mothers is classified as poor. Poverty brings other difficulties with it. Inadequate housing, crime, and health and emotional problems such as depression are all more common in disadvantaged areas. Large numbers of children in OECD countries are being raised in poverty.

Unemployment also puts stress on families. Income differentials have widened in most European countries, and unemployment in Europe has risen from a standardised rate of 4.3 per cent in 1975 to 11.4 per cent in 1994 (OECD, 1995b). When parents do have jobs, both of them sometimes have to work long hours – which puts a different kind of pressure on the family. Mobility too has increased enormously – both within and between countries – as economic circumstances force people to move to where the jobs are. And all these stresses are growing at a time when traditional sources of support – such as the extended family, religious practices and a long-standing local community – have been left behind or are declining in their influence. So for some families the school becomes a key source of support.

These changes are both a cause and an effect of the fragmentation of the consensual values of the past, which is making the family's task of raising children much more difficult and complicated. And there are other competing influences too – the mass media, personal computers and the Internet, and, in some countries, a pervasive and commercial youth culture which manipulates the values of young people and celebrates the judgements of the individual and the peer group above those of the family. Freedom and individualism are key values, to be sure – but, faced with increasing crime, poverty and alienation among certain groups within the population long after the rebellious years of youth are past, governments, policy-makers and parents in many OECD countries are now reasserting the importance of communal and co-operative values and social cohesion.

The school, therefore, has a much broader socialisation task than in the past. It needs to reach out to many different types of family. While in most countries the size of the middle class is increasing and the old manual working class is much smaller, unemployment combined with immigration means that many families with disadvantaged socio-economic backgrounds exist outside the mainstream. In seriously impoverished inner-city areas, the local school may be the only remaining institution which still represents the communal values of the wider society – as opposed to the unfettered competitive individualism of commerce and the mass media, from which, in any case, the disadvantaged are excluded.

Need for higher levels of education

At the same time, the levels of education (skills, knowledge and understanding) which schools are expected to deliver need to be higher than ever before. The disappearance of manual jobs and the reality of global competition, mean that governments are putting their schools under pressure to become more effective (OECD, 1995e). National and individual expectations are rising, which means that in most OECD countries more and more young people are continuing their education and training well beyond compulsory schooling. It is no longer acceptable for young people to finish their schooling with few qualifications or inappropriate skills; the jobs are not there for them, and high unemployment is a drain on a nation's resources. High quality education must now be made available to groups who in the past survived economically without it.

So one answer to the question as to why governments are becoming interested in the educative role played by parents is that for good economic and social reasons the children of working class, ethnic minority and other excluded families[3] now need to be drawn into the circle of education, which in the past tended to keep them out. If such excluded groups continue to underachieve educationally, OECD countries will not only find that their economies suffer from the wasted human potential, but that marginalised groups will become a serious problem to society as a whole. As it is, schooling young urban males successfully is one of the biggest challenges facing education systems today.

If these problems are to be addressed, parents who themselves did not have an effective education must nevertheless learn how to support their own children's learning – especially in the early years. The French sociologist Bourdieu (1977) postulated that privileged and high-achieving parents pass on "cultural capital" to their offspring as surely as they pass down financial capital.[4] Cultural capital represents the values, ways of communicating and patterns of organisation which are characteristic, in most societies, of the middle classes. If children are already familiar with these ways of thinking, behaving and communicating when they start school they are likely to be more successful – because schools are essentially middle class institutions which value these attributes. What's more, unless schools make a real effort to be welcoming and communicative, middle-class parents often feel more at home there than do working-class parents – although the latter may value education and want to support their children just as much. Middle class parents – who usually achieved well at school themselves – are more likely to share a social and intellectual framework with the teachers, to feel at ease taking part in school activities, and to use effective strategies in supporting their children's learning at home.

HOW SCHOOL-FAMILY CO-OPERATION RELATES TO OTHER ASPECTS OF GOVERNMENT POLICY

In many OECD countries, a key development of the last 15 years or so has been the rise of what has been called "new public management" in many aspects of national and regional administrations, not only education. Eight key features of the approach were identified by Boston (cited in Likierman, 1993). The most relevant in relation to the current study are:

- a shift from the use of input controls and bureaucratic procedures and rules to a reliance on quantifiable output measures and performance targets;

- the devolution of management control, coupled with the development of new reporting, monitoring and accountability mechanisms;

- the disaggregation of large bureaucratic structures into quasi-autonomous agencies;

- a stress on cost-cutting and efficiency.

These elements may seem a long way from the school and the family, but they are part of a political philosophy which has seen decentralisation and devolution in many OECD countries, including Denmark, England and Wales, France and Spain. In three of these countries (though not England and Wales) this has meant decentralising power from central government to local government. And similarly, in all of them, it has meant giving the schools more autonomy.

In Canada and the United States, too, there has been a move to deregulate and give schools more freedom. In these two countries, and in England and Wales, there have also been experiments with detaching schools from state, provincial or local government and funding them as free-standing institutions (charter schools in Canada and the United States, grant-maintained schools in England and Wales). Parents have a stronger role to play in these schools. Charter schools are often founded by groups of parents who want a different type of schooling from that offered by the state. In England and Wales, the parent body of any school administered by a local education authority (LEA) can vote to remove it from the LEA's jurisdiction (*i.e.* to "opt out"). However, the United Kingdom research suggests that although parents in these grant-maintained schools tend to be very satisfied with them, they do not necessarily feel a stronger sense of "ownership" – and, surprisingly, are slightly *less* likely to be involved in activities such as fund-raising than the parents in local authority schools (Power *et al.*, 1994).

This type of devolution, as suggested by Boston, requires new forms of monitoring and accountability – which fits in with the move towards involving parents in school governance as a new form of accountability. In most countries, however, parents are only slowly growing into their new role.

23

The new forms of management also represent a shift away from large bureaucratic organisations to smaller, more autonomous units where decisions are made according to local needs. This political philosophy chimes in with the desire of some governments to reduce the power of public sector trade unions, including the teachers. In England and Wales, where this tendency is particularly marked, decentralising power to the schools and putting school governing bodies in charge of their own budgets as well as appointing teachers has made for a wide variety of *ad hoc* salary decisions within the national pay scales.

It is noticeable that Spain and Ireland, which have most recently reformed their education systems (indeed, the Irish legislation is still in progress), have chosen to give parents a voice at every level. Denmark, which has a longer stronger tradition of parental involvement, is now attempting – not entirely successfully – to deepen and intensify it. In Canada and the United States, a number of provinces and states are reformulating their regulations to give parents a stronger voice at state, local and school levels. But in France, despite the recent decentralisation of administration, modes of thought associated with centralisation still seem to be prevalent. Although there is a long tradition of parental representation, it is not clear how far grassroots opinion is genuinely represented by the traditional parents' organisations.

WHY INVOLVE PARENTS?

Changes in the relationship between school and family

Moves to develop the partnership between the school and the family are coming, in most countries, from policy-makers (at government, local or even school level) and also in the other direction – from the parents and families themselves. The upbringing and education of children has always been shared among several institutions – the immediate family, the extended family, the Church, the school and the local community. The exact mix of influences changes over time, and still varies widely from country to country. There is, currently, much anxiety concerning the fragmentation of communities and their associated value systems; yet the breaking up of traditional ways of life has been happening for generations. Although social change is now ubiquitous, the ligaments which bind together the family and the community are still strong in many areas of many countries.

What are not so strong, sometimes, are the links between the family, the community and the school. Relationships tend to be complex and patchy – and not without tension. Although interactions between the three institutions vary widely from country to country and take many different forms, it is possible to trace their broad development over time.

In most countries, the advent of compulsory education for all children had a marked effect on the relationship between family and society. Until then, parents, community and Church had been responsible for children's education – which in any case was not normally expected to reach a high academic standard. Then a new stakeholder – the state – became involved. Whether or not parents wanted their child to spend every day in school, the law now obliged them to conform. Conflicts of interest could and did arise, especially when the labour of children was important to the family economy. Ensuring regular attendance at school became an indicator of being a "good parent"; it meant that the families under most economic pressure acquired a further stigma – that of not caring about their children's education.

At the same time, since the vast majority of parents had not themselves had much schooling, the teachers were very much seen as the experts when it came to academic education. Parents were not encouraged to involve themselves in such matters, and the rapid expansion of schooling after World War II represented a fairly clear division of labour in many countries: schools were responsible for education, with the parents' role more-or-less confined to socialisation, moral training and leisure activities. The churches had begun to withdraw from their former educational function, or had gone into partnership with the state. In some systems – especially those which were developing a welfare state – schools moved into the sphere of social and moral education as well, and even took responsibility for physical health. From being central to the overall development of their children, families risked being pushed onto the sidelines.

But now the relationship between families and schools is changing again. It is now widely recognised that parents play a major role in the informal education of their offspring, and should be seen as "partners in pedagogy" with the school. With ever-higher and more complex academic demands being made on schools, young children need to arrive "ready-to-learn".[5] A sound foundation laid down by the family is becoming a *sine qua non*. Schools in many countries have moved away from the strict and sometimes brutal disciplinary methods of the past. They need well-socialised but independent children who can learn through exploratory and active learning, as well as through more formal methods.

But, at the same time, the changes in the family make it harder for some families to prepare their children adequately. In very small, single-parent or immigrant families (especially those who do not speak the language of the host country), appropriate social and intellectual development may be difficult to achieve – particularly in the absence of a supportive community. Poverty and unemployment make the parents' task more difficult – and economic pressures may still be intense when the parents are employed. Low wages or fear of losing a job may lead to overwork – and when both parents are working, they may be too tired to support their children emotionally or educationally.

However, schools in many countries are less able – and maybe less willing – to make up for shortcomings in children's early learning and socialisation. They will not be able to achieve the required rise in educational standards without the co-operation and support of parents. Families and schools need to rethink their roles – which will probably not be the same in all countries – and forge new partnerships. But they cannot do it without support – from central and local government, and from their communities.

The key reasons underlying parental involvement

Although there is a widespread movement to involve parents across all OECD countries, there are a number of different reasons why countries may decide this is desirable – reasons which arise from values deeply embedded in the political culture. Broadly, the reasons given by officials and policy analysts during the research for this report tend to fall into the following interrelated categories:

- *Democracy*: In many – though not all – countries in the study, parental involvement in education is seen as a right, or as an outright democratic value. Some, such as France, Germany and Denmark, have had such a right enshrined in their laws for decades. The nature of this right varies according to the country. In Denmark and England and Wales, parents have a right to be represented on the governing bodies of schools; in France, they have a right to representation on a whole range of policy-making bodies; the Parent's Charter gives English and Welsh parents a number of rights – including the right to certain information from the school; in Spain, the Constitution recognises the right of teachers, parents and students to participate in defining the scope and nature of the education service; forthcoming legislation in Ireland will place parents at the centre of the education process, and give them a wide range of statutory rights in relation to education.

- *Accountability*: This is a more market-oriented concept than democracy, and is embraced most enthusiastically by England and Wales, Canada and the United States. Parental involvement – especially in school governance – is not seen primarily as a right of the parents, but as a means of making schools more accountable to the society which funds them. School-family partnerships are viewed rather like business partnerships, through which the two parties receive mutual and complementary benefits which enable them to operate more effectively.

- *Consumer choice*: Again, this is an idea borrowed from market theory, and is based on the belief that parents, as consumers, should have the right to choose schools, and also to influence the way in which they operate. The underlying assumption is that when parents think of themselves as consumers, they are likely to conceptualise more clearly what they want and to be more critical of what they are offered, thus pushing schools into meeting their needs more effectively.[6]

- *Lever for raising standards*: Findings from large-scale studies in Australia, the United Kingdom and the United States show that schools in which pupils do well (in terms of both academic attainment and positive attitudes) are characterised by good home-school relations (Brighouse and Tomlinson, 1991). In the more market-driven systems, parental involvement may be viewed as a way of improving school performance since (so the argument goes) parents may have higher expectations than teachers, and be more concerned about under-achievement and discipline problems.

- *Tackling disadvantage and improving equity*: This reason is related to the above, but refers more explicitly to the raising of individual children's performance by enabling their parents to support them more effectively at home. This is particularly important when there are cultural differences between the education system and the family (European Commission, 1995).

- *Addressing social problems*: In some countries (particularly Canada, England and Wales and the United States), policy-makers are turning to the schools for solutions or help in relation to issues such as drug and alcohol abuse by teenagers, sexual promiscuity and teenage pregnancy, child abuse, violence, and the gang-based street culture.

- *Resources*: Not only do parents raise extra funds for schools, but they can be a cost-effective way of mobilising resources – whether as helpers on school visits or field trips, coaches or assistants in sporting activities, or teachers' aides in the classroom. This reason can be highly controversial in countries where public spending on education has been held down.

From the point of view of the parents, there is a range of other reasons for getting involved. The reasons for participation – and its nature – change according to the age of the child, and the school sector concerned. Although this relatively brief report is not the place to analyse in detail the differences between the different levels, it is clear that effective parental involvement at the pre-school stage will often be very different from parental support at, for example, upper secondary level. Most of the reasons which follow are relevant at all levels:

- *Improved achievement*: The wish to improve the performance of their own child, and the need to find out how best to do it.

- *Parental education*: The need to support a child's learning can encourage parents to attend classes (at the school or elsewhere) covering aspects of the curriculum, for example, or good parenting, or joint literacy activities. A positive experience in this context can lead parents on to further education on their own account – and result in increased, and more effective, involvement in the school.

- *Communication*: A desire to find out more about what happens in school and to increase its openness.
- *Influence*: The wish to influence the curriculum or the transmission of values in the school.
- *Support for the school*: The recognition that schools are often underfunded and teachers overstretched, resulting in parents offering help – either fund-raising or assistance of other kinds.
- *Support from the school*: The need for individual help and advice during a family crisis, or a general interest in attending – with other parents – lectures or workshops on common problems (drug abuse, health issues, the difficulties of adolescence).

In virtually all countries, parent involvement with the schools is stronger at primary level. This does not mean that parents are not equally interested in their children's secondary education, but rather that their support demonstrates itself in other ways at later stages – in taking trouble to choose the right secondary school, paying for extra tuition, or taking their children on educational trips. They are, however, less likely to be closely involved in helping their children learn, because teaching at this level is more specialist (although many parents still supervise homework at the lower secondary stage).

Although it is important that school students know that their parents care about their progress, adolescents do not necessarily welcome parental "interference", and may be embarrassed by their parent's presence in school. Often they prefer to make their own decisions and mistakes. An exception, though, is career guidance, in which parents and other members of the family often play a key – though informal and sometimes unrecognised – role. One way of improving the quality of advice which young people receive during their transition from school to work (or further training or education) would be to brief parents on local job and training opportunities – since young people do not always find their way to official sources of information (OECD, 1996d).

2

A COLLECTIVE VOICE FOR PARENTS

INTRODUCTION

Governments which are attempting to increase parental involvement in schools tend to legislate for various forms of collective action by parents. Individual relationships, inevitably, are much harder to control through the law – although giving parents certain rights to be involved or consulted regarding the education of their own children is an important aspect of co-operation between family and school.

Collective parental decision-making takes two main forms: representation on policy-making bodies at national, regional or local level (or at least formal consultation on key policies); and involvement in the governance of individual schools.

Since, for the reasons explored in Chapter 1, more parental involvement is seen as highly desirable by many OECD countries, most countries participating in this study have recently legislated to increase the number of parents on school governing bodies – or even to create such bodies from scratch.

THE ROLE OF THE LAW IN ENCOURAGING PARENTAL INVOLVEMENT

There is, of course, only a limited amount that governments can achieve through legislation when it comes to changing the attitudes of individuals and encouraging co-operation between different groups. But they can alter the climate of opinion through such means as "orientation" laws, and by authorising funding for certain types of project – and of course by various forms of information-giving, publicity, advertising and propaganda.

There are a number of ways in which governments can have a legislative impact:

- parents can be given more power in policy-making and governance, both at national and regional level and at school level, by being fully represented on government committees or school boards;
- the setting up of parents' associations can be mandated, again at different levels of the system;

- parents can be offered more choice of school – although complete freedom of choice (even if desirable) is never in fact possible; popular schools cannot expand *ad infinitum*, and an unpredictable number of surplus places would be required to accommodate parental preferences;
- both local authorities and schools can be required to communicate specific information to parents regarding such issues as the curriculum, the performance of schools, and their children's progress.

With regard to the legal right of parents to have a policy-related input at different levels in the system, the nine countries in this study vary enormously – from Japan, where they have no such influence, to France, Germany, Spain and (potentially) Ireland, where they have some form of permanent representation at every level.[7]

As can be seen from Table 1, the nine countries in this study differ substantially as to the power they give to parents at different levels of the education system. At national or state level, Denmark, France, Germany, Ireland and Spain all have parents represented on key policy-making committees. In Canada, a number of provinces have recently set up parent advisory committees, and similarly some states in the United States have parents represented on district school board advisory committees. In England and Wales and Japan, parents are not represented on any national policy-making or advisory committee.

Table 1. **Parental involvement in policy-making bodies at different levels**

	LEVEL			
	National	*Province or state*	*Local authority or district*	*School level*
Canada	N/A	Some (A)	Some (A)	Some (A)
Denmark	Yes (A)	N/A	No	Yes (D)
England and Wales	No*	N/A	No	Yes (D)
France	Yes (A)	Yes (A)	Yes (A)	Yes (A)
Germany	Yes (A)	Yes (A)	Yes (A)	Yes (D)
Ireland	Yes (D)	N/A	Yes **	Yes (D)
Japan	No	No	No	No
Spain	Yes (A)	Yes (D)	Yes (A)	Yes (D)
United States	N/A	No	Some (varies)	Some (varies)

A   = Advisory role.
D   = Decision-making role.
N/A = Not applicable.
*   Some consultation documents sent to national parents' body for comment.
**   Legislation not yet in place.

SCHOOL GOVERNANCE

Recent OECD research on education indicators, which estimates the extent to which parents are involved in decision-making processes within primary schools, shows a very varied picture (OECD, 1996a). Across the twelve countries involved in the survey, about 60 per cent of primary pupils are thought to be in schools which involve parents in school planning, and 57 per cent are in schools in which parents participate in financial or organisational decisions.[8] Fewer than one in four attends a school where the parents have influence over staffing. The countries which have parents involved most extensively in all categories (using this definition) are Italy and Spain. In Spain, parent participation in school planning and financial decisions is particularly high: over three-quarters of pupils are in schools which involve parents in these issues. Countries in which parents play a less significant role in school decision-making include Greece, Belgium and France. French parents are particularly unlikely to have a say in how the school is organised; only about one in three pupils are in primary schools where this is the case.

So far as the governance of schools as individual institutions is concerned, countries differ as to how far they see their schools as autonomous units – rather than as elements in a system. In Japan, which has a rather centralised education system, the individual schools do not have governing bodies – so of course parents cannot be represented on them. Schools are run by the prefectures and the municipalities, in which parents have no direct representation (although they influence policy from time to time through various forms of political lobbying). The local authorities do have a fair amount of discretion when it comes to policy-making, and it is assumed that members of the local school board represent parental views, but in practice few are actually parents. In Germany and France, the schools similarly do not have governing bodies; parents in both countries belong to class councils and school councils, but these have limited decision-making powers – although in particular instances they can be highly influential. In Germany, school councils can influence the appointment of a school principal, for example, and can have a substantial effect on expenditure.

Until recently, all public schools in the United States were administered by district school boards; but now in some states – whether as a result of local action ("bottom-up") or by the state itself ("top-down") – school site boards have been set up to run individual schools. In Denmark, Ireland and Spain, the schools are seen as more autonomous, and their school boards or councils have real influence on decision-making. The process is probably most advanced in England and Wales, where individual school governing bodies make virtually all the significant decisions with regard to schools – and are encouraged to compete for pupils with other local schools.

Although school governance is very much a collective activity, individuals can of course become very powerful within any committee or management group. So individual parents on particular governing bodies can have a disproportionate influence – normally in one of two ways. They may develop a fruitful partnership with other governors and the principal, or they may dominate the proceedings through being well-informed, articulate, persuasive and determined (or, occasionally, through being opinionated and generally difficult). While most school principals would secretly put the "ability to manage the school board" high on their list of desirable qualities, not all of them are skilled at doing it.

Another difficulty built into the system is that parent governors sometimes find it hard to voice the complaints of other parents, for fear of alienating their own children's teachers. True accountability may be threatened, if parent representatives are reluctant to "pursue a point disinterestedly, on behalf of all parents, when their own interests and intense feelings are at stake" (Cordingley and Harrington, 1996).

Parental involvement in appointing and dismissing teachers or principals

The degree to which parents are involved in these procedures depends first, on whether school governing bodies have this power, and secondly how much influence parents have on these boards or committees. In some countries, the administrative structures do not offer a role to parents. In France, teachers and principals are appointed by the Ministry or the local *académie*, according to the level of the post. In the United States, the district school board makes appointments. Japanese teachers are appointed by the local prefecture – and principals are moved from school to school every two or three years. Danish school boards are always chaired by a parent – but in Denmark the municipality, not the board, has the responsibility for hiring and firing. In Ireland, at primary level, the school's board of management is responsible for selecting and appointing teachers and principals. At post-primary level, they may be appointed by the school principal, or the board of management, or the local vocational education committee – or a combination of all three – depending on the particular sector.

In Canada, until very recently, the district school boards were in charge of appointments; but now that some provinces have set up parent advisory committees – sometimes even doing away with the district boards – parents are likely to gain more influence over school personnel. In Germany the careers of teachers – who are civil servants – are managed by the individual *Länder*. There are only two countries where parents can have real power in this area. One is Spain, where school principals are elected every three years by members of the school committee, on which parents are well-represented. The other is England and Wales, where school governing bodies are responsible – and have been for many years –

for appointing both teachers and principals. The chairpersons of these bodies may be parent representatives – since they are freely elected from among the governors; and in this eventuality, a parent can be in a position of significant power. But parents are not in the majority on English and Welsh school governing bodies, so in other cases they will not be influential at all.

The power to dismiss ineffective teachers or principals is perhaps the most controversial aspect of school governance. In Spain, the right of a school community to elect and then not re-elect the principal is seen as an important plank of the country's new democratic system. In England and Wales, some headteachers have short-term performance-related contracts with their school governing body, but these are not widespread.

The fact remains that teachers in most systems are very secure in their employment and even very weak teachers are hard to dismiss. Yet in any school the parents are very aware of which teachers are least effective, and what to do about them is a source of frustration to them and, sometimes, to principals and other teachers. But at the same time this issue – although often unspoken – underlies a lot of resistance to the idea of increased parental involvement.

Involvement of students in school governance

One important element in the relationship between the school and the family which is sometimes overlooked is the role of the students themselves. Only three of the countries in this study – England and Wales, Ireland and Japan – do not have secondary school students routinely represented at any level in the system.[9] In the United States and Canada, practice varies according to state or province.

Student representation on school governing bodies

In Denmark, France, Germany and Spain, the secondary schools normally have student councils, and students are represented on school governing bodies. A typical pattern is that found in Denmark: every school which has five or more form levels (that is, contains pupils above the age of 11 or so) must set up a student council. Each class (even, in some schools, the youngest classes) nominates two students to the student council, and the council sends two students to sit on the school board. They have full voting rights, along with the parents and teachers. In Spain, each primary school board has seven parents on it; in secondary schools, these seven seats are divided between four parents and three students – again with full voting rights. These boards have real power, and are responsible for electing the headteacher. The structure of German school councils (which are advisory bodies) varies from Land to Land.

In these countries, such student participation is taken very seriously as part of the educative process. In Denmark, for example, it is explicitly viewed as training for democracy – and students who have been elected to student councils and school boards normally undergo brief training sessions on how to represent the interests of their fellow students, and on committee procedure. The view in France, too, is that students, as they mature, should naturally take over some of the responsibility for their development from their parents – and that the power structure should reflect this. In Spain, it quite clearly does so.

Most Japanese secondary schools have student associations (*seitokai*), which are sometimes consulted by teachers. For example, they may participate in revising the school rules. But since schools do not have governing bodies, they cannot be represented on them. In the United States, too, virtually all the secondary schools have student councils. Those schools which have school site councils (which are the exception rather than the norm) nearly always elect student representatives to serve on them – at least from the seventh grade upwards.

In Ireland and in England and Wales, student associations or councils within the schools are relatively unusual (although see Irish case study), and students are hardly ever represented on school governing bodies – although occasionally they may attend as observers.

Student involvement in decision-making at national level

At national level, three of these countries involve students in their national consultative councils. School students take part in the deliberations of the Danish *Folkeskole* Council, and of the Spanish State School Council – where they share 20 out of 80 seats with the parent representatives. Germany does not have one of these councils at national level, but the *Länder* all have consultative councils. These have varying titles and compositions, but students are normally well-represented. In the state of Bavaria, for example, the consultative council is composed of eight teachers, eight parents and eight students.

In France, parents, pupils and family associations sit on the national *Conseil supérieur de l'éducation*, which is consulted in relation to all issues of national interest concerning teaching and education, and parents and pupils are also represented on similar councils at level of the region, the *académie*, and the *département*. A unique French institution is the *Conseil académique de la vie lycéenne*, which advises the rector of the *académie* on school life and school work in the high schools. Up to half of the 40 members are normally school students (parents are also represented).

A NATIONAL VOICE FOR PARENTS

In virtually all the countries in the study, national parents' associations of various kinds represent the views of parents at the national level. Most are built up on a system of parents' councils or associations at the school level. No country makes it compulsory for schools to form such associations or councils – although in recent years governments have encouraged them. (Most Danish schools have class councils and parents' associations, but they do not normally feed into the national parents' association in Denmark – *Skole og Samfund* – which is mainly made up of parent members of school boards.)

Some parents' organisations are very long-standing and – in France and Japan, for example – are part of the local political establishment, and an accepted way for people to enter the general political process. It is not clear, however, how far this model enables ordinary parents to express their views and have them listened to by government. Sometimes – in France, Germany and Spain for example – there is more than one organisation, representing the interests of different groups of parents.

In five of the participating countries (Denmark, France, Germany, Ireland and Spain) members of the national parents' associations have a right to sit on key national committees and give their opinion or advice. Some provinces in the Canada and some states in the United States also have parental advisory bodies. In the United States, the National Parent-Teacher Association is very active in lobbying for federal policy, but has no legally-enshrined method of influencing policy. In Japan, the 15th Central Council on Education, convened in 1995, includes (for the first time) a representative from the national parent-teacher association (PTA) – but this is not as of right. English and Welsh parents are not represented at all at the centre – although key policy documents are normally circulated as part of the routine consultation process. Through this mechanism, the National Confederation of Parent-Teacher Associations has an opportunity to transmit its response to government; it is not clear, however, how far this organisation genuinely represents parental opinion.

CO-OPERATION BETWEEN SCHOOL AND COMMUNITY

Along with policies to increase the involvement of parents in education, most governments are also keen to encourage closer relationships between schools and local communities. As the Education Ministers of the 26 OECD Member countries all agreed in January 1996: "Schools are a major social asset and should become 'community learning centres' offering a variety of programmes and learning methods to a diverse range of students, and remain open for long hours throughout the year" (OECD, 1996b).

In most countries, though, in spite of good intentions, the policy has not moved much beyond the level of rhetoric. Every country has an array of impressive pilot projects and local links between school and community, but these are rarely built into the fabric of the system. Mainstream schools are already carrying out a large number of social functions for their pupils but often are not well-supported, and teachers are frequently overstretched. What's more, the community itself rarely takes the initiative; especially in disadvantaged areas where the community is weak, most of the effort comes from the school.

An important source of resources, energy and goodwill, however, even in deprived areas, can be local employers and businesses. These are not often recognised as relevant to the work of the schools, but school-business partnerships can offer support to both teachers and pupils – in terms of teaching materials, workplace visits, work experience placements and even jobs (OECD, 1992). They can also provide expertise in career guidance programmes, motivating students to achieve (perhaps through "compacts"), and easing the transition from school to work. Such arrangements are particularly strong in Canada and the United States. It is important that local employers – sometimes very critical of the products of schooling – come to understand the role of the school today, and the difficulties of the teacher's task of schooling and socialising alienated young people. Employers have a significant part to play in offering mentors or role-models for ethnic minority pupils or others in danger of dropping out or under-achieving; at the same time they become more informed about the work of the schools.

School governing bodies in most countries do not include community representatives – but in England and Wales, governors can co-opt individuals from the local community. Most often, this opportunity is used to bring in a representative of an ethnic minority group, or to recruit someone with financial expertise (since governors are responsible for the school budget). In Canada, Japan and the United States, local school boards are made up of elected members of the community – but how far they take a real interest in forging links between schools and community is uncertain.

According to Michael Hacker,[10] the idea of the community school embraces three key principles:

- Education is a continuous lifelong process and is not confined to the childhood years of compulsory education.
- Educational attainment is closely related to the support and understanding of parents and the wider community. This indicates a need to remove the walls, both physical and institutional, between schools and the societies they serve.

– There are significant economic advantages to be gained from the joint provision and more intensive use of school and community facilities.

The school can be a very appropriate centre for building community spirit – offering facilities for sports, meetings, adult education classes, and other forms of personal and social development. One OECD study focusing on rural areas cites several examples of schools acting as community resources, and contrasts the approaches employed in the Canadian province of Québec and in France: "In Québec, many schools provide a wide range of services for children outside school hours (including day-care before and after classes, at lunchtime and in the summer holidays) as part of a 1989 government policy which also provides grants. Similarly, the Education Act confers on school boards not only an educational mission but also responsibility for encouraging the use of school premises by public or community bodies within the area. In France, on the other hand, school premises are rarely used outside school hours, although this is specifically provided for in the legislation. However, there have been signs in a number of regions that this situation is changing, with lower-secondary schools (*collèges*) opening up to the public and offering a range of educational and cultural services. The *collège* is becoming a centre of activities and injecting a little vitality into otherwise culturally deprived areas" (OECD, 1994a).

As well as offering services to the community, schools can improve their own links with parents if they have a strong relationship with other groups. According to Mansfield (1995): "It is easier for parents to become involved in the school, and to overcome any inhibitions they may have, if the school is connected to its immediate surroundings through links with the local community". She gives a number of suggestions for strengthening such connections including: letting out school premises to local clubs and societies; fostering links with nearby museums and libraries; cultivating a regular contact at the local newspaper; distributing school newsletters, and notices of events to sympathetic shopkeepers and businesses; co-operating with other schools to form links with community organisations; at secondary level, allowing parents, the elderly and others to take part in classes along with the older students – a policy which has been found to improve students' behaviour and reduce truancy, graffiti and vandalism.

Such collaborative enterprises – which are often very cost-effective – mean that school buildings need to be more flexible and accessible, both in terms of opening hours, and their architecture and design. "Successive economic crises have eroded investment budgets to a remarkable extent. Schools of whatever level are increasingly asked to fulfil satellite educational functions: sport, cultural activities, specific programmes for local or regional industrial apprenticeships. They are seen as poles of local development. This means that their premises must be more freely available and they must constantly increase their adaptability" (OECD, 1996e). For example, a new Tokyo primary school has been designed to play an important part in the local urban community "by offering a wide range of social, sporting and cultural facilities [including] an indoor swimming pool, gymnasium, library, concert hall and medical centre".

All these developments cannot, however, be expected on a significant scale without specific strategies. Recent work which has been carried out on integrating services for children who are at risk of failing in school (estimated at between 15 and 30 per cent) contains policy lessons of much wider application – and numerous examples of successful co-operation between schools and a variety of community services (OECD, 1996f). If the schools are to be fully used to benefit all members of the community, their purpose, ethos and structure need to be rethought. Although much can be achieved – and often is – through the enthusiasm and commitment of individuals and groups, a coherent nationwide policy cannot depend on this; at the very least it needs planning, funding and trained personnel.

Ireland's Home-School-Community Liaison scheme (which serves pupils and supports parents who come from disadvantaged socio-economic backgrounds), the Danish policy of designating about one in ten *Folkeskole* as local cultural centres for the community, and the French ZEPs (*Zones d'éducation prioritaires* – education priority zones)[11] are good examples of innovative central government initiatives. It is clear from the Irish experience – and from the United Kingdom's more limited Family Literacy Programme – that educational initiatives based in schools can raise the educational level of the adults involved, and result in a general sense of empowerment in the local community. Parental involvement, especially in areas of socio-economic deprivation, does not just benefit the children and the school – it is a crucial aspect of lifelong learning.

PARENTAL INFLUENCE ON THE CURRICULUM

The curriculum at national or state level

Apart from Canada and the United States, every country in this study has a national curriculum which lays down what should be taught in the schools, but the extent to which it is fixed varies a great deal. Countries which in the past have not had one (such as England and Wales) have recently established a comprehensive and detailed programme. But some which have had a detailed centralised curriculum for a long time (Denmark, France and Spain) have now rethought it in terms of frameworks and targets, rather than the detailed regulations of the past. This gives local authorities and individual schools more chance to adapt it to suit their own situation.

In Denmark, Ireland[12] and Spain, parents are represented on the national curriculum committees which establish or revise the curriculum; and in Germany, every *Land* has a state parent council, made up of elected parents' representatives, which advises the Ministry of Culture on educational issues including drawing up curricula and authorising textbooks.

In other countries, such as England and Wales, France and Japan, parents have no say in the content or structure of the curriculum at national level. In Canada and the United States, curricula are established at state or province level, without, normally, any input from parents. But many of the Canadian provinces are restructuring at the moment, and some are setting up parent advisory committees which will be consulted on such matters.

The curriculum at regional level

Once the curriculum has been worked out at the highest level, it can sometimes be modified by the regional education authorities or local school boards. This is the case in Canada, Denmark, Japan, Spain and the United States, but not in England and Wales, France or Germany. Ireland currently has no local education authorities, except in the second-level vocational sector. However, regional education boards are due to be set up under the current reform plan and such boards will address the management of all schools, irrespective of sector, on a regional basis. In Canada, Spain and the United States, parents can have a local voice in modifying the central curriculum, but in Denmark they are not represented at the level of the municipality – a surprising gap in the Danish system. Although in Japan the prefectures have only limited scope for adapting the curriculum to suit local needs, the superintendent of Shiga Prefecture is interested in involving parents in curriculum development.

The curriculum at school level

Figures from the OECD's education indicators project (OECD, 1996*a*) suggest that – averaged across the 12 countries which participated in the relevant survey – about one in three primary pupils attends schools in which their parents can influence the curriculum. The range is exceptionally wide, from 1.4 per cent in Greece to 92 per cent in Finland. In France and Ireland the proportion is low (4.3 per cent and 16 per cent respectively); in Spain it is around the average.

The amount of difference parents can make to the curriculum of an individual school depends on both structural and personal elements. If schools have a governing or advisory body on which parents are represented (and this is true of eight of the countries in this study), it depends on whether this body is able to make curriculum-related decisions or give advice in this area. In Canada, Denmark, Spain and the United States it can, but not normally in France, Germany, or Ireland. In England and Wales, school governing bodies have no jurisdiction over the curriculum except with regard to religious education and sex education.

It also depends on how much power parents have on the school's governing body. In Denmark, parents are in the majority, and the chair is always a parent. In theory, Danish school boards can adapt the curriculum laid down by the local municipality to the needs of the individual school, but in practice the board's sphere of influence is very variable. Sometimes municipalities prefer to keep most of the power to themselves – and if a headteacher is not committed to partnership, he or she may reserve curriculum decisions as a pedagogical matter. Spanish parents have the power, through the school council, to adapt the curriculum to the needs of the school, especially with regard to optional subjects.

Class councils

Class councils are a common form of parental participation in countries such as Denmark, France, Germany and Spain. But in Canada, England and Wales (though see case study), Ireland, Japan, and the United States they are barely heard of. The usual structure is simple: all the parents of the children in a particular class form a group, and have regular meetings with the teacher. In Denmark, where teachers stay with the same class of children throughout the Folkeskole, parents and teachers come to know each other very well. French class councils include all the teachers who teach a particular group of children, and meetings usually focus on students' performance. In Germany, the class council is very influential, and can be a forum in which parents have an opportunity to criticise the performance of teachers.

Sometimes, the class council elects representatives to the parents' association or school governing body – which means that the views of ordinary parents are more likely to be represented than when a whole-school election takes place. Attendance at meetings, of course, varies, and sometimes a small group of active parents do a disproportionate amount of the work. A way of spreading participation is to adopt a more complex version of the model, such as that recommended by Skole og Samfund, the Danish national parents' association. This involves dividing each school class into several small groups of parents, each including a "contact parent". He or she acts as a link person, passing on the views of parents in the group to the class council as a whole. In this way, parents who otherwise might be too busy, shy or otherwise unwilling to attend regular meetings can still make their opinions heard. As yet, not many schools in Denmark have adopted this model – but the association hopes that it will spread.

At all levels of decision-making, in fact, "collective" action may not always be as broad-based as it seems. In many cases, only a few active parents are involved – and they may or may not genuinely represent the views of the mass of non-participant parents. Similarly, the bodies on which they are represented will vary as to how seriously they take the views expressed by the parent representatives.

3

INVOLVING PARENTS AS INDIVIDUALS

INTRODUCTION

Fullan (1991) identifies four different kinds of involvement by parents: involvement at school (as volunteers or assistants); involvement in learning activities at home; relationships between home, school and community; and governance. He notes that: "The first two forms of involvement have a more direct impact on instruction than do the other forms". And it is the first two forms which, essentially, represent individual rather than collective involvement.

In the end, the reason for most parents becoming involved in education has to do with the schooling of their own children. But in the past, unless parents were very devoted and motivated, they generally only became involved with the school when there were problems. So teachers sometimes had most of their dealings with two types of parents – those who were educated, ambitious and tended to be critical, and those with problem children. Now the aim is that all teachers and parents should try to develop working partnerships together as a matter of course – in the best interests of all children.

The involvement of parents as individuals falls into two main categories: their involvement in the life of the school or classroom in general, and their involvement as support to their individual child. These two types of activity are connected, in that the relationship a parent has with a school is likely to affect his or her child's attitude, commitment and even level of achievement. Often parents become involved on behalf of their own offspring, and then get drawn into a wider sphere of activity.

Parental involvement is particularly crucial as OECD countries move into an era of lifelong learning, in which everyone will need to update his or her skills and knowledge throughout life in order to keep up with economic change and the current explosion of information through new technology. "Ensuring that our children not only have a grounding in the basics but also have a commitment to a lifetime of learning will require an agenda for education unlike any we have seen before. To achieve this reform, we are going to have to raise our expectations for our children and for ourselves" (United States Department of Education, 1994).

PARENTAL INVOLVEMENT IN THE CURRICULUM, ITS DELIVERY AND THE LIFE OF THE SCHOOL

The curriculum, normally drawn up at national or state level, does not come to life until it is put into practice in a school. Delivering this curriculum to the pupils in the classroom is, of course, the teacher's professional task. Trained and experienced teachers are often hesitant to have volunteers closely involved in their work, but those involved in a well-planned scheme often find that parents can be a real resource and that their aid does not lead to a deprofessionalisation of the trained teacher's role. Parents benefit enormously from the increased understanding they gain of the educational process. Children, too, begin to real-ise that school is not an isolated world cut off from everyday life, and also that other adults, as well as teachers, value the learning that takes place in school. It can be particularly important for young boys who lack strong male role models to see adult men, by their presence, confirming the importance of what their teacher (who is often female) is trying to achieve.

Although a number of initiatives (particularly in Canada, England and Wales, Ireland and the United States) demonstrate that, especially in the early grades, both teachers and children can benefit if parents are available to support the teacher in the classroom, this may not necessarily be true in other systems. Primary education in, for example, France, Germany and Japan is delivered very effectively with virtually no parental involvement in the classroom – so it is clearly not a necessary condition for successful schooling. However, these three countries are relatively homogeneous societies with a strong consensus as to the purpose and processes of education. It may be that in more pluralist societies where such a consensus is breaking down, or perhaps never existed, parental involvement in the classroom is more crucial, especially in areas of socio-economic disadvantage. The importance of this strategy resides in the signals it gives to children, the help it offers teachers, and personal growth experienced by the volunteers. All these benefits, however, can be delivered in different ways in cultures where teachers and education are traditionally well-respected – and where the education system is well-funded.

To a certain extent, encouraging parents into the classroom means blurring the distinction between family and school, and between lay person and profes-sional. The fact that parental help is more common in primary school classrooms may be related to the fact that the academic knowledge of primary school teach-ers is less specialised than that of secondary school teachers (although their teaching skills may be superior). This means that, by and large, parents are less in awe of primary teachers – and have more to offer them since specific academic knowledge is less important in the primary classroom.

There is no doubt that this is one of the most sensitive areas of relationships between schools and parents. In many countries most schools are unwilling to accept parents in the classroom during lessons. There are a number of different reasons for this – which often vary according to the country involved. A representative selection of reasons (both admitted and unadmitted) would be: parents in the classroom would distract the children or might make the teacher feel uncomfortable; they might say or do inappropriate things – perhaps misinform children or in some way make their learning less effective; the use of parents as classroom aides could in the long run mean fewer jobs for trained teachers; employing parents in an educative role devalues the hard-won skills of teachers; parents should not be used as a way of saving money in underfunded systems; they might be used as "spies" to identify ineffective teachers; learning how to work with parents is yet another task for teachers who are already overburdened.

So, not surprisingly, in some of the countries studied, the presence of parents in the classroom is a rarity. It is least common in countries where the professional status of teachers is high and teacher unions are strong. In France and Germany, it is unusual – although in France some schools in the ZEPs are becoming more flexible in this regard (see case study). A few German *Länder* are exploring this approach. In Baden-Württemberg, for example, members of the community (who may be parents) can act as paid teacher's aides. But in Spain, in spite of moves to get parents more involved at all levels, tradition keeps them off the teachers' territory. Japanese parents are generally not welcome in their children's classrooms, but the Japanese custom of "observation days", is unique; schools hold special sessions, when parents and (occasionally) members of the community are invited to watch demonstration lessons. This is mainly so that parents can observe the behaviour of their offspring, rather than evaluate the teacher's expertise – so the stakes for teachers are not so high as they might be in other systems. Parents no doubt form their own opinions, but are unlikely to be overtly critical of the teacher's performance.

In Denmark and Ireland, individual schools are sometimes involved in reform projects or government initiatives to increase co-operation with parents. Teachers in these schools have in some cases received special training – and many have become accustomed to working with parents in the classroom.

In Canada, England and Wales and the United States, however, parents supporting teachers in the classrooms has almost become a hallmark of good primary school practice. Mothers and, sometimes, fathers coming in to hear children read, or to help with specialist lessons such as music or computer studies, is a widespread practice. Less common is training for parents so that they can offer more specific curriculum-oriented help. Parents in some areas can take courses in the early stages of the national curriculum, for example (see case study). And a number of special projects for parents from disadvantaged backgrounds in both

England and Ireland include training in how to act as a classroom aide – mainly so that parents become more knowledgeable about what the teacher is trying to achieve. But even in this context, teachers have found that the parent becomes a genuine help, and that a real partnership begins to emerge.

Helping children with school work at home

Probably the most widespread and acceptable form of co-operation between school and home is the practice of parents supporting their children at home – either directly through helping them with tasks such as learning to read or completing homework assignments, or indirectly through offering a rich cultural environment in the home. Research from a number of countries over the last 20 years or so has demonstrated that there is a clear link between socio-economic disadvantage, and poor performance in school. Conversely, an active partnership between parents and teachers can improve children's achievement. Tizard *et al.* (1982) showed that children's reading improved as a result of parents' involvement, as did Hannon and Jackson (1987) and, more recently, Wolfendale and Topping (1996). There is also substantial evidence that parents can also have a favourable impact on their children's early learning in mathematics (Merttens and Vass, 1993).

Helping children with their schoolwork falls into two main categories: supporting very young children, particularly in language development and learning to read and with early mathematics, and assisting with homework. Many pre-primary and primary schools now encourage parents to read aloud to their children from the earliest years, send children home from school each afternoon with a reading book and notebook for parental comments, and introduce parents to teaching techniques such as "paired reading". Some parents are uncertain as to how they can best help their children in the early stages, and look to the school for guidance. Classes for parents on child development, parenting skills, educational toys and books, are often popular, and schools or parents' associations who want to improve co-operation sometimes organise this kind of meeting or workshop. Experience suggests that there is a widespread unmet need in this area – but teachers do not always have time to arrange such events, and in schools without an active parents' association there may be noone else to do so.

New figures collected for the OECD's education indicators project (OECD, 1996a) suggest that about three-quarters[13] of primary pupils go to schools which regularly engage parents in actively supporting their children's learning at home. Evidence gathered from headteachers in 12 countries shows a wide range of practice; this approach is most widely used in Finland, Norway and Spain, and is least popular in Austria, where only about half the primary pupils are in schools which regularly employ this practice. In French and Irish primary schools, the figures are 86.3 per cent and 87.1 per cent respectively.

Older children often have specific homework with which they may need help, or project work which demands books, pictures, library visits or other resources. In most countries, of course, helping children at home, especially with homework, is a crucial aspect of good parenting. In Japan and France, in particular, this role is taken very seriously. Many Japanese parents, indeed, supplement the state system by paying for their children to attend private "cram schools" (*juku*) after school and at weekends. In England and Wales, where some children may not have anywhere suitable to do their homework, some schools have set up various forms of after-school study, including homework clubs. Such initiatives – which seem to be taking over the parent's role – can in fact can help parents from disadvantaged backgrounds to support their children. The experience of workers for Education Extra, a British pressure group which campaigns for improved after-school provision, is that "after-school activities can build bridges between schools and families by providing unthreatening access points to the school, ensuring that parents are valued and making a real contribution to school life" (Andrews *et al.*, 1996).

A more intangible form of support is the general cultural environment in which a child is raised: whether or not the parents read for pleasure, what kind of television programmes they watch, whether the family visits museums, theatres, art galleries and sporting, musical and community events, if the child meets people who play musical instruments, or paint, or dance, and so on. Teachers may arrange for pupils and their parents to attend cultural events, or encourage them to do so during their leisure time. They may indicate desirable limits on television viewing, for example, or encourage parents to keep up the tradition of a family meal in the evening – so that children can talk about the events of the day. But how far teachers are seen as having a right to recommend family activities in this way varies from country to country. In Japan, for example, such advice is not only accepted but requested; in other countries, parents may feel that it is intrusive, or represents a criticism of their family life.

COMMUNICATION BETWEEN SCHOOL AND HOME

Updates on children's progress

The most widespread form of communication between school and home is, of course, reporting to the parents concerning the progress of the individual child. Data from the OECD's education indicators project (OECD, 1996a) shows that virtually all primary pupils in the 12 countries surveyed attend schools which inform their parents regularly as to how they are progressing.[14] In most of the nine countries which participated in the present study, the schools must report by law two or three times a year. The minimum number of communications which parents are entitled to receive in each country is:

- *Canada*: Varies according to the province, but normally a report card once per term.
- *Denmark*: A conversation with the teacher, normally once or twice a term, up to seventh grade; after that stage, marks are given in writing at least twice a year, and are normally discussed with the parents.
- *England and Wales*: A written report at least once per year.
- *France*: Report card (*bulletin*) three times a year; an individual diary communicates marks regularly to parents throughout the year; minimum of one meeting per year with the teacher.
- *Germany*: Written report two or three times a year (depending on *Land*) including marks (after the first two grades) and a comment.
- *Ireland*: Normally at least one report per year at primary school, and two reports per year at second level – but there is no statutory minimum.
- *Japan*: One report card per term, often with space for parents' written comments.
- *Spain*: One report card per term, one interview with the teacher per year.
- *United States*: Varies from state to state, but normally between two and four report cards per year.

Individual schools often give parents more frequent updates on their children's progress, and in every system examined here, parents can request a discussion with their child's teacher. The frequency and importance placed on verbal communication vary a great deal; in the United Sates, for example, most parents have to be satisfied with a report card. In Denmark, the verbal feedback which teachers regularly give parents is considered a crucial element in the triangular partnership between parent, teacher and child – and part of the accountability process.

Homework notebooks/journals/agendas/diaries

Especially at secondary school, when parents are often less closely involved than when their children were younger, two-way (and sometimes three-way) communication is through the medium of the student's notebook – usually the notebook in which he or she keeps track of homework assignments. Parents normally have to sign the book to demonstrate that they have read it and supervised the homework, and they can write messages to the teacher who then replies. In Japan, a clear distinction is made between this notebook and the student's diary. The latter is where the student is encouraged to keep a daily record of events – including his or her thoughts, reactions and feelings and hands it in regularly to the teacher, who returns it with comments. This is seen as an educative activity, but also offers the teacher an insight into the lives of his or her charges. This interesting practice suggests that a feature of the relationship between teachers and parents in Japan is that the teacher has a large amount of privileged information about individual children – of which the parents may be unaware.

Home visits

A form of communication which seems very much accepted in some cultures but not in others, is the practice of teachers visiting pupils' homes. In Japan and Denmark, home visiting is widespread and part of the normal communication between home and school. In Japan, for example, homeroom teachers visit the homes of every one of their new students at the beginning of the academic year during Home Visit Week. During this brief (10-15 minute) visit, teacher and parents meet each other, and exchange information on school policy, and on the individual characteristics of the pupil.

In other countries – such as Canada, England and Wales, France or the United States – home visits are rare, and a sign of serious problems. Exceptions in all these countries are a range of special projects, usually for disadvantaged or ethnic minority parents, which include home visiting as one of the strategies for building up trust between family and school.

PSYCHO-SOCIAL SUPPORT

The challenge for many schools in involving parents in their children's education resides in the lack of confidence and know-how exhibited by many parents when confronted by the demands of the school. It is likely that much success in school is related to the possession of the "cultural capital" and "social capital" which some children – mostly middle class – inherit from their parents. Adaptation to school life, the mode of discourse used by teachers, and the academic content of the curriculum are much easier for these children than for those who lack this basic orientation. Working class children, and those from ethnic minorities often find adjustment to school more difficult.

These difficulties tend to be of two kinds – which often go together. First, parents may themselves not be very well-educated; they do not know what to do to support their children, they are unfamiliar with educational toys and books – indeed, they may not be literate. Secondly, they often have unpleasant memories of their own schooling, and may feel uneasy in the presence of teachers, or even hostile to the school. These difficulties are likely to affect the response of the children as well – and the teachers, who often have little training in interacting with parents in a manner which genuinely makes them feel like partners in the process.

This can be particularly true of immigrant parents, or those of ethnic minority origin. According to Tomlinson (1993): "There is evidence that teachers are still not well-informed about the lives (...) of ethnic minority parents and are still willing to stereotype such families as 'problems'. Ethnic minority parents are less likely than white parents to be involved in day-to-day school activities, and to be represented on governing bodies". Research she carried out among Bangladeshi parents in London showed that "such parents were not well informed about new curriculum and assessment arrangements and other educational innovations intended to raise achievements". She concludes that teacher education for all teachers should include a course in which they learn about their ethnic minority fellow-citizens, and that: "Teacher concepts of their professionalism should include a willingness to consult with, offer information to, and involve all parents, but especially ethnic minority parents, in the process of schooling, on a basis of equality. This will require an enormous change of attitude".

Parental education

Most parents, whether or not they are aware of research which shows how important is parental help at home, want to support their children's learning – but many do not know how to go about it. Parental education is an idea which some policy-makers greet with some suspicion – there is an element of superiority about it. But the fact remains that i) some parents are better able to support their children than others, mainly because they themselves are well-educated; and ii) many parents who would like to involve themselves in their children's school lack the confidence and know-how to do so.

Parental education can have a real impact in two directions: raising the level of children's achievement through, for example, literacy classes for parents, or workshops explaining aspects of child development or the use of educational toys; and raising the levels of knowledge, understanding and confidence of parents who, after taking some classes, often become more involved with the school, and begin to feel at ease with the teachers. Some may go on to take more courses at college or even university.

In many countries, the involvement of parents is complicated by issues of social class or ethnic origin (see Tomlinson, 1993). In order for parents to become effective partners, a lot of work needs to be done. Ultimately, this work is a powerful tool for increasing equity and reducing exclusion, and teachers often find it rewarding. There is a risk, though, that a "deficit" model of parenting may be adopted, condemning such parents to remain forever in an inferior position. Some teachers may find it more congenial to work with parents who do not threaten their self-esteem, and thus avoid the challenge of developing a more equal partnership.

When resources are put into various types of education for parents from disadvantaged socio-economic backgrounds, it is important that such schemes operate on a small local scale even if they are funded nationally. First, they offer information and short courses (usually based in the primary school so that the surroundings are not too intimidating) on topics such as child health, how children learn, how to support the child at home, or the problems of parenthood. Some schemes also offer general interest classes (ranging from cookery and hairdressing to keep-fit and stress reduction) designed to increase parents' general competence and self-esteem, and to "hook" them onto further education.

A further development is to improve parents' own literacy and mathematical skills so that they can better support their children – but such interventions must be approached sensitively since many parents are embarrassed by such difficulties, and have felt humiliation in the past. A particularly successful initiative has been the Family Literacy Programme in England and Wales. The project was based in four deprived urban and rural areas, and involved young parents with poor basic skills and their children. Over 12 weeks, the parents worked on their own literacy and on how to help their children, while the children received, separately, intensive teaching with a strong emphasis on writing and talk, as well as reading. Then they worked together in joint activities. In 1996, the National Foundation for Education Research (NFER) evaluated the four demonstration programmes, and concluded that the children made significant gains in early language, reading and writing – and continued to improve after the project had finished. For example, the proportion of children likely to be struggling in school because of poor reading fell from 67 per cent to 35 per cent over the 12 weeks. The NFER researchers described the project as one of the most effective initiatives they had encountered.

Experience shows that such programmes are welcomed enthusiastically by parents, who often then become more confident with the teachers and more able to help their children – who also benefit from seeing their parents at ease in the school. Some may join the parents' association or school committees which they avoided previously. Parents sometimes continue to develop academically, usually in one of two directions. As they find out more about the educational process, they may move on towards further courses on supporting teachers in the classroom (such as the Chatsworth Computer Project in Liverpool, see case study); or they may begin further education courses, perhaps at a local college. There are examples of parents from very deprived backgrounds moving onto university courses in, say, law. This can have a marked effect on the local community, empowering its residents through education.

Special educational needs[15]

One of the most crucial areas for parental involvement relates to children with special educational needs. The parents of such children are often very active in lobbying for improved services, and form advocacy groups which politicians cannot ignore – and which are often well-supported by the mass media. Research carried out by the OECD's Centre for Educational Research and Innovation has found that it is often the parents who "force ordinary schools to implement already existing legislation in providing integrative programmes". Parents in some countries form support groups, meet regularly to discuss how to improve the situation for children with disabilities, and become involved in efforts to "educate members of the community about disabilities and to promote awareness of the rights of disabled people. This type of involvement allows parents opportunities not only to affect policy at local and national levels but also to influence procedural guidelines and perhaps ensure that there are means of monitoring them" (OECD, 1995c).

The success of such pressure groups is partly a result of the fact that articulate middle class parents with professional knowledge and useful political contacts can have children with disabilities – and they then proceed to fight for their rights. Parents who are marginalised by the school system for socio-economic, cultural or ethnic reasons – especially those whose children are deemed "at risk"[16] – are in a much weaker position. Yet involving these parents is particularly important. "Effective education necessitates bringing together the school, the family and the community. Those who are 'at risk' are likely to have had unsatisfactory experiences in one or more of these areas" (OECD, 1995d).

Although such parents can sometimes be successfully drawn into school-based projects which encourage them to support their children's learning, it is particularly hard to involve them in school governance. "The parents of children 'at risk' may be doubly disenfranchised. The poor, possibly without such facilities as personal transport, telephone, etc., will find committee membership hard to sustain. In addition, their attitude to school may not be positive. They themselves often do not possess a history of school success, and their memories of school may be unhappy" (OECD, 1995d).

Special needs work with parents raises matters (of both principle and practice) which have a wider application and significance. For example, in the United States (and in other countries) parents participate in developing and approving – or not – individual educational plans for their children. Often it is one of the strongest arenas for effective home-school work, and, at its best, offers good examples of a real partnership between parent and professional which could usefully act as models in planning for children who do not have special needs.

4

DEVELOPING PARTNERSHIPS

AN IDEA WHOSE TIME HAS COME?

Verbal support for more parental involvement in the schools is now widespread among OECD countries – from governments, parents and the public – although there is still a long way to go when it comes to practice. However, a survey carried out in 12 countries (OECD, 1995b) showed that the public sees "keeping parents informed and involved" one of the most important tasks for schools. So much so that public opinion in the United States put this task at the top of a list of seven possible priorities; in seven other countries (including Denmark and Spain) it was seen as the second most important task of the school today. (The top priority was "helping with difficulties in learning".) The key exception, interestingly, was France, where respondents to the survey rated parental information and involvement as less important than: help with learning difficulties; careers advice and guidance; maintaining discipline; and strong leadership from the headteacher.[17]

Meanwhile, the governments of virtually all the developed countries are now developing policies for involving parents in their children's education – and parents too are exploring new forms of partnership. After years of declining membership and influence, the National Parent-Teacher Association in the United States now reports an increase in membership and activities. The European Parents' Association (EPA), which celebrated its tenth anniversary in 1995, represents over 100 million parents in the European Union. The association supports parental participation in education by gathering and disseminating information throughout Europe, highlighting innovation, promoting training courses for parents, and supporting research into aspects of parental participation and partnership.

The EPA's aims are: to pursue education policies at European level which will ensure the highest possible quality of education of all children; to use the influence of the EPA to promote in a European context the active participation of parents at all levels of education; to develop a dialogue between parents in Europe; to work to support effective partnership in education throughout Europe through the sharing of good practice. And the mission of the association is to: "work in partnership with other educators in the creation of an educational community of parents throughout Europe" and to "give a strong voice to parents in the development of all educational policies and decisions at European level". This emphasis on shared policy-making, put the association in the vanguard of thinking on parental involvement.

At the same time, involving parents as partners in school governance fits in with other aspects of government policy and educational reform in many countries. For example, in countries which are decentralising their educational administration, the increased participation of parents fits in with the philosophy of local autonomy – whether at community level or in relation to the school itself.

IS TRUE PARTNERSHIP POSSIBLE?

"Partnership" is a key concept in the analysis of relations between home and school (see Wolfendale, 1992); but it is a slippery term and often means different things in different systems – and sometimes to different people. The word itself suggests a static, already worked-out relationship, but in reality partnership is more of a *process* – learning to work together, and valuing what each partner can bring to the relationship. Clarity is important, especially since power in a partnership is rarely equal, and ground rules need to be established. As Macbeth and Ravn (1994) put it: "Should school teachers educate children while parents humbly support the schools? Or could it be the other way round? Are parents the main educators of their child, while schools supplement home-learning with specialist expertise?".

A further survey finding (OECD, 1995b) is related to the partnership issue. The public in virtually all the 12 countries surveyed thought that responsibility for the personal and social development of young people should be shared equally between home and school. Some 81 per cent of respondents in the United Kingdom were in favour of this equal division, as were 79 per cent of the French. The exception in this section was Denmark. Only 43 per cent of Danes thought that this duty should be shared equally, while 55 per cent believed that the home should have more responsibility than the school. This is particularly intriguing, since parent-teacher relations are probably closer in Denmark than in any other country in the current study, and communication between the two is not confined to the school environment but may legitimately take place in the home, the street, the shops – anywhere in the local community. *Folkeskole* teachers are rarely "off-duty". Does this closeness mean Danish teachers and parents have more opportunity to discuss and internalise the complementary roles of teacher and parent, and separate out the relevant rights and responsibilities to their mutual satisfaction?

When it comes to partnerships between parents and teachers, it is important that each party recognises the special skills of the other. Pugh (1989) suggests a definition which has proved popular (see Irish case study). She defines "partnership" as: "a working relationship that is characterised by a shared sense of purpose, mutual respect and the willingness to negotiate. This implies a sharing of information, responsibility, skills, decision-making and accountability".

So far, most of the emphasis – justifiably – has been on the need for teachers and schools to welcome parents, draw them into the joint educative enterprise, celebrate their role as children's first educators, and so on. But parents, too, should be sensitive to the complexities of the teacher's task and, in particular, refrain from indulging in ill-informed criticisms. Over-critical parents can damage relationships by forcing teachers onto the defensive, making them unwilling to be open and reflective about their practice. Yet most parents benefit from exposure to the realities of classroom life; normally, the more a lay person knows about the classroom, the more he or she is impressed by the teacher's ability to carry out a sometimes very difficult task. Far from wanting to take over the teacher's job, most parents respect the teacher's skills increasingly as they come to understand what goes on in the classroom. This is also often true of employers, who – on the rare occasions when they are invited into school – usually leave with a higher regard for the professional competence of the teachers.

But teachers may be doubtful – although those who have taken the plunge into partnership, whether willingly or not, tend to find that parents become valued partners and an extra resource. Even countries with long tradition of social partnership can find this change of gear difficult to achieve. Most professions, such as doctors or lawyers, are very unwilling to allow lay influence, and teachers' professionalism should be respected. The key characteristic of communication between teachers and parents is that the stakes are perceived as being very high for both parties. Parents may believe that the future of their child is at stake, and teachers often feel defensive. They lead very stressful, demanding and exposed working lives, and schools have not always developed good support strategies which do not depend on closing ranks against outsiders. The leadership qualities of individual headteachers and principals are often crucial in developing partnerships between teachers and parents.

Principals, teachers and parents need more experience in working together – and training in how to do it, especially since some teachers find it hard to relate professionally to adults rather than children. In some countries, joint training programmes and workshops, such as those organised by Ireland's National Parent Council-Primary, have been set up by parents' associations.

Schools, too, can take the initiative in creating good working partnerships where each side trusts the other – after all, however overworked, teachers are the professionals, and this is an area where their professionalism is crucial. Parents cannot be expected to make all the running – and would probably be resented if they did. However, if governments are serious in putting these policies in place, they need to support the schools. A key challenge for both teachers and parents is to overcome barriers to communication which may have their roots in class and ethnic differences, so that they together can identify areas where they can work productively in the interests of the children.

Enabling partnership to develop in this way is an important aspect of lifelong learning, and binds the school more closely to its community. As Ranson (1994) points out, a key purpose of educational reform is to bring into being "a learning society, one in which parents are as much committed to their own continuing development as they are to supporting their children's education, in which women assert their right to learn as well as support the family, in which learning co-operatives are formed at work and in community centres, and in which all are preoccupied with the issues of purpose and organisation of learning enough to get involved in the public dialogue about reform".

HOW FAR IS PARENT POWER DESIRABLE?

A distinction needs to be made between the notion of partnership – which implies equal commitment by both parties, and sensitive and subtle strategies for working together – and the idea of "parent power". The latter makes an arresting political slogan, and performs the important function of reminding parents of their rights. Its usefulness, though, is limited – partly because it sounds combative and gives out negative signals to schools and local authorities, but also because successful change needs to be negotiated and thought through, rather than driven along on the basis of one party's "power".

In particular, governments need to bear in mind that unfettered parental power can have effects which may run counter to other aspects of education policy – or to overall policies such as holding down public spending. In particular, choice of school can lead to a widening of the gap between the most and least effective schools (OECD, 1994b), and intensify social divisions (Ball et al., 1996). Some parents – often the most influential and articulate – may be in favour of various forms of segregation – which has become a contentious political issue in Canada (see country summary).

As is usual with government policies, some results – such as parents supporting their children's learning more effectively, or pressurising schools into raising their standards – seem eminently desirable to politicians; but others – such as creating a powerful parental lobby for higher spending on education – seem less so. Truly empowering parents does not mean simply enlisting their support for government policies. And parental advocacy is a weapon which is not yet being used to its full extent in most countries. But there are signs that organised parents are a powerful group – especially when it comes to campaigning for education spending. Governments which attempt to hold down public spending on education can expect strong lobbying from newly-empowered parents.

According to Golby (1993) we should concentrate on the idea of "winners and winners". Involving parents in school governance, he says, need not entail the loss of power for other parties (teachers or local education authorities). "School governors can be seen as adding power to the whole system, over against other competing social and political priorities, rather than causing a redistribution of a finite quantity of power within the education service".

But a central issue in relation to parent power is the fact that some teachers *are* vulnerable. The underlying but unspoken anxiety in many schools is that parents will use their new power to identify ineffective teachers. This is indeed an issue in which parents themselves are very interested; although in most systems, even when they have the power to do so, other considerations often prevent them from acting. However, the two most contentious policies – allowing parents into the classroom, and giving them some influence over the curriculum and how it is delivered – do not just infringe on the territory of teachers, but may well expose weak teachers to parental scrutiny. Of course, inadequate teachers need to be identified, and retrained or otherwise dealt with. But most teachers are well aware of the weaknesses of their colleagues – as are principals and, often, inspectors. The undoubted problems which exist in weeding out those who are not performing adequately relate, in most countries, to legal and political considerations. Parents on the warpath are unlikely to make any difference, and trusting partnerships need to be established if they are to play an effective role in relation to teacher quality without destructive or demoralising consequences for the teaching body.

Interestingly, the country in which parents are most able to use parental representation to talk to teachers about any problems which arise in connection with their teaching (such as difficulties in terms of the methods they are using) is Germany – although German parents have only limited formal opportunities to share in decision-making, and the line between lay and professional people is very clearly drawn. In Denmark, on the other hand, this rarely happens, in spite of the fact that Danish school boards are dominated by parents, and that there is currently some anxiety with regard to standards of achievement in the *Folkeskole*. This intriguing paradox suggests that, so far as improving the quality of teaching goes, involving parents in school governance is not necessarily an effective strategy.

Parents as participants in the inspection process

Of the nine countries in the study, four (Canada, Denmark, Japan and the United States[18]) do not have a national system for inspecting either teachers or schools. Schools and individual teachers are both inspected in France, but parents are not involved in the process. In Germany, school inspectors focus on the performance of teachers rather than schools as institutions; they may consult parents in the class council when assessing a teacher, but this tends to be unusual and only in special circumstances.

In two countries, however – England and Wales and Spain – inspectors solicit the views of parents as an integral element of the inspection process (OECD, 1995e). In England and Wales, the registered inspector from the Office of Standards in Education must send a questionnaire to parents concerning their opinion of the school, and hold a meeting at which parents can express their views. In Spain, inspectors' reports are publicised through the parents' association, and parents are involved in drawing up the school development plan which follows such a report and must address any weaknesses identified by the inspectors. Although Irish parents are not currently involved in school inspection, proposals for a system of "Whole School Inspection" are currently under consideration. Under these new arrangements, parents would be consulted as part of the process.

Involvement of mothers

It is very evident in all the countries in this study that virtually all the parents involved in co-operation initiatives with schools are women: parent power means "mother power". Normally, the reason given is that fathers are too busy and tired from their jobs to be able to spend much time in school activities. However, even in areas where large numbers of men are unemployed, the women are often the only ones to form links with the school. This can be very positive for the women, of course, and in some cases is leading to a revitalisation of local communities as hitherto disadvantaged women get themselves an education and begin to explore their power.

But it is not clear what effect this lack of symmetry may have in the long run, as women begin to outstrip men in their eagerness to educate themselves and also to support their children's learning. Negative attitudes can be passed down to boys if their fathers do not value learning. In some disadvantaged areas, many boys do not have academically successful male role models with whom they can identify. In some countries, teaching (especially at primary level) is a mainly female profession, and there is some anxiety that the schools are becoming "feminised" – leading to the underachievement of boys who do not take education seriously, perhaps because for them it is associated with being female.

CONCLUSION

There is now a range of new statutory obligations in many countries, which are likely to change the relationship between families and schools – and parents and teachers. And it is clear from the experiences of the nine participating countries that involving families more intimately in the education process has real benefits – educational, social and financial. Children, parents, teachers and the community can all achieve more if they co-operate with each other. It is also clear, however, that individual schools and even whole systems can function very effectively without such links – but this would tend to be in circumstances where the population involved is relatively homogeneous, and where there is already a great deal of shared understanding, and agreement on goals.

In more heterogeneous societies and systems, different sections of the community may not understand each other well, or the values of one group may not be shared by the other. With increased economic mobility and migration, along with the development (particularly in countries with high unemployment) of an excluded class, pluralist societies are becoming the norm. This means that if the young are to be educated to play their full role in society, and if their parents are to be given the chance to continue learning, partnership is the only way forward. If different parties learn to understand each other's background, aims and aspirations, there is more chance that agreement can be reached – but this cannot be achieved without tolerance from both sides, sensitive negotiation, and conceptual clarity.

In France and Germany, it is probably fair to say that both parents and governments would like to move faster and further, but the pace of change is held up by powerful teacher interests. Even in Japan, where parental involvement has traditionally been limited to supporting individual children in the home, the schools – at the government's instigation – are encouraging parents to become more involved (within well-understood limits). Since the government and the teachers alike are afraid that Japanese children are not developing into well-rounded citizens, and that small families and crowded urban living mean that children no longer learn spontaneously how to get along with each other, more parents – especially mothers – are being encouraged to work in partnership with the school.

The most successful approaches, it is clear, are those which focus on enabling parents to support their children's learning – particularly in the early years. Numerous case studies demonstrate that parents – even those with significantly disadvantaged backgrounds – can not only develop educational skills but often, in the process, become highly committed to the school itself – and that this development often has a valuable spill-over into the local community. Effective techniques have been identified for encouraging such parents, making schools more accessible and teachers less intimidating, and proving to them that they can not only improve their children's life chances, but make up for lacks in their own education.

Less obviously successful – although still significant – are efforts to involve parents in various forms of policy-making and governance. Few countries attempt to do this at all levels, but all espouse different forms of participation. Sometimes parents may, should, for example, help run the schools – but are excluded from decision-making at the national level. In another country, they participate in drawing up the curriculum, but are not given any say in how it is taught. Given that all these forms of participation have a generally positive effect, it is not clear why they are not more universal. Whether parents' rights are seen as part of a democratic society, or rather as an aspect of consumerism, logic demands that partnership can – and should – operate at all levels of the system.

In deciding whether or not to involve parents more closely, it is important for policy-makers to clarify (to themselves, if not to others) exactly why they want to put such a policy in place. Certainly, the nine countries in the study demonstrate a whole range of reasons, some articulated, and some not. And, as always, if a government adopts a policy without analysing it sufficiently, some unexpected – and undesired – consequences may be the result.

Some political aims – such as encouraging teachers to take the lead in developing innovative relationships with parents and the community, while at the same time criticising them and attempting to reduce their power – risk being mutually contradictory when put into action. Governments need to consider which of their objectives are really most likely to lead to an improvement in the education of children, rather than to some other – perhaps more ideological – end.

There are also hard questions to be answered as to whether what is good for individuals is also good for the greatest number. In most schools in most countries, the number of active parents is not large – a small articulate group often does a disproportionate amount of the work. Of course, the energy and commitment of concerned, well-educated and socially stable members of the community are of great importance and need to be harnessed by the schools – yet it is not their children who are most in need. In most OECD countries the real educational problems concern those from disadvantaged backgrounds – whether they live in the inner city, in suburban housing projects or municipal estates, or in impoverished rural areas. Without successful educational experiences to reconcile them to the values of mainstream society and to allow them to gain qualifications, their employment prospects – and their socio-economic futures – remain bleak.

However, there is now enough research evidence[19] from innovative projects being developed in many of the participating countries to conclude that building partnerships between parents of all kinds and the schools their children attend is perfectly possible – though still quite rare. Given that partnership looks like a desirable means of achieving worthwhile ends, what are the most effective way of making it a reality?

POLICY IMPLICATIONS

To a large extent, we now know what works – but are not putting it into action. There is no doubt that family and community involvement with education – in all its manifestations – is potentially an exciting strategy for developing schools which can meet the needs of learners in the future (although not, of course, a panacea for all the problems suffered within education systems). Energy should now be put into transforming what has been learned into more widespread practice; and strategies need to be developed for moving good practice out from among a small band of enthusiasts into the mainstream parent/teacher population. Currently, much of the impetus is already coming from parents themselves. In some countries there has recently been a surge of interest in parents' associations, and volunteering to help in school is becoming more popular.

Parents are anxious as never before concerning their children's employment prospects, and in many countries, they have been frustrated in their attempts to understand the qualifications system and their efforts to inform themselves about what happens in school. In some cases, they have been intimidated by the professionals. But if governments were to smooth their paths and spend quite modest sums on encouraging partnership, the results of mobilising parental energy could raise educational achievement among both children and adults – and make the teacher's task easier.

Governments which want to maximise the positive effects of involving parents in schools, should consider the following issues:

- *Publicising and disseminating examples of successful practice is a crucial step.* In those countries which have committed themselves to increasing parental involvement, there is now an impressive range of successful one-off projects or experiments (see case studies).

- *Strategies and funding mechanisms should be developed so that successful innovations can be continued.* Most of the successful projects have remained confined to their original context, or have even come to an end through losing their funding – despite demonstrable achievements. This means that much painfully-developed expertise is lost, and committed teams are broken up unnecessarily.

- *Methods of replicating successful strategies should be developed, so that parents, students and teachers across the country – and in other countries too – can benefit from them.* Too often, the lessons learned from successful innovations are not adequately disseminated or built into the system as a whole; much time is wasted in re-inventing wheels.

– *Governments should be clear about what they really want to achieve.* There is currently a great deal of pious rhetoric concerning parental involvement – and in some countries parents' hopes have been raised but not satisfied, leading to apathy and cynicism. If governments only want to empower parents as a means of forcing change upon reluctant schools, they are unlikely to succeed. Building genuinely productive partnerships is a long-term project, and requires planning and strategic thinking.

– *The aim should be to establish interlocking policies which ensure that all schools will build strong programmes of partnership with all their families in all six types of involvement.* Further work needs to be carried out on the relationship between top-down and bottom-up approaches in establishing a coherent system-wide strategy.

– *Questions of power cannot be ignored when considering the building of productive partnerships.* The political culture of some countries encourages issues such as the respective interests of parents, teachers and government to be faced head on; others feel that exposing the realities of power too brutally is counter-productive. Countries in the first group risk demoralising or alienating their teaching force – unless discussion of the pros and cons of increased parental involvement is sensitively and honestly handled. Countries in the second group risk obscuring the underlying lineaments of the policy and allowing entrenched interests to manipulate it – thus making it far less effective.

– *Genuine partnership entails mutual respect among the different partners, and a recognition of what each can bring to the collaboration.* Much successful parental involvement comes down to a question of individual teachers and parents learning how to negotiate, to handle differences of opinion and to understand the importance of each other's role – without losing confidence in their own. Training – which need not be extensive – is often necessary if successful partnerships are to be built. The most fruitful approaches often involve teachers and parents training together.

– *The support of school principals is crucial in establishing such partnerships – but they need to be convinced of the benefits.* Charismatic headteachers who are in favour of parental involvement can create extremely successful partnerships, but even in systems where parental involvement is built into the routine, a principal who is not really committed to the idea can defeat the policy by keeping parents at arms' length.

– *Parental involvement is potentially an important and exciting policy for empowering the dispossessed, and strengthening communities.* This is possibly the greatest challenges faced by OECD societies. Teachers, far from feeling threatened, can become very committed to this approach.

– A *key reason for wanting performance at school to improve is, at bottom, economic.* Every country is anxious that, without a highly skilled population, they will slip behind in the unremitting global competition. But it is also clear that the schools in most countries cannot do the job without extra support – and money is short. One way of releasing fresh resources into education is to draw on parents, who, at the very least, have a natural drive to help their own children.

– *In order to make best use of the energy and resources of parents, the parental agenda needs to be identified clearly.* Making assumptions about parents' needs or desires may lead to speedier policy formation – but can backfire when the consequences of the policy are working through. Such an agenda would need to involve consultation with a wide range of groups and agencies, and tap into a broad cross-section of views and experience of different groups of parents. Governments should not assume that parents will always want what they want.

Post-script

"Home-school partnership cannot be left to quietly evolve, unaided, in its own good time! Neither should it be left to individual schools, teachers and parents to foster on their own, without help. It is a major task that calls for imagination and commitment, initiative and direction; it also needs management, understanding and support" (Bastiani, 1993).

Part II

COUNTRY SUMMARIES

CANADA

OVERVIEW

Canada has a decentralised education system, and education is entirely under the jurisdiction of the provinces and territories. Although there is little formal collaboration among the individual provinces, and no organised movement to increase co-ordination, there has been a surprisingly consistent wave of educational reforms across the country and developments in parental co-operation need to be seen in this light.

Schooling is considered an important instrument in addressing a wide variety of social, economic and educational issues from early intervention to adult literacy. Parental involvement in schooling, from providing the right home environment to supporting children's learning, to working on fund-raising projects, to participating in decisions that affect the operation of schools, are all considered as essential strategies towards making education more effective. So, among Canada's 10 provinces and two territories, involving 700 or so school districts, there is increasing action to enrich parent-school relations.

Compared with the parents in most other countries, Canadian parents have, potentially, a remarkable degree of power over the functioning of the school system – although it is so new that it is not yet being used to its full extent. In particular, in some provinces they can have a say in the appointment and dismissal of the school principal and other teaching staff, and can influence both the content of the curriculum and its delivery in the classroom – all elements of involvement which in many countries are the sacred territory of either the education administrators, or the teachers (usually stoutly defended by their trade unions). Canada bears watching to see how the balance of powers regarding educational decision-making is achieved amongst professional educators, provincial governments, parents and other stakeholders.

Even though support for the concept of parent-school involvement is now virtually universal in Canada, there is a considerable gap between proposals for action and the realisation of widespread and consistent co-operation between parents and schools. Many different forms of successful co-operation, however, demonstrated in individual schools and classrooms throughout the country, show that it can be done.

SOCIAL BACKGROUND

One of the most important aspects of the social context for education in Canada is the multi-cultural, multi-lingual and multi-racial nature of the country. Unlike the "melting pot" of the United States, Canada prides itself on the "mosaic" quality of its diverse population. The nature of this mosaic has resulted in a national sensitivity to issues of equity and social justice; the goals of universal schooling in a democratic society.

In particular, Canada's First Nations people are strongly expressing their desire for changes in the decision-making processes. Historically, native people have not fared well in the education system and have not felt that the system responded adequately to their needs. They now want to increase their control over the education their young people receive so that it is more culturally appropriate, and they see the increased involvement of parents and elders as a vital component. This issue is particularly significant in Western Canada, where First Nations people make up a larger proportion of the population.

Questions of poverty, literacy and truancy are some of the main issues that are challenging present education reforms; the Senate Standing Committee on Social Affairs, Science and Technology has estimated that over the next 20 years some 187 000 young Canadians will drop out of school because of poverty, and that this will cost the taxpayer C$620 million in unemployment insurance and C$710 million in social assistance payments. In the recent International Adult Literacy Survey (see OECD and Statistics Canada, 1995), over 10 per cent of Canadian youth (16-25) scored in the lowest category of literacy, compared with only 3.1 per cent in Sweden. In this international survey, Canada did not fare much better than the United States, even though it does not have the extreme levels of child poverty found in many areas of the United States. Yet at the same time, all provincial governments are concerned with reducing deficits – and in most cases they have drastically reduced funding for education. There is little money to support initiatives that might increase home and school co-operation.

As in many countries, in Canada there have been marked changes in family structure over the past decade, which, alongside changes in the economy, have led to an increase in the number of children living in poverty. Levels of child poverty rose from 15.2 per cent in 1981 to 18.3 per cent in 1991, which the Vanier Institute (1994) attributed to "a slow economy, high divorce rates, high unemployment, inadequate education, lack of sufficient child care options, low wages (especially for women) and cutbacks to social programmes". In this context, increased family-school co-operation is viewed by some policy-makers as a way of addressing these social problems, as schools attempt to grapple with the problems of disadvantaged families, and parents, under increasing pressure, find it hard to give their children the support they need. While good relations between school and family are of course vital in such circumstances, they need also to be recognised as an essential element of effective schooling for children of all backgrounds.

POLICY CONTEXT

Canada is a vast country with no centralised educational system; educational policy is under the jurisdiction of the provinces and territories. The federal government's primary role is to provide a block grant to the provinces and territories to help in the funding of primary, secondary and post-secondary education. Unlike the reforms of the 60s, which expanded and upgraded the system by creating more secondary education institutions and raising the qualifications and salaries of teachers, the current reforms are attempting to adapt the school system to changing social and economic circumstances.

Given the autonomy of the provinces, there is no nationwide policy-making or research that sets the agenda for greater home-school co-operation. At the provincial level, policy-makers recognise a variety of roles parents may play in co-operating with schools. The majority of policies to date, however, are concerned with the role of parents in school governance.

Within the provinces, the legal authority for education is highly centralised. The Minister is responsible for administering the various legislative regulations and acts – mainly called School Acts. Within each province, the administration of schools is carried out in districts (in some cases called divisions, units or counties). School districts are defined geographically and in most cases are contiguous areas, but in some provinces there are separate districts serving denominational and non-denominational schools, or English- and French-speaking schools, some of which overlap geographically. In most provinces (and until recently all provinces), the population of each school district elects a school board which is accountable to the Minister of Education for carrying out the statutes and regulations contained in that province's School Act. The school board typically hires a superintendent – the chief executive officer in charge of carrying out the duties of the board.

An important aspect regarding the authority of school boards is that legally they exist "at the pleasure of the provincial legislatures". Recently, in a move to decentralise power, give the schools more autonomy, and involve parents more closely in school governance, a number of provinces have reduced the number of school boards by amalgamating school districts, and, in the case of New Brunswick, dismissed them. The impetus for these changes, however, stems also from a desire to reduce costs. At the same time, as provincial governments are decentralising control over the processes of schooling, they are increasing their control over the outcomes of education by developing stronger systems for monitoring school performance. So, educational policy in Canada is shifting its emphasis from provincial and district reforms to initiatives at the school level. The key to reform is now seen as being how teachers and school-site administrators mobilise schooling resources in their particular context. The main strategies for reforming schools in the 1990s have been to increase "parental choice" and to restructure schools in ways that give parents, teachers and students greater autonomy.

The motivation for greater involvement of parents in schools is not so much that present relations are poor, but that they could be improved. An opinion poll conducted by the Canadian Education Association (Williams and Millinoff, 1990) found that most Canadian adults felt that schools responded well to parents' concerns about their children – in the elementary grades at least. However, the responses of parents at secondary level were less positive and schools in large urban areas received lower ratings than schools in smaller cities and rural areas.

WHY INVOLVE PARENTS?

The main rationale for involving Canadian parents in schooling is to improve educational outcomes for students. These objectives are perhaps best expressed in a publication issued by the Canadian School Boards Association (1995), a national non-profit organisation that aims to give school boards across Canada the opportunity to share experiences and expertise on federal government policies and programmes affecting education.

The association points out that one impetus to increasing parental involvement in school governance has been in the political arena, where school reformers consider that decentralisation – with parental participation through mandated local advisory bodies – will help solve some of the problems facing the Canadian school system. A second reason for encouraging parental involvement across the country is based on research evidence which indicates that involvement by parents in the education of their children has a significant impact on students' achievement.

THE LEGISLATION

Since every province or territory draws up its own education legislation, there are no national policy-framing laws in Canada. But the increased importance of parental input can be seen in reforms around the country which are adding parent committees that will co-exist with district school boards, or in some cases are even replacing school boards with parent committees. To increase parental participation at the higher levels of decision-making, all provincial governments have either established parent advisory committees (at provincial or district level), or are in the process of doing so. Virtually all the provinces have passed legislation that specifies the roles and responsibilities of these higher-level committees – although the Departments of Education tend to approach the issue in different ways.

For example, in New Brunswick the school boards have been disbanded, and the province's School Act is now implemented directly through eight district superintendents (five English-speaking and three French-speaking). In future, education will be administered through two provincial boards of education, district parent advisory councils, and a school-parent committee for every school.

Each school will have a school-parent committee comprised of parents elected by the parents/guardians of children attending the school. The principal and one teacher elected by the staff will serve as ex officio members, and in high schools a student will be elected by a student committee. The explicit role of this committee is to advise the principal. This entails direct participation in establishing the school mission statement, developing a school improvement plan, developing school policies that will enhance school climate, assessing school performance reviews, and encouraging family and community involvement. The committee chair (or designate) participates in selecting a new school principal.

The new district parent advisory councils will advise the superintendents – taking over what was part of the former district school board's mandate. However, these councils will have much less influence than the school boards did. The line of authority from the provincial Minister of Education now flows directly to the superintendent of each of the school districts, rather than through a school board elected by the citizens of the district. Two provincial boards of education (one English-speaking and one French-speaking) will also be established. These will be composed of one parent from each of the district parent advisory councils, and will advise the Minister of Education.

This legislation seems to strengthen the power of the provincial government, by centralising control and authority. However, the former school boards only existed by courtesy of the provincial government, and New Brunswick parents should find that their informal authority over school matters has now increased. This may make for less cumbersome channels for expressing views about their schools.

In New Brunswick's recent reform (Excellence in Education), parents, along with the teacher and the student are considered as essential partners in education. The report "Schools for a New Century" states that parents must assume a large part of the responsibility for the education of their children and the school system must show how it values their participation.

KEY ELEMENTS OF CO-OPERATION BETWEEN SCHOOL AND FAMILY

Parental involvement in school governance

The most significant result of the reforms designed to increase parents' power is that many more schools in Canada now have a parent committee or school council than was the case five years ago. In most instances the traditional structure has not altered; the provincial government still administers the system through school boards, and parent councils have largely an advisory function pertaining to local issues.

For example, in the province of Ontario, the New Foundations for Ontario Education aim to reduce the number of school boards by 40 to 50 per cent. Within the recommendations of the recent Royal Commission on Learning, the provincial Ministry of Education has proposed legislation to create individual school councils as "the next logical step towards giving parents a greater say in how schools are run and strengthening partnerships with the community". The Ministry will require all schools in Ontario to establish school councils to provide advice to principals on school-related issues, and to improve links between schools and communities. All school boards, and the minority-language sections of boards, will have to develop a policy that will ensure that a school council is set up in each school and operates according to school board policies.

Parent councils in Nova Scotia have perhaps the strongest degree of control and authority; they have direct responsibilities concerning school improvement plans and accountability reports. In this capacity they may be in the best position to influence school climate. In British Columbia and Quebec, parents may decide to form a school council rather than being obliged to do so by legislation. However it is encouraged by the provincial government.

Most councils are made up of parents, school staff, often community members and students. British Columbia and Quebec have more parent-based councils. In some provinces, council members undergo training, and manuals are produced. Newfoundland, for example has a facilitator in each district, and Manitoba has a Department of Education employee who provides information through workshops and brochures. The decision-making ability of councils varies; sometimes the councils are strictly advisory, whereas others have more direct input into decisions.

In New Brunswick, the Ministry assists school boards and schools in developing school councils by providing guidelines for development, a handbook containing information and resource materials for schools, and sponsors a School Council Forum to enable people to set up school councils and to share information and effective practices.

Various new forms of governance are also being proposed to give First Nation Canadians more control over the education offered to their children. Suggestions include autonomous control by Indian and Metis bands, collaborative joint control between the provincial government and bands, and community-based control.

A national voice for parents

The national voice for parents in Canada is the Canadian Home-School and Parent-Teacher Federation (CHSPTF). The CHSPTF, which celebrated its centenary in 1995, is a broad umbrella organisation representing the interests of all parents and has its national office in Ottawa. From there, it co-ordinates the work of its provincial and territorial affiliates.

While the CHSPTF's continuing mandate is to serve the general well-being of children and youth, it views the expansion of school councils as an opportunity for a new level of parental participation and furthering of its mandate. Furthermore the federation believes that the historical involvement of parents in Home-School Associations has contributed to present developments in the creation of school councils.

Currently the federation is actively involved in analysing the various models of parent-school councils from the different provinces. Given the extent of recent changes across the country it will take some time before the nature of the new relationships becomes clear. The federation does, however, make the following recommendations regarding councils:

- Councils should represent a cross-section of the population; it is essential that marginalised segments of society be included.
- It is important to find solutions at grassroots level and engage large numbers of the population if the current rapid changes in education, are to be well-managed.
- Councils should provide a forum for open discussion about educational issues. Participants should not be accountable to any governing body.

The CHSPTF is optimistic that problems experienced in Canada's schools (which they believe stem primarily from social roots) can be solved, once agreement is reached on the type of action needed. They advocate the involvement of the whole community and recommend more parenting education as part of this process.

Other national organisations also exist in Canadian education devoted to special interest groups where parents have an active voice. Notable among these is Canadian Parents for French. With its more than 18 000 members, these parents are recognised as the driving force behind the French immersion programmes across Canada.

The school and the community

The interface between school and community is increasing in most provinces. Because school district budgets have become much leaner over the past decade, local communities are contributing to funding sports grounds, leisure-time activities and school outings. A number of newly built schools in New Brunswick, for example, do not include equipment for playgrounds; the parents are expected to raise money from the community to finish the school. In return, schools are increasingly contributing to the community by offering resources such as information technology networks, and offering courses on effective parenting. Students across Canada contribute to their community in many ways by helping to clean and maintain parks and neighbourhoods, offering art or music to the elderly and canvassing on behalf of community organisations.

Schools also co-operate with the community by sharing their facilities; most Canadian schools open their doors to outside agencies after regular school hours, and a number of schools identify themselves as "community schools". A good example is the Alex Taylor Community School in Edmonton, Alberta. It is located in an area with a large immigrant population, and runs cultural programmes, social and health programmes, continuing education programmes and fund-raising activities on its premises in which the whole community participates.

One strategy to raise the level of "social capital" in a community is to strengthen social relationships that facilitate action – that is where members of the community can do things for one another, creating an atmosphere of trust by building up expectations and fulfilling obligations. An example of capacity building of the school and community can be seen in the ongoing reforms in Halifax, Nova Scotia, where parents are being invited to work with schools to plan change. In one difficult inner-city school with a high black population, parents invited business sponsors to adopt the school and tried to improve its profile in the media. A number of companies in all parts of the country have "co-operative education" links with local schools, offering students various forms of work-based experience designed to ease their transition into the working world.

Partners for Youth in Fredericton, New Brunswick, is a community programme[20] that aims to improve the self esteem of young people who are experiencing difficulty in family or peer relationships, have poor academic performance, or may be at risk of dropping out of school because of early sexuality or alcohol and drug abuse. The adventure-based programme, staffed by local teachers, involves challenging activities such as rock climbing or winter camping, which give the children an opportunity to experience success (sometimes for the first time), to build trust, to meet challenging goals, and to work co-operatively with each other. Partners for Youth is a good example of how investment from the school can further community goals and at the same time advance the interests of the school.

Parental influence on the curriculum, its delivery and the life of the school

A core curriculum for the schools is usually established at the provincial level, and here parents could have an input through an advisory council at the provincial level – where such councils exist. But it is not clear how often this happens. At the district level, school boards and parent advisory councils have the most authority on staffing, some curriculum decisions and school policy. Under the new legislation, parents in most provinces – through district parent advisory councils – can participate in the hiring of new staff (including principals), in decisions regarding the appropriate number of instructional hours at different ages and in the allocation of funds for such purposes as hiring a school librarian, a business manager, or a special educator. Again, given the fact that the reforms are very recent, it is not clear how widespread real participation is.

At the individual school level, parents are likely to contribute – through the parents' committee – to decisions concerning the development of certain curriculum subjects outside the provincial core curriculum. In some cases, school staff might decide to adopt a particular teaching strategy or orientation towards teaching, and usually its successful implementation requires the support of the parents. (The adoption of a "whole language" approach to instruction in the language arts is an example that has engendered considerable controversy in some schools.) Parents' expectations can have also a marked effect on daily routines and processes, sometimes referred to as the instructional "climate" of a school. School discipline is usually a major concern for parent committees. They may also make policy concerning truancy, the dress code and general conduct.

Parental influence on segregation – between and within schools – is an important and contentious issue in Canada. Some parents, especially those with academically gifted children, strongly favour it, whereas others do not. Students are often allocated to different schools, classrooms or instructional programmes through various formal and informal mechanisms, which can lead (intentionally or unintentionally) to segregation – according to ability, academic achievement, social class, gender, race or ethnicity. Segregation between different schools usually stems from residential segregation, but private schools, denominational schooling and charter or magnet schools[21] which offer parents more choice of school can lead to the increased segregation of different populations.

There is considerable research which suggests that when children are segregated, either between schools or within them, those with lower than average academic ability achieve considerably less, while those with above average ability achieve only marginally better. Because of this, Ontario has required schools to "destream" their academic offerings at the secondary level.

Within schools, students can be segregated between classrooms either formally by streaming into academic and vocationally oriented programmes, or informally through selection mechanisms such as standard-based test scores for entry into certain programmes. Programmes for gifted children and French immersion programmes contribute to segregation both between and within schools. There is potential for conflict here, because some members of parent committees may see segregation as a positive move, while others do not. For example, children with emotional and behavioural problems risk being segregated, because of the difficulties they pose to teachers; and other parents are often reluctant to have their children educated in a situation which they feel will impede their learning. A number of educators and policy-makers in Canada fear that influential parents may push for more segregative practices in the future.

The curriculum itself also represents an important medium for communication between school and home. Teachers find many ways of increasing communication – maybe by using interactive methods with students' parents, or through interviews with other family members or people in the community. Sometimes teachers in Canada use "student-led conferences" as part of their assessment; the student presents his or her work to both teacher and parents, and the group together evaluates the work.

Volunteering is another important way for parents and other family members (such as grandparents) to participate in school. In 1987, 26 per cent of Canadians from age 15 years and up volunteered in 9.2 million positions; 14 per cent of this work was connected to education or youth activities. A considerable amount of this work occurs in schools. Although the amount of volunteer support is considerable, the range of activities is limited and most of it occurs in the early grades. A survey in British Columbia found that the majority of schools have more than 8 parents volunteering each week.

The main types of services provided by volunteers are assistance to the teacher, for example in teaching small groups, in library resource work, remedial teaching, clerical work and supporting special education. The results of the surveys in British Columbia and Ontario showed that in many cases volunteers have moved beyond their traditional roles into a number of curriculum areas. The majority opinion was that the quality of school life and instruction was enhanced by volunteers and justified the organisational responsibilities of having them.

Communication between parents and schools

A key challenge to Canadian schools is to find appropriate ways of communicating with parents from extremely diverse racial, cultural and linguistic backgrounds. Schools need to be highly sensitive to the fact that successful communication needs to involve parents from different backgrounds – not only those from the middle classes or from favoured ethnic groups. In Halifax, Nova Scotia, the Department of Education has trained facilitators from outside the immediate community to carry out team building between schools and parents, and to explore more egalitarian methods of communication. Educators in British Columbia, especially those in urban areas serving large diverse immigrant populations, have also developed initiatives to increase communication between parents and schools.

One of the most important aspects of home-school communication concerns the evaluation of student progress. Methods of assessing students and reporting their results to parents are included in a number of provincial reforms. Neither parents nor teachers have been fully satisfied with the traditional report cards that reported only letter grades in each subject area. In the early 1990s, British Columbia attempted to reform this system by asking teachers to write anecdotal comments describing student progress – but the reaction from parents and local business groups was negative. They wanted standards-based information. This led to a new education plan to provide "clear, complete communication with parents about student progress, and public reporting of the school system's progress toward meeting educational goals". The idea is that the student reports (three formal and two informal per year) will form the basis for individual meetings between teachers and parents, and further co-operative action. In Ontario, a new standardised report card in all schools gives parents and students consistent information about student achievement three times a year.

Canada's important position in the telecommunications industry has encouraged schools to expand the use of technology in communicating with parents. A considerable number of schools in Canada already use the Internet and by 1997 virtually all 13 692 Canadian schools will be linked through "School Net". Besides telling the world about their school, community and students, schools will be able to provide electronic newsletters to parents and solicit volunteers. However, until computers become as widespread as televisions and telephones, this form of communication is not practical for most elementary and secondary school staff to communicate with families.

Another technological innovation available across New Brunswick and being considered by other provinces is a voice-mail telephone system which allows a sender to phone a message to selected homes to inform parents – about meetings for example. The provincial telephone company offers this service to schools, and gives instruction and support in setting up the system. This enables a teacher to make one phone call and leave a message for all students and parents in his or her class; to inform parents of upcoming events, clarify information about homework, and to provide ideas for home-based parent-child activities. A special dial tone indicates to parents that a message has been sent which they can retrieve by dialling a specific code. This technology has been available in New Brunswick since September 1994, and although not all schools use it the method is spreading.

Psycho-social support

Not all parents are equally able to support their children's learning at school. Significant research has shown that differences in class, race, and linguistic background have an effect on how well they can support their children. Increasingly, Canadian schools are becoming aware that partnerships between parents, school and community can contribute to helping parents acquire the necessary "parenting" skills to be able to establish a home environment that helps children develop in their work. Parents often need to be encouraged to express their needs, so that school staff can understand their concerns, values and views concerning their children.

An important aspect of school-based support for parents involves parental education of various kinds – particularly with regard to literacy skills, workshops related to aspects of the school curriculum, parenting skills (including topics such as child development and the problems of adolescence, and various forms of health education including sexuality and drug abuse). In Canada, however, such initiatives are not widespread; schools seem rather reluctant to enter this sensitive area. Success in this aspect of family-school co-operation requires the building up of long-term relationships of mutual trust; workshops, meetings and information are seldom sufficient.

However, there are some good examples of successful innovation, such as Ontario's "Family Learning Programme". Based in an urban working class neighbourhood, it enables the parents of young children to receive credit towards a high school certificate by taking various courses in literacy and parenting. The aim was for them to use their enhanced literacy in their parenting practices, and to this end they engaged in discussions and written reflection on a variety of issues. The programme was judged a success, in that the young parents began reading more at home, and half continued to work towards a high school diploma. They also adopted a wider range of parenting strategies during the programme.

Maternal Literacies, a project based in rural New Brunswick, encourages schools to give greater recognition to the important roles that rural mothers play in their younger children's learning, thus making parents feel more supported. In Manitoba, the Dauphin Ochre School Area encourages positive parenting practices through a "Parenting Page" on their Internet web site. The project is overseen by a school psychologist, and includes question and answer forums and discussion groups.

Some initiatives have been set in motion by parents themselves. For example, parents in some British Columbia high schools have established a system to contact other parents regarding student absence from school. The way that teachers handle student bullying, especially in adolescence, also concerns many parents.

Special needs

Provincial legislation requires school boards within each province to provide special needs students with educational services. However, local school authorities are left with decisions regarding *how* the services will be delivered. Provincial education legislation faced dramatic implications when the Charter of Rights and Freedoms was entrenched in the Canadian Constitution in 1982. The statement that Canadian citizens have the right not to be discriminated against because of colour or physical or mental disabilities put added pressure on the educational systems to make a commitment of full inclusion, and more importantly, the Charter gave parents (or guardians) a legal basis for their demands for inclusion.

Since the 1982 Charter, parents of children with special needs are increasingly advocating full integration for their children, with the legal backing of the Canadian Constitution to support and defend them. Inside the classroom, parents of special needs students have no extra legal rights than parents of other students; however, parents of students with special needs are often considered by teachers as a source of support for the integration process. Parental involvement in this process is an important factor in its success.

Consequently most Canadian schools have adopted "full inclusion" policies for children with special educational needs. The goal is to have all children taught in regular classrooms. These policies recognise that parents are integral partners in deciding how the needs of their children can best be met. Parent advocacy groups have also pushed for changes to the education system, and the parents of children with special needs are well-organised. In Ontario and Quebec, the school advisory committees normally include parents of students with disabilities.

The Charter is the primary tool that parents are now using to pressure governments to change. The view of a national survey of school principals was: "The education of special needs children has become very politicised and the extent to which students will receive equitable treatment mainly depends on the effort of lobby groups and whether the parents are articulate and well-versed in Charter guarantees" (Mackay, 1987).

Some children receive part of their schooling in special schools, which may be characterised by very full parental involvement. At the Montreal Oral School for the Deaf, for example, parent participation in the children's pre-school is mandatory, and communication with the school extends throughout the child's education. When a child is ready to enter a local mainstream school, parents are encouraged to function as advocates and to maintain their active participation with the new school. At the Centre for Gifted Education in Calgary, Alberta, school staff organise continuing education courses for parents with gifted children and publish a newsletter.

CONCLUSION

There has been considerable policy development and legislation aimed at increasing parents' involvement in the governance of schools across Canada. These measures have been successful, in that there are parent advisory committees in the majority of schools and by the year 2000 probably all schools will have them. Although these committees have only an advisory role and little legislative authority, parents can potentially have a strong influence on aspects of school climate, particularly those pertaining to discipline, expectations for academic success, student-staff relations and the allocation of students to schools, classrooms and curricular programmes.

Canada is also a world leader in advancing new forms of communication and will be the first country to link every school to Internet. Reforms aimed at integrating the curriculum and making instruction and assessment more authentic and transparent have also provided more opportunities for communication among students, parents and teachers. Better communication will likely ensue as reforms take hold.

Other aspects of co-operation between teachers and parents are less developed. Volunteering is common in some areas – at elementary school level more than at secondary. But, despite some very successful experiences, many teachers still do not feel comfortable having parents in the classroom while they are teaching – and there is little training available for either parents or teachers to support their efforts to work together. Yet teachers who spend the time to recruit parent volunteers and train them, however, often find their investment is well worthwhile. As parent committees across the country begin the process of defining their school's mission and setting long term plans, they could consider how their efforts at restructuring their schools could involve parents at all grade levels, and in a wider variety of roles.

One of the most important aspects of parental involvement is encouraging parents to help their children with school work. Canadian schools are increasingly coming to understand parents and schools need to communicate effectively if parents are to have the necessary information and understanding about what is expected of their children. Understanding and appreciating the role of parents – especially those who are disadvantaged – as their children's "first educators" is also an important step towards building up co-operation.

One way for schools to achieve more home and school co-operation is to ensure that parents are informed about teaching objectives, skill requirements for each subject, homework policy, a schedule of major assignments and information on how best to assist their children.

A number of innovative and effective programmes across Canada are exemplars of "what works" – parental involvement in the wider process of education is not yet widespread. For example, schools seem to be reluctant to get involved in helping parents develop better parenting skills or to extend their education mission much past the students enrolled in the school. If family-school co-operation in Canada is to increase, policies and practices need to move on to support the training of teachers and parents to work together in a productive partnership.

CASE STUDIES

Garden Creek School, Fredericton, New Brunswick

Garden Creek School is an elementary school situated on the outskirts of Fredericton serving a very diverse student population. It includes kindergarten to sixth grade, and all classrooms are fully integrated with students of varying ability levels. The school uses a variety of learning strategies which promote group learning activities, and all the pupils' activities, from desk work to free play to school events, are viewed as learning situations with an emphasis on co-operation, not competition. Teaching itself is seen as a learning process, and the staff are committed to professional development.

Parents are highly involved in school activities. Some volunteer to work with teachers in the classroom, tutoring students who have fallen behind or helping others with reading, or accompanying classes on field trips. The Methods and Resource teacher, who is in fact in charge of special educational needs, co-ordinates the parent volunteer programme. Parents tape books for children who cannot yet read, and come into school to speak to students and teachers on a variety of topics (for example, a father recently gave a lecture on Australia), while others speak about their occupations, or forthcoming cultural events.

The Lions Club, an association to which a number of parents belong, also supports the school. They have organised a series of training workshops for parents and teachers on subjects such as "Skills for growing", drug prevention, health care, and "Making choices in working life".

Parents participate in the school-parent committee, which has a fair amount of power; for example, the chair sits on the selection committee for hiring the principal. The committee's first meeting is in the autumn each year, combined with a social gathering to break the ice between staff and parents. Its official role is to: participate in setting the school mission and establishing school improvement plans; collaborate in school policies related to education, culture and language; and review results of the School Performance Reviews. The committee ensures that the language and culture of the school reflect the language group for which it is organised and provides suggestions on improving the physical plant and facilitating the use of the school by the community.

Community Academic Services Programme, New Brunswick

The Community Academic Services Programme (CASP) is a non-governmental organisation set up in New Brunswick to combat adult illiteracy. It was supported by the Minister of State for Literacy and Adult Education. Some 700 CASP programmes in 123 communities around the province have been established to upgrade adults' reading and writing skills. Many centres are based in schools and are attended by parents needing to raise their level of literacy to help their children with school work.

The programme had to invent an aggressive marketing approach to help overcome the stigma attached to illiteracy and returning to school. (Roughly one in ten students drop out, and many do not want to experience the anxiety of failing tests ever again.) The term "literacy" was found to be more acceptable than off-putting concepts such as spelling and grammar.

CASP is now seen as being as important for adults as Head Start is for pre-school children. Companies can "adopt" a community and help set up a CASP for unemployed workers. In the Acadian Peninsula, a CASP was established for workers in the fishing industry during the off-season. At the end of the programme, adults credit towards a graduate education diploma, which allows them to pursue further training at a community college. The programme has been found to have significant effects on the children of participating adults.

DENMARK

OVERVIEW

The Danish education system is undergoing a long process of reform which has a twofold underlying rationale: a general political impetus towards decentralisation, and a specific desire to develop the Danish *Folkeskole* and raise educational standards which have been causing concern in recent years. Overall responsibility for the *Folkeskole*,[22] including their funding, has been pushed down from the Ministry of Education in Copenhagen to the 275 local municipalities, and parents now dominate the school boards which oversee each individual *Folkeskole*.

In most *Folkeskole*, there is a very close relationship between parents and their children's teachers, and the system of class councils makes for a high degree of parental involvement at the classroom level. Teachers are responsible for both the academic and the social development of their charges, and are expected to get to know them and their families well – a real strength in the Danish education system. As part of the recent reform movement, they have been encouraged to build partnerships with the local community as well.

The Danish system offers parents quite a high level of influence. No other country, for example, has a majority of parents on its school boards,[23] and the boards have recently been reformed with the aim of increasing their involvement in making policy for the school. But there is disappointment in some quarters concerning the degree to which parents are genuinely exploring the possibilities of their new powers of governance, and by the fact that – after a brief surge in interest around the time of the reforms – parental participation in school boards elections remains low. Parental fatigue (since in most families both parents work), a certain passivity, and the unwillingness of some headteachers to share their power are all cited as reasons.

There is also some concern that some municipalities are not delegating enough power to their school boards, and that the new law does not give parents sufficient hands-on involvement in running the schools. For example, teaching methods, standards of achievement and assessment are seen as the business of the teaching profession, and as outside the remit of the school boards – yet these are aspects of education in which parents are highly interested and regarding which there has been some criticism of the Folkeskole. The teachers' union is strong in Denmark, and in many cases, the school board still tends to follow the lead of the headteacher, accepting (sometimes reluctantly) that he or she knows most about the inner workings of the school.

If the head is in favour of involving parents – and some are very committed to the policy – a fruitful partnership can be built up. Indeed, an alliance between the board and the headteacher can be a powerful combination, especially if a head wants to move faster than his or her staff. But if there is no genuine commitment to working with parents, it seems fairly easy in Denmark for the headteacher to withhold information from the board, or in other ways prevent it from exercising its full influence.

SOCIAL BACKGROUND

Danish families have a wide choice of school; private schools, which are attended by 11 per cent of Danish children, are heavily supported by state funding, and if a group of parents wants to set up their own school, the government will pay the cost. The state covers 80-85 per cent of the cost, and the parents pay 15-20 per cent. This degree of freedom means that close parental involvement in their children's education has for many years been taken for granted as a right. Today, however, patterns of work and family life in Denmark are very different from in the past. For example, only 10 per cent of women of child-bearing age are not involved in the world of work, and in 1995, 16 per cent of children under 18 were living with a single parent – two thirds of whom were in employment.

In particular, there seems to be a widespread conflict between the demands of work and family life. Although three out of four Danish men play their part in housework, both parents are often tired and have less time to spend with their children. The changing nature of children's experience results in new tasks for the schools. According to the White Paper on education published in 1987: "Young people have insufficient contact with their parents, and [this] poses new challenges for the Folkeskole. It is not that the teacher should take over the role of parents, but the daily contact between teacher and pupil does offer the children an extension of adult contacts. For this reason, the necessary time must be allowed for this process, especially in the case of the class tutor".

Until 20 years ago, Denmark was a very homogeneous culture. Now – although compared to many other countries immigration has been modest – Danish society is more pluralist than it used to be. In 1992, about 3 per cent of the population were immigrants, mostly from Turkey, the Middle East, Bosnia and Pakistan. Most are concentrated in Copenhagen. In 1995-96, nearly 36 000 pupils come from families who did not speak Danish as a first language. This has caused some stresses and strains in a system which very much runs on taken-for-granted tradition and consensus, but is also committed to "bottom up" change. Schools have their well-established methods of communicating with parents, and are not accustomed to "outreach" work, or to soliciting contact with parents who may feel uneasy coming into school or communicating with the teachers – who may not speak Danish or understand the way the system works.

POLICY CONTEXT

Since the late 1960s, the Danish political system has tended towards decentralisation, and this tendency has recently been intensified by an overt shift of power from the central government to the 275 local municipalities. The idea behind the most recent moves towards decentralisation is that central government should govern through "goals and frameworks" rather than through the control and supervision of details.

In any decentralised system, there is of course a risk of significant differences in standards from area to area – in this case from municipality to municipality. But throughout Denmark there is a strong sense of consensus with regard to education – and a long-established national curriculum. This makes for an unusually coherent system and set of educational values in comparison with many other countries, even if local manifestations differ. However, there is some anxiety among Danish educationists that unacceptable variations are developing between schools in different municipalities.

The liberal politicians who came to power in 1982 were dissatisfied with the amount of real power exercised by parents, and distrustful of the grip that the teaching profession had on the system – which they saw as somewhat complacent and underperforming. In 1989, the Danish Parliament passed a new set of administrative regulations which, when they came into force in 1990, gave parents new responsibilities through the school boards – which were themselves given more autonomy. The Danes themselves seem to feel uneasy using the vocabulary of power; they prefer to conceptualise such shifts in terms of talk about managing the consensus.

The heart of the Danish education system is the Folkeskole – the network of comprehensive schools which are attended by all Danish children[24] for between nine and ten years, usually from the age of seven until 16 or 17.[25] Folkeskole are the essence of the Danish educational tradition, having been in existence since 1814, when Danish children were first given the right to seven years of education – with a national curriculum consisting of religion, reading, writing and arithmetic. Since then, only five major changes have been made to Denmark's education legislation[26] – in spite of its history of frequent minor adjustments and adaptations.

The current reforms have been based on a nationwide research and development programme which began in 1987.[27] The approach which has been taken is in tune with the Danish educational tradition of developing new initiatives "from the bottom up". The aim of the reforms is not only to improve the running of the *Folkeskole* and to raise academic standards, but to promote the building up of local cultural centres based on the schools, so that children, parents and grandparents, as well as other members of the community, can meet on the school premises and carry out activities together.

WHY INVOLVE PARENTS?

Although Danish teachers and policy-makers agree that parental support helps children to achieve academically, this reason is rarely cited in the policy documents. Most of the thinking behind the policies aimed at encouraging parental involvement in schooling is related to a wish to extend democracy, and to increase the participation of the ordinary citizen in all aspects of public life.

Compared with some other OECD Member countries, the Danes often seem relatively relaxed about levels of academic achievement. There is little doubt, however, that an underlying aim of the reform programme – in which increased parental involvement is a crucial element – is to improve the quality of education offered by the *Folkeskole*. What's more, Danish students have recently been coming out rather badly on international surveys of reading achievement. In 1994, the results of research which compared reading standards of 10-year-olds led to a certain amount of shock in Denmark and some questioning of standards in the *Folkeskole*.

There is particularly a strong tradition in Denmark of involving children and young people in the schools. For example, the law provides for every school which includes pupils above the fifth grade (aged about 11 years) to set up a student council consisting of two students elected from every class in the school – in some schools right down to 7-year-olds. Student councils normally meet quite frequently – meet about once a month. Those who have been elected are given a preparatory training programme which explains the function and structure of the council and its meetings and how they can take part. Such participation is seen as important training for citizenship. The council elects two pupils to represent it at meetings of the school board. In some municipalities, such as the City of Copenhagen, the students on the board have voting rights. In others, they do not.

THE LEGISLATION

Parents in Denmark have been legally responsible since 1814 for making sure that their children are educated – although this education need not necessarily be in school. Over the last 30 years or so, legislation has increasingly given parents rights with regard to the running of schools. The most recent legislation offers a broad framework rather than a great deal of detail, in order to make room for local differences:

- The **Law of 1970** gave Danish parents the right to be represented on the school board of their children's school.
- In **1975**, the Basic School Law ruled that schools should co-operate with parents in relation to all the tasks of the school.
- In **1990**, a set of new regulations decentralised decision-making in education from the central government to the municipalities, and from the municipalities to the school boards. The composition of the boards was altered so that parents dominated, and their sphere of responsibility was extended.
- The **Law of 1993** confirmed the structure and purpose of the *Folkeskole* and reformed the content of reaching and learning. Under the new legislation: "The *Folkeskole* shall – in co-operation with the parents – further the pupils' acquisition of knowledge, skills, working methods and ways of expressing themselves, and thus contribute to the all-round personal development of the individual pupil". The expression "co-operation with parents" is central to the act, and is expected to be taken seriously and put into practice.
- The **Law of 1993** also established the *Folkeskole* Council, to oversee the development of the schools. This is a body of 15 members, of which two must be parents and two students.

KEY ELEMENTS OF CO-OPERATION BETWEEN SCHOOL AND FAMILY

Parental involvement in school governance

The law of 1990 has given Danish parents new powers in the management of *Folkeskole*, through the school boards. In the past, they had jurisdiction over the day-to-day aspects of school life. The reformers concluded that such responsibilities were too time-consuming and trivial, distracting parents from thinking about the real role of the school and discouraging them from coming forward to serve on boards. So today their role is to establish aims, objectives and policy directions for the school, while managerial and administrative issues have been handed over to the headteacher.

Legislation since 1990 has given Danish parents, potentially, a strong voice on individual school boards. Each board consists of either five or seven parent members, two student members, two teachers, and a co-opted member if the municipality so desires. The headteacher is not a voting member, but attends each meeting and acts as secretary. The chairman of the board is always a parent.

School board members are elected every four years, in the same year as the municipal elections. The school board elections take place in the individual schools, and the parent representatives are elected from and among the parents and guardians of children at the school. Other members of the board (teacher, other school staff, and students) are elected annually. Along with some of the municipalities, Skole og Samfund (see below) offers training to parents elected to school boards. Parents who – for whatever reason – become board members in mid-term often do not receive any training.

Concern that parents were not coming forward onto school boards in sufficient numbers resulted in legislation changing the duties of the boards. But the numbers of parents standing for election, after a brief surge when the new law was passed, has fallen back to the previous disappointing level. The power of the boards, many people consider, depends on individuals grasping the opportunity presented, and testing the limits of what they can do. For example, although school boards cannot hire or fire teaching staff (as some would like), they have a great deal of influence with the municipality. They can interview prospective headteachers and make recommendations, and there are examples of boards complaining about staff – even principals – who are then removed.

But there is also a body of opinion which believes that the law should be reframed in order to return to boards the responsibility for everyday matters. Passing these over to the principal, it is argued, gives him or her too much influence over the inner workings of the school. The new legislation, which sought to give more power to parents by strengthening the rights of the school board in relation to the teaching body, seems in effect to have taken power from the teachers only to give it to the principal. And, the argument goes, drafting the overall philosophy and aims of the institution is ultimately dissatisfying, when school boards have no way making sure that their words are translated into practice. Not everyone agrees with this interpretation, however, and a governmental committee is currently reviewing the workings of the act, and recommending how parents could be encouraged to participate with more enthusiasm.

Upper secondary schools, which offer a general education to about 45 per cent of post 16-year-olds, normally to prepare them for university or further education or training, are under the jurisdiction of the counties. Their school boards are made up of: representatives of the county council and the municipal councils of the catchment area; parents; staff; and students. Total numbers vary according to the county, but the member who come from outside the school must outnumber those who are elected from inside. Parents are not in the majority. Other stakeholders, such as local business people, can also sit on the board. The headteacher participates, but does not have a vote.

The board's duties include setting the school's budget (within a framework drawn up by the county council), fixing class sizes, establishing the rules of the school, and deciding (on the headteacher's recommendation) which optional subjects should be taught. The board is also expected to play its part in encouraging co-operation between the school, the students' homes and the local community, and to contribute to the solution of any social problems which arise within this relationship. The headteacher is not only the pedagogic and administrative leader for the school, but is also the local representative of the Ministry of Education. He or she is responsible for all matters connected with the teaching in the school and its management, and plays a stronger role *vis-à-vis* the school board than is the case in the *Folkeskole*.

A national voice for parents

Danish parents have the ear of the Ministry of Education through *Skole og Samfund* (School and Society) – the national organisation of parents' associations. This organisation represents 96 per cent of parental groups, including school board members, parents' associations and individual parents. *Skole og Samfund* co-ordinates parents' views, and, by law, must be consulted by the government on certain policy issues. It also receives information and documentation from the Ministry of Education on a regular basis.

Parents are fully represented on governmental working parties and committees, notably the *Folkeskole* Council, which was set up in 1993. Parents recommended by *Skole og Samfund* are elected to the council for a three-year term. Employers are supposed to give parents paid leave to attend such meetings, and school board meetings too, but in reality workers often find it hard to ask for this right.

The goal of the organisation is to strengthen the *Folkeskole*, and increase the amount of co-operation between school and home. It offers its members support and education – through offering courses on subjects such as co-operation between home and school, the effective operation of school boards, and financial decentralisation. The organisation also runs meetings for parents, and provides information through its magazine, leaflets, educational games, specialist book service, and telephone hotline. Help is offered in solving problems – particularly with regard to interpreting the law.

The school and the community

An important aspect of the recent reforms is the aim that schools should develop into local cultural centres, offering adult education and leisure options to local residents. So the relationship between schools and parents in Denmark should be seen in the context of this development. The main idea behind it is that of coherence. The aim is to create "coherence between generations, and between local activities, through which local identity is strengthened and the division which characterises society in general is counteracted. The school is intended to become a focal point for the local society which in turn could improve students' learning processes by broadening them" (Hogsbro *et al.*, 1991).

Schools now have a legal duty to solicit feedback from pupils and their parents, and the Ministry is also encouraging them to take the opinions of the local community into account as well. About 50 of the reform projects mentioned above involve linking the school more closely to its community – but so far only those schools involved in the projects are developing this approach.

Evening classes for adults, covering a wide range of subjects, are common in Denmark and enthusiastically followed by large numbers of people. Often they are held in *Folkeskole*, or in other local institutions. The vast majority, though, are organised by private promoters, so although the *Folkeskole* buildings may be in use, these classes do not act as a real link between the school itself and the community. Except in schools involved in pilot projects, real openness seems to be the exception rather than the rule. There needs to be further thought and planning concerning how far communities see their local *Folkeskole* as being as a natural part of the community, and also what the school might offer to it.

Parental influence on the curriculum, its delivery and the life of the school

There are three main aspects of parental involvement in the curriculum and its delivery in the classroom. The first involves the establishment of the Danish curriculum at national level. The Parliament (*Folketing*) and the Ministry of Education set the targets for each subject. Under the new law, the Ministry has established a national curriculum framework of "central knowledge and skills", rather than seeking to control the curriculum through detailed regulations. Parents can influence this procedure through their representation on the various committees which establish the national curriculum framework (the central knowledge and skills), but it is not clear how much notice, in practice, is taken of their views.

Secondly, the municipalities and the schools between them are responsible for deciding how best to achieve these targets. The headteachers in each municipality meet regularly – often as frequently as once every two weeks. Parents, on the other hand, do not have any say at municipal level, and the school boards only meet a few times a year. This is an important gap in the system, and sometimes results in parents being excluded from important curriculum decisions.

In some areas, parents serving on school boards have become very much engaged in interpreting the curriculum framework to suit the needs of their school – but municipalities do vary a great deal as to how much freedom they are prepared to give their school. What's more, school boards are normally excluded from influencing aspects of the curriculum such as classroom practices and teaching methods, which are explicitly outside their remit, being the business of the pedagogical council.[28] Yet this type of issue is frequently one which parents want to explore.

The third aspect of involvement in the curriculum concerns its delivery to the students. Although parents are encouraged to be involved and help in the work of the class, and often play a key role in curriculum-related activities outside the school, they are rarely seen assisting in classrooms. This is partly because the Danes emphasise, justifiably, that "education" does not necessarily have to happen in school. But since most parents work, it is hard for them to get involved during the day. A number of reform projects, however, involve parents as guest teachers, especially when classes go on expeditions outside the school. In some project schools, parents and teachers have planned aspects of the curriculum together. The 1993 Alcuin Award was won by a Danish *Folkeskole* teacher who for more than ten years has been involving parents in curriculum development. The jury noted that "Mrs. Rolsted actually discussed, planned and set up her entire programme in close consultation with the parents of her students".

As in many other countries, parents are – as the Danes say – "partners in pedagogy". Schools encourage parents to help their children at home, and may offer suggestions on how to support their learning. One favourite is the strategy of using the evening meal as a forum for discussing school progress or for exploring topics which are being studied at school, which is also seen as a way of strengthening communication within the family. But whether parents are seen as genuinely equal partners is another question. Most Danish teachers welcome the involvement of parents when it is focused on supporting them and the school – but are perhaps less willing to concede that parents have a right to challenge classroom practices.

Communication between parents and schoolds

Denmark has a long tradition of co-operation and contact with parents, especially when children are younger. The education of children is seen as a collaborative matter, requiring a continuous dialogue between parents, teachers and pupils. Class teachers hold meetings every year to discuss with parents the curriculum plan for that year, and sometimes meet again to consider how far it has been fulfilled. Many also produce newsletters (sometimes written by pupils) or write to parents regularly.

Danish parents have a legal right to be informed at least twice a year concerning the academic and social progress of their children – but not necessarily in writing. Verbal reports, interviews and conversations are seen as an important part of the process. Danish children do not receive marks before the age of 13 or 14 (eighth grade). From then, they must receive a written report at least twice a year, giving their level of attainment, in terms of both academic achievement and application, on a 13-point scale.

Assessment is not always focused on academic achievement. Social and emotional development is highly valued in the Danish system, and parents and teachers work together in supporting their children. Since most class teachers stay with the same class of children throughout their school career, teachers and parents come to know each other well. Each set of parents normally forms a "class council", and chooses three or four "contact parents" who, ideally, act as a link between the parents and the teacher, and pass on information in both directions.

However, it can be hard to get all parents involved, and often the burden falls on a few committed individuals whose very enthusiasm can then put others off. The President of Skole og Samfund believes that if class councils were restructured to make them more representative, parental influence could become a more vital element in schools. He suggests that each class should choose five or six contact parents for two to three years, with half being changed annually. The class would be divided into five or six groups, each with a specific contact parent, which would meet regularly to discuss school matters. Over the nine years most Danish children spend in the Folkeskole, parents would become closely bonded, forming a "social and educational village", and the real agenda of the parents would emerge more readily. Skole og Samfund is encouraging schools to use this model; only about one in ten does so currently, but a much larger number are now moving towards it.

There is an impressive amount of individual, informal contact in the Folkeskole. Teachers will call on parents at home if they need to discuss something, and it is normal for Danish parents to be given teachers' home telephone numbers, and to call them out of school hours – even at the weekend. Each teacher's salary includes an element representing paid hours for working with the class and the parents – in groups or individually. This includes informal contacts with parents – even discussions in, say, the street or local shops. A survey[29] carried out in 1989-90 showed that Danish parents telephone their children's teachers very frequently. One reason why this high degree of contact is acceptable to teachers is that classes in the Folkeskole are very small by international standards; the number of pupils may not exceed 28, and the average number today is about 19.

Psycho-social support

The close relationship established between parents and teachers in the Folkeskole means that parents and children with problems receive a great deal of support. Teachers are responsible for making sure that pupils develop acceptable attitudes and values, in partnership with the parents. Denmark has fewer social problems than many other OECD countries, and intervention to help disadvantaged families improve their parenting practices and general level of education – which has become widespread in countries such as Ireland, the United States and England and Wales – is not, however, very common in Denmark.

Special needs

Children with special needs are identified at an early stage (before the age of one year) by a local health visitor who carries out developmental testing in the home. Virtually all those who are identified as needing special educational help are educated in mainstream classes; in 1993-94, about 1.3 per cent of the school population (6 597 pupils) suffered from a severe handicap of one kind or another. Of these, almost half were being educated in special schools, and about one in three was being taught in special classes within the Folkeskole. Some 22 per cent were interested into mainstream classes. This policy – which is often more complex from an educational point of view – is a result of the wishes of parents, and has developed into a general "principle of nearness", whereby children with special needs are taught, as far as possible, close to home and their peer group.

The close attention paid to the individual child's development by his or her class teacher, in partnership with the parents, means that a wide range of problems[30] are identified relatively early. About 13 per cent of the school population is receiving some sort of special education at any given time, and overall about one in four pupils will receive additional help at some stage during their school career (ranging from a few extra lessons over a couple of months to extensive specialised help).

CONCLUSION

The great strength of the Danish system is its sense of coherence. Virtually everyone – parents, teachers, students, the general population – seems to share in a broad consensus as to what education is for, and the direction in which it should be going. Parents are accustomed to being involved at every stage of the education process, and forms of participation which would be seen as very radical in other countries are taken for granted in Denmark as part of the fabric of normal life.

At the same time, however, in spite of vigorous efforts at reform, there is a danger of drift and, perhaps, complacency. Denmark has a generally homogenous and well-educated population and long-established traditions. This gives rise to a public perception that the system works well and can almost be left to run itself.

This works against real liveliness and activism and there is a risk of passivity and withdrawal from civic responsibility.

As the population changes and becomes more pluralistic, new forms of reaching out to ethnic minority parents and community will need to be developed. The shift towards making schools into community cultural centres is an imaginative move. Such changes, as Danish policy-makers are well-aware, need to grow from the bottom up in order to make an impact at the grassroots; but as yet there is still a feeling that they are "top down".

CASE STUDIES

Matthoeusgades Skoles Kulturcenter

This small *Folkeskole* (250 pupils) is situated in one of the most ethnically-mixed and deprived areas of Copenhagen – indeed of the whole of Denmark – and in 1990 was earmarked for closure. However, following the appointment of a new headteacher, it was decided to transform the school into a local cultural centre – a particularly innovative notion in an inner-city setting. Within five years, pupil numbers had markedly increased. Today, the school has more applicants than it has room for, and is no longer at risk of closure. The initiative was initially funded for three years with development money from the central government. Since then, the City of Copenhagen – the local municipality – has covered the main costs (11 extra teacher hours).

This brightly-decorated and lively school, under its active and charismatic principal, has developed close relationships between the school and its parents, and draws imaginatively on the resources of the local community. About 40 per cent of the children are from ethnic minorities, mostly Muslim. The headteacher, Lars Bjorner, is particularly concerned that all parents and children should feel that they belong to the school, and that the school belongs to them.

The school has established itself as a gathering place in the afternoons and evenings. During the winter, more than 400 local people of all ages attend each week, to take adult education courses, to join in cultural activities, and simply to meet each other. The children, their parents, and all school employees – the school secretary, the caretaker, the cleaners and the medical staff, as well as the teachers – are automatically members of the cultural centre. More than 700 others have paid a small fee to join, and receive the school newspaper ten times a year.

Parents and members of the cultural centre are welcomed at any time, and the school has developed strong links with the two social centres in the same street, and with a centre for senior citizens which is situated next door. There are a large number of co-operative activities. For example, elderly people from the centre can – and do – join school classes. They also act as guest teachers, telling students about their school days, or about their wartime experiences. On Fridays, half a dozen senior citizens from the centre join forces with ten children aged between 6 and 9, and together cook a hot lunch for all 75 children in the three youngest grades. This means that the whole group ends the week by sharing a meal (unusual in Denmark, where packed school lunches are the norm). Every year, the whole school goes for a week to the seaside along with parents and senior citizens, and three generations get to know each other better.

The principal is quite sure that the school as a whole, and the quality of learning which it offers, have benefited enormously from these links. He is not afraid to state his belief, however, that the parents and community members are not equal partners with the teachers, since they are not education professionals.

Hummeltofteskolen

In this school, a group of the teachers have been working on a project to improve communication between parents and the school. Teacher, parent and child form a triangle, the teachers point out, and each one of the three must play its part. Class teachers write to the parents five or six times a term giving them news of school events, details of the curriculum, and advice on how to help their children. Normally, they meet each set of parents twice a year for 15 minutes to discuss the child's progress.

The teachers have been experimenting with assessment forms, especially for the younger pupils, which parents and children can fill in and discuss before meeting the teacher. In particular, the children have been asked to assess their own progress and development by colouring in a series of happy, sad or indifferent faces for different elements of their school life – including aspects such as feeling at ease in the playground. This approach – which has been approved by the school board – offers a more focused starting point for the conversation between parent, child and teacher.

The students' council is particularly active in *Hummeltofteskolen*. The students agree that, as pupils get older, parents should naturally hand over responsibility to them – and that the system works well. The chairman is a member of the school board, which meets once a month, and has a vote, so he can speak for the pupils in the school. Every class has two representatives who contact him with suggestions or complaints, and there is also a student council mail box. The student council's most recent achievement has been the installation of a soda machine, whose profits go to the school. There is a certain amount of discontent over the curriculum; several students would like more say over, for example, what themes are studied in English lessons. Since the reforms, teachers have been encouraged to co-operate more in planning their lessons – and one effect seems to be that less attention is now paid to the opinions of students.

Grantofteskolen

This *Folkeskole* of 575 pupils is in the municipality of Ballerup, about 20 kilometres from Copenhagen, which has the reputation of being a forward-looking municipality. Many local authorities tend simply to adopt the curriculum laid down from the centre, but Ballerup has taken advantage of its freedom within the framework to construct its own local curriculum based on the national guidelines. Parents, teachers, education advisors and students have all been involved.

Each school board (consisting of parents and students) must approve the new curriculum, and most will modify it slightly, putting their individual stamp on it. In Ballerup there is a strong common culture, which is encouraged by the local director of education. He meets the headteachers of Ballerup's ten *Folkeskole* every two weeks, so that they can discuss developments, share problems and make decisions together. All the school boards meet at least four times a year.

Grantofteskolen has been designated a local cultural centre, and is open to the community every Monday night. These Open Evenings are run by parents, and attract between 50 and 100 people for recreation and a meal. Teachers who are attending meetings may come too. Part of the social administration for the municipality has been decentralised to the local neighbourhood, and these meetings too take place at the school.

Parents are influential through the school board, and receive a weekend of training, paid for by the municipality, after they have been elected. Students, too, are offered a two- or three-day course to learn democratic procedures – then they elect two of their number to the board. This process is taken very seriously as part of the education of a citizen in a democracy.

The school board at *Grantofteskolen* is currently in the throes of discussions as to whether to modify the school timetable. Students, the headteacher and the board are unanimous in wanting to release four or five weeks a year from the strict timetable. For the last ten years, one week per year has been spent in students working in the workshops of their choice; and another has been spent exclusively with the class teacher. The principal is convinced of the educational benefits of such flexibility, and would like the number of free weeks to be increased; but a group of the more conservative teachers are not in favour of the plan. In the past, the teachers' pedagogical council would have had the final word. But now, the new-style school board, which is responsible for the overall direction and philosophy of the school, has the right to approve it.

ENGLAND AND WALES

OVERVIEW

There is currently a great deal of emphasis on parental involvement in England and Wales – especially in terms of government policy, which has undergone a revolution in the last 15 years or so. But as well as a whole raft of national legislation, there is also a plethora of local authority and individual school-based initiatives, funded from a variety of sources (see Bastiani and Wolfendale, 1996).

Overall, four key elements are characteristic of national school-family policies. First is the shift towards viewing parents – and encouraging them to see themselves – as consumers making choices, and having the right to a certain quality of service. Secondly is the involvement of more parents in the governance of schools, in order to make the schools more accountable to the local community. Thirdly is the emphasis on improving the achievement of children, especially young and disadvantaged children, by developing more effective partnerships between school and parents. And fourthly – very characteristic of the English and Welsh approach – are moves to encourage parents to get involved in classroom activities and around the school, especially at primary level, to support the teachers and their children's learning.

In comparison with some other countries, it is noticeable that parents in the United Kingdom do not have a recognised national voice or form of representation which is influential at the policy-making level – particularly with regard to decision-making committees, the new agencies, or the national curriculum. Similarly, at local education authority (LEA) level they have no legally-endorsed means of influencing local decisions – although they do have some form of representation in about one third of LEAs (O'Connor, 1994).

As well as the national push towards increased parental choice and influence on the schools themselves, there is an enormous amount of locally-funded home-school work going on across the country, especially with disadvantaged parents – to enable them to support their children's learning more effectively, develop their own skills and qualifications, and move into a more equal partnership with teachers. And overall it is clear that progress is being made; the key emphases are now shifting away from the preoccupations of the early days (the need to tackle long-established resistances to new ways of working, for example) towards issues of quality and effectiveness, the need to maintain and further develop the work, and "second order" questions such as "where do we go from here?".

SOCIAL BACKGROUND

Efforts to foster co-operation between home and school need to take account of the rapidly changing nature of British society. Life for many is increasingly urbanised and controlled, and many children – living in flats or near to busy roads – have less opportunity than in the past to socialise freely with their peers. What's more, according to the latest available evidence,[31] only one in four children currently in British classrooms comes from a long-term two parent "traditional" nuclear family, in which the father goes out to work and the mother stays at home while the children are young. Many children of school age, therefore, are experiencing in varying degrees: single-parent, multi-generational or "combined" families; pressurised working mothers; the effects of parental separation, divorce and remarriage; difficulties associated with speaking English as a second language and/or belonging to an ethnic minority; being fostered or in care; long-term unemployment of one or both parents; inadequate accommodation. Many of these phenomena are associated with stress, poverty and dependence on state benefits. At the same time, parents who are in work often have less time than ever to spend with their children.

These changes mean that schools need to develop flexibility in order to meet a wide range of family needs – at a time when educational standards and the demand for skills and qualifications are rising. Many schools under pressure do realise that their parents could be an important resource – with the potential for making their teaching more effective and the lives of their staff less difficult – once teachers have learned how to work in partnership with them and draw on their strengths.

POLICY CONTEXT

Education policy in England and Wales has seen many changes since the early 1980s, notably those enshrined in the 1988 Education Reform Act, which centralised education standards by establishing a national curriculum and regular assessment procedures, while at the same time reducing the power of the local education authorities and transforming schools into semi-autonomous units in charge of their own financial affairs. Schools are now funded on a per capita basis, so the pressure is to compete for pupils by offering what parents want.[32] Brown (1990) describes education policy dictated by the needs and wishes of parents as a "parentocracy" – and suggests that it will be the next phase to follow the current meritocracy.

Not only were LEAs required to delegate their school budgets to the schools, but parents were encouraged to vote that their schools should "opt out" of local council control entirely and become Grant Maintained (GM), receiving their funds directly from central government through the Funding Agency for Schools.[33] About 7.8 per cent of pupils attend independent fee-paying schools, and through the government-funded Assisted Places Scheme parents who could not otherwise afford private schooling for their child can get help with the school fees.

All these policies reflect the British government's intention to encourage parents to see themselves as consumers, and to increase the choices available to them. Much parent-related legislation has involved increasing the amount of information which schools must provide to parents, so that they can make more informed choices.

At the same time, another – and more long-standing – influence has been at work. During the late 1960s and early 1970s, academic research revealed wide-spread and persistent inequalities of opportunity and achievement in British education. Since parental attitude, level of education and socio-economic back-ground were key features in such inequalities, a number of major initiatives have since then been introduced, at both national and local levels, focused mainly on parents living in multiracial inner-city neighbourhoods and on large municipal housing estates, and aimed at raising the attainment of their children. More recently, research has shown good home-school relations to be a characteristic of effective (*i.e.* high-achieving) schools. As a result, home-school activities, rather than being peripheral to the life and work of the school, have moved to centre stage and increasingly involve the key processes of teaching and learning.

WHY INVOLVE PARENTS?

So, the key reasons for involving parents in their children's schooling in the English and Welsh context tend to fall into three categories:

- parental choice and involvement is seen as a lever for raising standards in schools, and encouraging parents to act (with government backing) as critical consumers;

- mobilising parents was one way of trying to change the "education establishment";

- if children – especially those who are disadvantaged – are to achieve their full potential, their parents need to understand and be involved with their learning and confident in their relationship with the school.

97

THE LEGISLATION

- **1980:** The Education Act allows parents to express a preference for the school of their choice, and established the Assisted Places Scheme.

  Parents are given increased representation on governing bodies, and the right to information concerning the curriculum and organisation of the school.

- **1981:** The parents of children with special educational needs (SEN) were given the right to participate in the assessment of those needs, and in an annual review of the statement of special educational needs.

- **1986:** The Education Act (No. 2) describes parents' responsibilities within school governing bodies, and institutes an annual school governors' report to parents at an obligatory meeting.

- **1988:** The Education Reform Act, through establishing open enrolment, strengthens parents' rights to choose their children's schools, and to appeal should a school refuse to admit their child. Schools are required to give parents more information concerning a child's programme of work, and his or her progress within it. Parents are given the right to vote their school out of local education authority control.

- **1989:** The Children Act gives priority to the welfare of children, and outlines parents' rights and responsibilities.

- **1991:** The Parent's Charter (see below).

- **1992:** Parents to be consulted before schools are inspected by the Office for Standards in Education.

- **1993:** New code of practice for the assessment of special educational needs, including extension of parents' rights in SEN assessment and decision-making.

- **1994:** The updated Parent's Charter.

KEY ELEMENTS OF CO-OPERATION BETWEEN SCHOOL AND FAMILY

Parental involvement in school governance

As the result of successive Education Acts, all schools in England and Wales must have an individual governing body which works within a clear constitution and wields considerable power. Each governing body consists of parents (elected by the parents of children in the school), teachers (elected by their colleagues), the headteacher (normally), political representatives of the local education authority, and community representatives (usually co-opted).

The governing bodies of schools in England and Wales have more power than similar bodies in most other countries. The school governors must:

- be accountable for the performance of the school;
- plan the school's future direction;
- select the headteacher;
- make decisions on the school's budget and teaching;
- make sure the national curriculum is taught;
- decide on how the school can encourage pupils' spiritual, moral and cultural development;
- make sure that the school provides for all its pupils, including those with special educational needs (Department of Education and Employment, 1996).

Parent governors, although in a minority, are potentially very influential members of school governing bodies. They are likely to be most effective if: they represent the whole range of parental background, culture and experience; they are supported through training programmes; they can communicate with other parents through newsletters and school "surgeries"; and if they genuinely canvass other parents' views. Naturally, these ideal conditions are rarely all present in the same governing body.

A national voice for parents

The issue of giving parents an official voice is both unclear and problematic in England and Wales. Unlike many other countries, particularly in Europe, parents do not have any legal right to form a collective body to represent their views, at national, local or school levels. Neither are parents consulted officially, or regularly, by governments or their departments. Many school parents' associations and parent-teacher associations are affiliated to the National Confederation of Parent-Teacher Associations (NCPTA), which is active, frequently quoted, and normally responds to consultation documents issued by government. It is not clear, however, how far its pronouncements reflect the overall view of parents – as opposed to teachers – and it has no official status or recognition. The National Consumer Council has recently convened an Education Forum of some 16 organisations (including the NCPTA, the Advisory Center for Education and the National Home-School Development Group). The agreed remit of the Education Forum is "to promote a wider discussion of current issues among the whole range of organisations representing parents and pupils, and to improve arrangements for communication, consultation and liaison between the education consumer lobby and other professional and political groups, especially government".

Recent research has established that fewer than one in three local education authorities has parent representatives on their education committees. Just over one third of LEAs has some kind of system for consulting school governors, parent governors and/or parents about policy issues, or bringing them into the decision-making process in some other way. A small minority of authorities are "enthusiastic supporters of parental involvement, and are putting significant effort into encouraging participation".

Similarly, there is no legal right or requirement to form a parents' association or parent-teacher association within a school, and the most effective structure for such an organisation is nowhere officially defined (although the NCPTA and other bodies offer model constitutions). Class councils on the German or Danish model, though still unusual, are becoming more common (see case study). Most English or Welsh schools have some kind of parent or joint parent-teacher association, and many are very active. Their activities, though, are often dominated by fund-raising, and the relationship between such associations and the parent governors is often unclear.

The school and the community

England and Wales has for decades had a community school movement – and certain local authorities (notably Leicestershire) have taken it very seriously, building schools which included community services such as public libraries or swimming pools, sports halls, or senior citizens clubs, or rooms for local meetings. In Cambridgeshire, virtually all the secondary schools have been community schools or "village colleges" since the 1920s, a concept which is at least 50 years old. Unfortunately, such initiatives (which are normally funded from Adult and Community Education Budgets) have been harder and harder to fund since local authority spending has been cut or controlled by central government.

School governing bodies in England and Wales, unlike those in most other countries, can have community representatives, and the ability to co-opt governors of this type means that local people with important skills of benefit to the school (such as the ability to speak a community language, for example, or experience in drawing up budgets and managing money) can be drawn onto the board of governors.

The relation of an individual mainstream[34] school with its community works in two directions. So far as the community's involvement in the life and work of the school is concerned, most schools hold open days, when parents, families and members of the community can visit the school and displays of children's work. Some are open one morning a week for visitors to observe the school during a normal working day. Students regularly study aspects of their local area or family history as part of the curriculum, and many schools celebrate the festivals of their local community – which may represent a number of minority cultures. Schools normally draw on a range of community agencies, such as the school library service, educational theatre, and sporting clubs and organisations (which encourages the participation of fathers). Increasingly (and controversially) such links are fostered or sponsored by the commercial sector.

The use of school premises for activities such as shared daytime classes, evening classes, clubs and societies and other meetings is sometimes positively encouraged – both from a social and a financial viewpoint. School governors are responsible for letting out the premises – but while some are forward-looking and the school is well-used by the community, in other cases the buildings are shut outside school hours and remain somewhat remote from community life.

Schools involve themselves in the life and work of the community through community service schemes, and local companies can co-operate with secondary schools in offering work experience or work shadowing placements, or mentors for girls or ethnic minority pupils. Some businesses are involved in "Compact" schemes: they guarantee jobs to pupils who have fulfilled their side of a contract (in terms of attitude and achievement). Initiatives such as the Liverpool Parent School Partnership (see case study), by improving the skills and confidence of disadvantaged parents, can make a marked contribution to the regrowth of damaged communities.

Parental influence on the curriculum, its delivery and the life of the school

Parents in England and Wales have little or no formal voice in decisions as to what their children are taught. The curriculum is drawn up by central government committees (which do not include parents), and ratified by Parliament. The only exceptions are religious and sex education, where schools are legally obliged to consult with parents.

Parents are encouraged to help their children's learning (especially reading) both at home and, increasingly, in school. It is now common practice for parent volunteers (usually mothers) to be regularly involved in working alongside teachers and others such as nurses and classroom assistants in primary school classrooms. Some have had training paid for by the school, the local education authority, or a special local or national initiative (see case studies). Typically, they help individual pupils with their work; hear children read aloud; organise small group work; contribute their own skills and experience in, for example, crafts, computer studies, cookery, language work, making story books (often bilingual); run lunchtime and after-school reading clubs.

There are several well-established development programmes which offer a range of practical activities through which parents and other family members can be actively involved.[35] More and more schools are giving parents in advance an outline plan of the year's work, so that they can offer both encouragement and resources at home (through, for example, visiting local libraries, visiting museums, or collecting relevant material). Parental involvement in helping their children learn to read is virtually universal in English and Welsh primary schools. Homework, which fell out of favour during the 1970s and 1980s, is now promoted by politicians of all parties, and is receiving more emphasis for children at virtually every stage of schooling (reinforced by school homework clubs in socially disadvantaged areas). Some secondary schools ask parents – and sometime students too – to contribute to the formulation of clear homework policies.

Many schools in England and Wales – both primary and secondary – run evening curriculum workshops in subjects such as maths, computer studies and information technology, in which parents may lack knowledge and confidence. In this way, parents can learn actively about the work their children are doing, and pupils often contribute to the process by working alongside their parents.

Communication between parents and schools

Schools in England and Wales are legally required to communicate certain information to parents. The Parent's Charter, first published in 1991 and updated in 1994, informs parents that: "Under the government's reforms you should get all the information you need to keep track of your child's progress, to find out how the school is being run, and to compare all local schools. There are five key documents:

- a report about your child;
- regular reports from independent inspectors;
- performance tables for all your local schools;
- a prospectus or brochure about individual schools;
- an annual report from your school governors" (Department of Education and Science, 1991, 1994).

As well as fulfilling the legal requirements, many schools do some or all of the following:

- draw up "home-school agreements", which clarify what parents, teachers and pupils can reasonably expect of each other;
- produce newsletters for parents, often with input from the parents themselves;
- make sure that parents feel welcome in the school, using a number of strategies such as: clear and visible signs (including in any local community languages) so that parents can find their way around; displaying books, objects, or pictures which reflect the cultures of all the pupils in the school;

producing booklets (perhaps in several languages) explaining the school's attitudes and aims, and stating whether or not there is an "open door" policy;

– offering a range of opportunities for informal contact between teachers and parents through social and fund-raising events.

All schools give parents or carers two or three opportunities each year to discuss their children's progress with their teachers. The written report on the child's achievements must include:

– the child's progress in all subjects and activities;

– a summary of the child's attendance record;

– the results of the child's performance in the national curriculum assessments at 7, 11 and 14 years (parents also receive a summary of the results for the school as a whole and a summary of the national results);

– external examination results.

Two-way communication is encouraged in a growing number of schools through nursery records or home-school diaries which are taken home by the children at night. These encourage regular dialogue, and keep parents fully-informed on a daily basis. Secondary school parents often communicate with teachers through homework notebooks, which they are required to sign regularly to demonstrate that they are aware of what homework has been set, and that their child has completed it. It is also common for the parents of younger primary school children to speak informally to the teacher at the beginning or end of the school day. Teachers' visits to the homes of parents are not very common compared with other countries. Except when home visiting is part of a specific scheme, it is usually associated with problems such as truancy.

Home-school relations is one of the specific areas to be scrutinised during formal school inspections carried out by the Office for Standards in Education. Before a school inspection, the Registered Inspector must send a questionnaire to all the parents requesting their views, invite them to a meeting, and encourage them to express their opinions concerning the school and the quality of education it provides. This ideal situation does not always happen, though, due to language problems and the reluctance of some parents to speak up in public. Although serious parental dissatisfaction ought to come to light either through the survey or the meeting, it is not clear how far these channels of communication are effective for ethnic minority or very disadvantaged parents – especially those who were themselves disaffected pupils.

Another opportunity for parents to make their views known is at the legally-required annual meeting, when the school's governors present an annual report on the school and review progress over the previous year. Parents can discuss and, where appropriate, vote on key issues. But the real potential of these meetings, which generally attract very small numbers, has not yet been realised.

Complaints about schools are handled in various ways depending on the nature of the complaint. There are statutory procedures which cover:

- admissions (if a child is not offered a place at his or her preferred school);

- exclusions;

- special needs (which may be referred to a Special Educational Needs Tribunal);

- curriculum complaints (which are dealt with under section 23 of the Education Reform Act of 1988).

In other cases, the recommended procedure is to follow these steps in the order given: discuss the complaint with the child's teacher, if appropriate; discuss it with the headteacher; raise the issue with a parent (or other) governor or the chair of the school's governing body; approach the Chief Education Officer of the local education authority (in the case of LEA maintained schools); or, finally, parents can also complain to the Secretary of State for Education and Employment.[36]

Psycho-social support

Changes in British society – such as altering patterns of family life and the virtual disappearance of unskilled jobs for school leavers – and education policies which emphasise competition between schools in terms of examination results and pupil behaviour, have resulted in a more intense focus on matters of discipline and behaviour.

Within this wider picture there are several important features: increasingly difficult behaviour among younger, as well as older, pupils; a growing recognition that parents and families need to be involved, too, in tackling this issue; and the growth in a range of personnel and agencies to support teachers in the schools.[37]

So far as student behaviour goes, several projects have been initiated at national level with central government funding. These include the Attendance and Truancy Projects paid for through the GEST[38] budget, and free Guidelines on Pupil Behaviour and anti-bullying materials published by the Department of Education and Employment. Many schools are developing policies on pupil behaviour, to which teachers, governors, parents and, normally, pupils themselves have contributed. Such policies, especially if students of all ages have been involved in framing them, can have a marked effect on the overall climate of a school.

There is a growing recognition that parents should be involved as early as possible, and many schools (especially at secondary level) have developed semi-formal mechanisms for resolving conflicts and problems involving pupils and their families. These may include: special daily reports, to be signed by all the school staff involved with the young person; individually negotiated student "contracts", often discussed with parents, identifying the specific desired behaviour; case conferences involving relevant staff inside and outside the school (perhaps including an education welfare officer, health service professionals, local police, and youth or community workers).

The support offered to families and pupils by schools is regularly supplemented by:

- school-based workshops on topics such as health, sex and drug-related education;
- opportunities for parent support groups of various kinds to meet on the premises;
- careers education, guidance and counselling sessions;
- links with the local youth service (who, in England, have traditionally shared school premises);
- connections with other family-linked community organisations, such as locally-based health provision or religious groups.

There is currently much interest in the area of "parenting education", and programmes are offered by a wide range of educational, health and social services agencies. Some of this work is based in primary schools, targeted at local parents. The recently formed Parenting Forum, based in London at the National Children's Bureau, is currently aiming to co-ordinate and develop these initiatives. Other successful support measures include "befriending schemes", through which experienced and knowledgeable parents pass on their expertise and understanding to newer parents, and mentoring schemes, in which, for example, successful black parents act as role models for black pupils in inner-city schools.

Special needs

The recently introduced Code of Practice for education for children with special educational needs is making a considerable impact in England and Wales. It brings together a number of existing features and gives them a fresh emphasis. These include:

- a clear allocation of responsibilities;
- detailed recommendations – to both schools and local education authorities – for the "identification, assessment and provision" for all children with special education needs;

105

- the endorsement of, and continuing support for, existing good practice;

- above all, genuine recognition of the vital importance of the knowledge and understanding that parents have of their children, which is such a key element of developing the partnership which is essential to special needs work (see Wolfendale, 1997).

Individual schools are now responsible for working with children with special educational needs and their families. Each governing body must appoint one of its members to be responsible for the school's special needs policy, and make sure that it is working effectively. Schools must also appoint a special needs co-ordinator, who is responsible for keeping a register of needs within the school, and making sure that these needs are being met. The government has funded a three year "pump-priming" project to encourage partnerships. Every local education authority has appointed a parent partnership officer, and schemes are being developed to enhance partnerships between LEAs, schools and the parents of children with special needs.

CONCLUSION

In some ways, the involvement of parents in decision-making at school level in England and Wales differs from practice in other countries in that parents are seen primarily as consumers by policy-makers. They can have a strong influence on schools through school governing bodies but this is mainly because so much power has been pushed down to school governing bodies – on which parents in any case do not form a majority. There is no representation at national or regional level, and no real encouragement to form a representative national body which will represent the voice of parents.

A great deal of government effort has been put into developing the idea of the parent as consumer and encouraging families to become more critical of what they are offered – mainly as an aid to pushing up standards in schools. This approach has certainly stimulated many schools into examining their practice more carefully.

But this consumption model conflicts somewhat with the notion of parents and schools working together as partners – a concept on which most successful local initiatives are based. So, although parents without doubt are better informed than they used to be and there are very many examples of good practice, there is nevertheless a sense of uneasiness and the feeling that aspects of the policy are pulling in different directions. This means that local education authorities and individual schools who are not really committed to involving parents can continue to pay lip service to the idea but in reality ignore the issue. At the same time, there is in many areas a culture within which schools try to be responsive to the needs and lives of their pupils, their families, and the neighbourhood as a whole.

CASE STUDIES

Liverpool Parent School Partnership (PSP)

This is a long-standing project, which is based in a deprived area of the inner city, stricken by crime and unemployment. Some of its centres opened soon after the 1981 riots in the city. The project is based at 29 primary schools and one secondary school, each of which has a parents' centre and, ideally, two extra staff (a teacher key worker, and an outreach worker). Since 1990, the scheme has been extended; the original 30 schools now act as bases from which staff work with all 150 Liverpool primary schools. Each school-based centre is entitled to five hours of adult education a week, plus a crèche, and works to a development plan which dovetails with the school's development plan, drawn up in co-operation with the governors and parents.

The project is supported financially by Liverpool LEA (which is strongly committed to parental involvement), and the European Social Fund. PSP aims to involve parents in their children's education, provide opportunities for their own further learning, and offer them guidance and support of all kinds (especially with financial problems). Two of its most significant educational initiatives are the Family Literacy Project and the REACHOut scheme:

- *Family Literacy Project.* This national pilot project was funded by the Department of Education and Employment through the Basic Skills Agency. Four pilot demonstration programmes were set up in Liverpool, Cardiff, Norfolk and North Tyneside. They were aimed at improving parents' literacy skills, their capacity to help their children learn to read and write, and the children's acquisition of these skills. The programmes, which were targeted on parents with poor basic skills, lasted 12 weeks – six hours per week for parents and children separately, and two hours in joint sessions. Some 150 Liverpool families took part, and only 10 per cent dropped out. The children made significant progress, and 70 per cent of the parents signed up for further courses at the end of the programme.

- REACH*Out* enables parents who have returned to learning through the Family Literacy Project, or through other classes designed to help them support their children's learning, to progress to higher education. Based in local communities – normally at PSP centres – it offers a part-time route to a number of higher education courses, including degree courses (offered by Liverpool Hope University College in partnership with the Open University). Some 80 parents have now achieved access level and 50 have begun degree level study.

Rush Common Primary School, Abingdon, Oxford

This school, which caters for about 460 pupils aged between 5 and 11, is situated in a small country town outside Oxford. For the last eight years, it has had a highly successful parents' association based on class councils which ensures that the association is much more representative than is usual in English or Welsh schools, and enables the school to draw on the resources offered by parents thus freeing up teachers for teaching.

Each of the 17 classes has a home-school association, which builds up a close relationship with the class teacher and organises parental help in the classroom and both curriculum-related and extra-curricular activities for the children. Teachers hold class "surgeries" every week for parents who want to check on their children's progress.

School governors also belong to class associations, which ensures that they are more closely in touch with parents than many governors are. The class association also elects representatives to a social committee at school level which organises a wide variety of events (discos, quizzes, theatre, trips, celebrations), creating a feeling of unity in the school. Class associations run curriculum-related workshops for parents (usually with a crèche so that those with smaller children can attend) on subjects such as maths, reading, computers and arts and crafts. Twice a week there is an early morning "shared reading" session, when parents and grandparents come into school to read with their children.

As the result of a two-year Royal Society of Arts project "Parents in a learning society", Rush Common is working with its local secondary school, Fitzharrys, in an effort to keep this high degree of involvement alive into secondary level. Five "link parents" (two from sixth grade, the final year in primary school, and three from seventh grade, the first class in secondary school) are responsible for bringing together parents and teachers from the two schools and organising joint activities (both social events and curriculum-related workshops) for the parents and children in these two-year groups.

Home-school work in Coventry

The City of Coventry, in the English Midlands, is an example of a local education authority which has developed strong policies in this area. Home-school work is a well-established aspect of the Community Education Service. Schools are expected to recognise that "parents and families are usually the prime educators of children, and so provide opportunities for the involvement of parents and others from the community in the teaching/learning process". Every area in the city has a Home-School Worker responsible for a group of schools, whose role is to strengthen the partnership between parents, schools, and the local community. This is particularly important in areas where there are large numbers of ethnic minority parents who may not speak English, and parents are recruited to act as bilingual link workers, to encourage other parents to become involved.

Parents in the classroom (Liverpool, Oxfordshire, SHARE)

Parents helping teachers in primary classrooms has become one of the hallmarks of co-operation between parents and schools in England and Wales. Although some teachers (and their unions) have remained suspicious, others have found that parents can be a real resource and that their aid does not lead to a deprofessionalisation of the trained teacher's role. The next step is to train parents as teachers' aides, so that they understand the educational process better and offer more effective support. Initiatives are currently running in a number of areas:

- *Chatsworth Computer Project (part of the Liverpool PSP).* Through this scheme, parents (most of whom had no qualifications) are trained in computer skills in order to support primary teachers in the classroom. Since 1992, more than 900 parents have completed "Helping with Computers in School", and over 100 schools are now involved. Teachers and parents have become accustomed to working together, and the project is currently developing packs of materials for use in joint programmes. Some parents have continued their training, gaining further qualifications in word-processing, english and maths.

- *Parents in the Classroom (Oxfordshire).* This small project, funded by Oxfordshire County Council and the Centre for Parent-Teacher Partnership at the University of Oxford, ran from 1994 to 1996. Some 46 parents were trained to work in five Oxfordshire primary schools, supporting teachers in Key Stage 1 (pupils aged between 5 and 7). Parents spent six weeks per term on a module of study: first English, then maths and finally science (18 weeks in all), while continuing to gain practical experience in the classroom. Including sessions with a tutor, and private study, each module took up approximately 30 hours, and was worth one credit from the Open College Network. A report on the pilot stage (two schools) concluded that the school principals and teachers found the project very successful – although rather time-consuming. The parents gained a great deal of confidence, not only as educators, but as learners in their own right.

- SHARE. Based in Coventry,[39] SHARE is a demonstration project which began in September 1996. Teachers in four infant or primary schools in each of five LEAs (Birmingham, Gloucestershire, the London Borough of Southwark, St Helen's and Warwickshire) work with the parents of first-grade pupils. The key characteristic of the SHARE approach is the materials which it offers, to help parents support their children's learning in English and maths. By working through the materials at home with their children, parents will gain Open College Network credits. The scheme is designed to fit in with normal school life, and each participating school is allocated three teacher training days. The ultimate aim is that in 1998 SHARE should be adopted nationally by a wide range of schools and LEAs.

FRANCE

OVERVIEW

The French education system follows the guiding principles of the republican tradition: education as a public service, non-religious and democratic. This does not mean that there are no private schools – for there are many – but these must conform to the same norms and regulations as the public schools, and are considered as private schools "under contract" (to the state). There is a general consensus concerning the main objectives of education: the transmission of knowledge and general culture, the development of the individual (both for his or her own benefit and also as a citizen of France), and preparation for working life. The landmark *Loi d'orientation* (passed in July 1989) asserts that education is a key national priority, contributing to equal opportunity for all. An important characteristic of the French system is the dominant role of the central administration, and the role of the state. Under the Third Republic, the state was charged with creating social unity around republican values – through public schooling. But as the system grew it became too big and unwieldy to be run entirely from the centre, and during the 1980s, most of the administration was devolved to the local authorities – although central government retains the responsibility for, among other things, recruiting and paying teachers and controlling the content of the national school curriculum.

It is this decentralisation, perhaps, that has brought about new ways of conceptualising the role of parents in children's schooling. Decentralisation changed attitudes by proving that effective decisions could be taken at a local level in partnership with the local community. For a highly centralised system this was a big step towards altering normative assumptions about the way things should be done. Teachers have now begun to see the benefits of partnerships with others outside the school, especially parents.

Parents' attitudes have shifted too, as a result of the changing social and economic context. The increased importance of effective schooling, qualifications and diplomas in the search for work has put more pressure on families to succeed. Parents now tend to look more closely at the capacity of the school to equip their child with adequate knowledge, skills and qualifications for the future. Although French parents have no direct say in teaching methods or the curriculum, teachers and administrators now accept that for student success they need to be considered as partners in the child's education.

With increasing immigration into France, most schools cannot rely any longer on the traditional ritualised forms of communication between home and school. Teachers need to reach out to parents from different cultures to encourage them to attend meetings and support their children's educational progress, and some schools are beginning to identify innovative strategies for doing so. In particular – and this is true of many native French parents too – there is a need to change parents' fear of schools and teachers, and make them feel welcome. The new context encourages schools to see parents as partners in the construction of a new type of educational institution, capable of adapting to different needs of diverse population. But there is still a very long way to go before this vision becomes a reality.

SOCIAL BACKGROUND

Schooling in France has always been recognised as having a major role in the social and professional integration of the population. The Napoleonic idea of "republican education" as being universal, non-religious and egalitarian is still very much present in the French value system. The nature of education, though, is changing – and consumerist notions of the "marketplace" and school choice, with private and public schools competing for "customers", are increasingly creeping into the system.

The relationship between family and school in France has gone through many changes since the late 1960s. It was only in 1968 that parents were officially allowed into the institution. And the legislative evolution of co-operation between school and family needs to be understood in the social context of increasing mass education. The government's aim is that by the year 2000 at least 80 per cent of all students will reach baccalaureate level. This means that schools are having to adapt to offering high quality education to a much more heterogeneous student population.

Families in France are changing too. More are under pressure because of factors such as marital breakdown, the decline of the extended family, unemployment and immigration. As a result they are making greater demands on the school, and as their needs become more extreme and diverse the education system which is supposed to create social unity is experiencing strain. At the same time, middle class parents are beginning to treat the school as a service provided for consumers, rather than as a social institution. They demand that the school should equip their children with the knowledge and competencies (including personal and social skills) that will ensure employment later on. In former times it was considered that education was the function of schools and bringing up children the business of parents. Increasingly, schools are expected to educate children socially and parents to help in school work.

Many of these alterations in demand and attitude are rooted in the changing economic context – particularly increasing youth unemployment – which has accentuated parental worries about their children's chances for employability. Families are now looking at schooling more in "market" terms of what exactly is on offer, and how useful it will be. Teachers, on the other hand, are more concerned with the transmission of traditional knowledge and well-established methods of work related to their disciplines. Their tendency is to put socialisation, professional training and the question of what is taught at school more in the background. Often this makes for misunderstandings and difficulties in communication between teachers and parents.

POLICY CONTEXT

Co-operation between family and school in France can only be understood if a clear distinction is made between the traditional, formal measures at the legislative level and the more informal practices that actually occur in local schools. In the past, the role of parents in the French system has traditionally been a formal, legal one stipulated through various decrees – some of them very long-standing. The political activities of national parents' associations (right and left wing) have also given parents a significant voice in education at the national level – and have acted as the launch-pad for a number of political careers.

Systemic change started in the 1970s – by which time many politicians, local administrators and parents had begun to criticise the Ministry of Education in Paris as a monolithic "dinosaur". Reforming legislation to decentralise education was passed between 1982 and 1985, and much of the administrative decision-making was delegated to local authorities. The legal status of secondary schools was also modified; they became more autonomous and were encouraged to be outward looking, and to identify more with the local community.

The current official policy in France is to include parents as full partners in the educational community; this is confirmed through legal frameworks set up in the last ten years. The orientation law of 1989 demonstrates the concern of the policy-makers that parents should be given the role of responsible partners in the functioning of the schools, as well as in the success of their own children. Accordingly, they are now represented at every level – in class councils, school councils, local administrative councils, and on the "superior council for education" at national level.

Most French parents are extremely conscientious in supporting their children's school work at home, but their direct involvement in their local schools has, traditionally, been minimal – and not encouraged by teachers. However, new attempts are now being made to treat parents as "partners", or as "active parents", moving beyond the legal framework in an effort to keep them in touch with what is actually happening in school – rather than keeping them at a distance. This means involving them in school activities and considering them as an essential part of the education community.

WHY INVOLVE PARENTS?

Although French parents have formally been involved in education for many years, their participation has tended to be institutionalised and politicised. Dominated by a particular type of active parent, these structures have not really acted as a channel through which ordinary parents have been able to achieve decision-making powers. This form of involvement represents an aspect of local community activism through political institutions – and as such is an element in the democratic process in France.

The philosophy underlying the more recent moves to involve parents in the functioning of their local schools is related to the role which the education system is supposed to perform – that of welding the French population into a coherent social whole, through the unifying force of French culture and ways of thought as transmitted through the curriculum. Since changes in society and the family mean that French schools cannot now achieve this single-handed, the parents (especially those who are immigrants or disadvantaged in some way and therefore may not share the culture of the school) need to be involved as well. The resources offered by increased parental support (at home and in the school) are also crucial if young people in France are to achieve the high levels of education and training which a competitive economy requires – and to which the government has pledged itself.

THE LEGISLATION

The increasing importance given to the presence of parents in schooling can be traced through the progress of the legislation, as it gives parents the right to representation on a range of decision-making bodies:

- **1932:** First circular on parental participation is issued.
- **1945:** School administrative councils are created, but do not come into their own until after 1968.
- **1975:** The law of July 1975 defines the school community as consisting of "staff, parents and students", and underlines parents' rights to be informed

about their child's "orientation", *i.e.* the course their child is following, and the "type of career it is likely to lead to".

- **1976:** In December, a new decree creates the school council.
- **1982:** A civil service circular authorises parents to take time off work if they belong to a class council or an administrative council.
- **1985:** Article 33 of the Decree of August 31 regulates the participation of parents in class councils. These councils become obligatory in all *lycées* and *collèges* for each class. A further decree specifies the participation of parents in the administrative council of *collèges* and *lycées* (secondary level) along with principal and staff, local community representatives, qualified personnel and students.
- **1986:** A circular outlines the rights and responsibilities of parents' associations.
- **1989:** Article 11 of the law of orientation states that "parents are full members of the educational community", and that their participation in the life of the school, as well as their right to dialogue with teachers and other staff members, must be assured. The new law also created a "higher council for education" as a consulting body representing all the different partners in education – that is, ministry staff, teachers, parents, community members, associations and business. The council is presided over by the Minister for Education, and has both consultative and jurisdictional powers.

KEY ELEMENTS OF CO-OPERATION BETWEEN SCHOOL AND FAMILY

Parental involvement in school governance

Parents in France are involved in various forms of governance at different levels:

- At the national level, they are represented on the *Conseil supérieur de l'éducation* (CSE) (higher council for education). Nine represent the public schools, and three the private schools; the council is consulted on all issues of national interest concerning teaching or education (objectives, operations, regulations on the education system). Parents at national level can also belong to one of the main parents' associations.
- At the departmental level, parents participate in the *Conseil départemental tripartite de l'éducation nationale* (CDEN) (tripartite departmental council). Of 30 members, seven are parents, appointed for a three-year period. The departmental council consults on matters such as the structure of programmes of study, the provisional budget and school transport. Parents are involved in consultations that deal with appeals concerning the orientation

of students – for instance regarding promotion to the next grade – and any other decisions that were taken at the class council level. A similar council exists at the academy[40] level and has a similar mandate; parents may be delegated by the rector to this council but it is not obligatory.

– At the secondary school level, parents are represented on the *conseils d'administration* (administrative councils) of *collèges* (7 parents and 3 students) and *lycées*[41] (5 parents and 5 students) along with principal and teaching staff, local community representatives, qualified personnel and students. These councils have decision-making powers in relation to issues such as the organisational rules of the school and the choice of teaching method. They also approve the school budget and special projects. Parents who belong to one of the national parents' associations are elected to the council for one year by the parent body.

– Also at the secondary school level, parents are represented on *conseils de classe* (class councils). These councils are an important aspect of school life in France. The members of a class council are: the class's teacher or teachers; two parents; two students; the principal counsellor; and the orientation counsellor. The parents are elected each term by other parents in the class from a list prepared by the parents' associations. The class council meets at least three times a year, and examines the organisation of teaching and learning in the class, especially the progress of each individual child, his or her behaviour, marks and general demeanour. Proposals for future orientation, and the question of repeating a grade, are all discussed in the council. It is only after agreement by its members that the principal will inform the family of the decision. Although the legislation is there to guide parental participation, there is no guarantee that parents of children with difficulties, or immigrant parents will play their part, since it is hard to legislate sensitively enough to encourage this type of involvement.

– At the primary level there are no class councils, but many schools have a *conseil d'établissement* (school council) on which each class is represented by one parent. The council decides on issues such as the school rules, or the organisation of extra-activities for the pupils, and advises the principal, but it has no legal standing.

A national voice for parents

Institutionalised participation of parents is through the main parents' associations,[42] all of which were founded earlier in the century, and are embedded in French national politics. They differ both politically, and in the nature of the ideas they put forward about the role and nature of schooling. Parents' associations are consulted by the government concerning major educational reforms and changes in policies.

The *Fédération des conseils de parents d'élèves de l'enseignement public* (FCPE) (federation for parent councils in public education) was created in 1947. It is considered to be more to the left in its political views, having as its main agenda fighting school failure and elitist education, the development of project work in school and reducing school hours. The association has 320 000 members, is recognised by the Ministry of Education as a public utility, and carries out a number of services including publishing two periodicals for parents,[43] organising financial support, school insurance and language trips abroad.

The other main parents' association is the *Fédération des parents d'élèves de l'enseignement public* (PEEP) (federation for parents of students in public education), which was created in 1906 and has 400 000 members. The PEEP is looked upon as a more conservative association; its main agenda is to meet the needs of parents and reflect on the role of parents in the secondary school. It also edits a magazine *La voix des parents* ("The voice of parents"), and is planning to create a telephone service to answer parents' questions.

The *Union nationale des associations de parents d'élèves de l'enseignement libre* (UNAPEL) (national union of parents' associations in private education) was founded in 1935; and has 800 000 members; it also issues a magazine called *Famille et école* ("The family and education"). In 1972, the Catholic union split from UNAPEL to create its own *Association des parents d'élèves de l'enseignement catholique* (APEEC) (association of parents in Catholic education).

Participation in the parents' associations has been diminishing in recent years, although it is higher at secondary level (40 to 45 per cent in the lower secondary colleges, and 60 to 70 per cent in the *lycées*). In the Catholic schools it is almost obligatory. Some attribute the falling participation to the fact that increasingly school is considered from the consumer's point of view – that is, parents limit their involvement to choosing the best school and then expect not to have to participate in the child's education.

The school and the community

The tendency since decentralisation is to open schools increasingly to the local community, although classrooms traditionally remain closed to the public. Nevertheless schools are using local resources such as museums, libraries and even some local businesses for work experience for students. Because "project work" is now an accepted area of school experience, many teachers can use this space as an opening to invite parents and members of the community to bring in their talents, and resources as an enrichment of students. Traditionally, schools in middle class areas organise special open days in which different associations, local stores, and parents participate. Some schools run *ateliers* (workshops) where parents or other community members can pass on their skills to students.

Art and sport education also make use of local facilities outside the school and contribute to local entertainment by organising exhibitions and performances. This represents significant collaboration between ministries and the local community. A given *département* draws up a proposal to open up an "experimental site for artistic education" and presents it to the Ministries of Education, Youth and Sport, Culture and Higher Education and Research. The proposal, over and above its artistic goals, resources, budget and so on, must outline the existing local cultural resources and what kind of collaboration with the local community is envisaged. The "policy of artistic sites" is financed in part by the ministries: in 1995, the Ministry of Education spent FF 2 160 000 (FF 180 000 per site) and the Ministry of Culture, 5 636 000 FF.

Business and schools are not seen as natural partners in France. Their cultures are very different, and traditionally the two are considered as very separate, almost antagonistic domains. Businesses do not spontaneously offer work experience for students, and teachers often find it difficult to find work experience placements for their students. Similarly, there is no tradition of business helping schools with financial support – although special projects in schools may receive some resources from a company. Parents are often asked to help in finding work experience or training placements for students in their company.

Perhaps it is in the *zones d'éducation prioritaires* (ZEP), where, paradoxically, the communities are so diverse and the problems are the greatest, that the best use is made of local resources both human and material. Such disadvantaged areas receive extra resources of all kinds to facilitate, for example, the integration of immigrant children and their parents. One example is "linking-women" (*femmes relais*) wherein members of an ethnic community are employed to help parents link up with the school, explain administrative procedures, and translate when necessary – not only in terms of language, but also in cultural terms.

Special projects have been set up in ZEP to educate parents in hygiene and how to improve the health of their children. In some cases a nurse will visit the home to make sure that the children have been going for their medical check-ups. Another type of project aims to improve the image of children in their parents' eyes by showing them that they can succeed at school. One such effort involves a project entitled "I show who I am", in which children are videotaped in classroom situations while successfully carrying out a task. Parents watch the videos around a cup of coffee at the school. Other projects involve training parents to help with the school library; mothers may come to read to children, especially in primary school. Special workshops are also run by parents who have particular skills, such as painting, cooking, or mechanics. Local associations of various kinds may support children who need it, or explain the basic principles of the school system to parents, or help immigrant parents with working papers, residence permits and other official documents.

Parental influence on the curriculum, its delivery and the life of the school

Parents are not involved in any of the decision-making related to the French national curriculum. The programmes are prepared at national level by "technical groups for the disciplines" which are made up of university professors, general inspectors and teachers. Parents are not represented. However the present Minister, in keeping with the "new contract for schooling" wants greater transparency in this process. As a result, parents at national level were consulted in the revisions of the *sixième* programme (first year of lower secondary school). It was published in a popular edition, and sold widely.

Recent reforms at the school level have mainly addressed the problem of how children can best be "oriented" (or guided) so that their school education acts as an adequate preparation for their future career. The notion of "orientation" has evolved with the new diversity of the school population. The law of 1989 states that "the right to orientation counselling" and information about the curriculum and professional development are all an integral part of the right to education.

The final orientation choices are the responsibility of the family and the student. Any disagreement between the family and the school council concerning the necessity of repeating a grade, for example, are discussed with parents at a meeting before any final decision can be made. If the decision does not conform with the wishes of the family, it must be justified. The family can appeal against the decision.

The law insists that young people must actively construct their own plans rather than being passive recipients of guidance: "No-one can decide for him/her. To make a choice he/she must be informed, helped and receive counselling. Family and school are partners in the decision". The role of parents in this process can be complex, especially since students are legally adult at 18, and have the right to make decisions without the agreement of their parents.

Although it may not be evident in practice, the legal frameworks can be seen to increasingly involve parents in the curriculum orientation of their children: a 1990 decree (14 June) made it very explicit that parents must be in agreement with the school in deciding if their child should repeat a grade; decisions taken by the principle concerning the orientation of students at the end of a cycle (passing from primary to secondary or from *collège* to *lycée*) must be justified and explained to the parents in person. In 1993 another circular was added to specify that the homeroom teacher must make every effort to "develop a dialogue between the teachers, the orientation counsellor, the psychologist, the student and their parents".

When it comes to student learning, schools are eager to mobilise parental participation. Many different projects have been created such as: "Helping parents help their children"; "How to make parental participation a success"; "Students, parents, teachers, professions for college success". These illustrate the increasing efforts to building parental involvement in the curriculum. The presence of parents within the classroom is rare, however; only inspectors are allowed to be in the class, although some teachers accept the presence of researchers or special trainers.

Such projects concerning parents are often conducted within a general framework of "school projects" that were put in place by the orientation law of 1989 and are in principle obligatory for all schools. They are authorised by the school's administrative council and financed through the school's general budget. The projects are managed by the principal, who reports on them in writing at the end of the year.

Communication between parents and schools

The official guidelines speak in theory of informing and creating a dialogue with parents. In practice, communication is organised in each school through the parents' associations, through the elected representatives on the different councils outlined above. Therefore communication between parents and the school is highly institutionalised. Parents are informed of their child's progress in school through a *bulletin* or report card three times a year. An individual diary or notebook for each student is used to inform parents about daily progress, problems and marks throughout the year. Parents must sign it and can use it to make their comments in writing to the teacher. Usually there are two to three meetings a year for parents; the minimum is one and is usually held in October when parents meet teachers individually to talk about their child's progress.

Since 1989 general evaluations have been carried out at the beginning of the year in order to determine a student's level in basic subjects such as maths, reading, writing. At elementary level the results are discussed with parents at a meeting; at the end of primary school they are simply sent to the parents. At the end of lower secondary level (*collège*) they are discussed with the parents, since they contribute to choice of course in upper secondary.

Parents can have direct contact with schools especially through the parents' associations. The way this is done varies: parents come to the school, a meeting is organised in apartment buildings (this occurs mostly in poorer neighbourhoods), evening activities, dinners, outings and (more rarely) organised meetings on special topics, such as drug prevention or violence in school. The most common way to communicate with school is by writing, except among immigrant parents or those with literacy problems. In these cases, mediators and translators can be provided either by the school or the local neighbourhood. Traditionally teachers do not do home visits, and when this occurs it is considered to be innovative and largely the initiative of the individual teacher. The only formal visit from the school, when necessary, is from the social worker.

Psycho-social support

Although it is hard to institutionalise solutions to problems such as inequalities between social groups, it is clear that school legislation in France is trying to adapt schooling to changing social, economic and political realities. Parents and families are not a homogenous group. Some look on the education of their children as if they were consumers, developing strategies related to conscious and specific choices and plans. Another type of family, often working class or immigrant may become caught up in a cycle of school failure.

The 1989 orientation law has tried to bring some support to these families first of all by identifying a specific kind of public: "among the partners whose actions must come together in a global educational plan to fight against exclusion, there are first of all parents who need to be reconciled with school, welcomed and helped to gain the necessary skills to be able to help their children learn". In his speech in March 1996 on the prevention of violence in schools, the Minister of Education (François Bayrou) stated that one of the main elements in preventing violence in schools, is the strengthening of links between parents and schools. From 1997, all educational establishments, from *sixième* on, must organise a meeting before school begins, to enable parents to meet the teachers, counsellors, and the principal and to become familiar with the school.

Dialogue between immigrant parents and teachers is often made difficult because of language and cultural differences. Mediators and translators will be made available for those parents who find it necessary. Truancy prevention will also be made a priority, since it is often an indication of family problems. Families, social services and the youth squad will be mobilised when necessary.

School climate, helpfulness, co-operation cannot, however, be dictated through decrees. Support is often more effective given through grassroots activities, some organised through "parent schools" when parents are taught how to read a report card, how to deal with the administration, or learn how to read. The educational priority zones have been earmarked for extra resources, and alternative strategies, and some very motivated teachers and community workers currently support children and parents whose culture is not that of the traditional French school system.

CONCLUSION

The creation of a true partnership between family and school is an important policy issue today in France. The government has made considerable legislative efforts, especially in recent years, to ensure that parents are full members of the educational community. However, it is also clear that legal frameworks are not enough to make partnership a reality; much depends on local practices and grassroots experience that are developed in concrete situations.

Parents and schools are not "natural" partners in France. In fact there are many indications that prove the contrary such as misunderstandings, cultural differences and diverging interests. However the need to place students at the centre of the education system, and the conviction that children do better when parents are supporting them in partnership with the school, is gradually forcing both parents and schools to change their images of each other. The challenge is now a social one, not that of policy.

The question of "orientation" of students renders things more difficult. Pressures are from all sides: the family, the school, the work place. A recent survey found that the most successful students tend to be those whose mothers are teachers. Knowledge of the system seems to be a most favourable factor. Seemingly the relationship between parents and schools is one important aspect of a wider question: the role of schooling in the social and professional future of the child.

CASE STUDIES

"Priority zones" (ZEPs)

A collège in Amiens

The Collège Arthur Rimbaud is located in a "sensitive" area of Amiens, which means that the population consists mainly of immigrants, some recently arrived. The school staff, a local association called Femmes en mouvement ("Women on the move") and the municipality have decided to make a joint effort to involve parents in the school, in the hope that this will facilitate both their integration and that of their children, and help the school identify problems as they occur.

As most of the school population are immigrants from North Africa, one of the teachers on the staff is from North Africa and teaches Arabic language and culture. This allows Arabic speaking children to take Arabic as a first language right to the baccalauréat. The formal teaching of Arabic, learning about the culture in school, and learning to read and to discuss the Koran helps students feel proud of their roots. The teacher also helps other teachers to understand North African culture and its religious festivals. A member of the association Femmes en mouvement acts as a special "cross-cultural" go-between with parents and teachers, and the school has been allocated a Ministry of Education co-ordinator to set up special support in the French language.

"Women on the Move" was created in 1974 when North African families were able to come and join their husbands and fathers in France. Most of the association's members are North African women who speak French. Their task is to contact new families, identify their needs and help them with practical affairs such as schooling, health care, housing, and employment. Since the association has been working with the *Collège Arthur Rimbaud*, truancy has diminished, and families who were previously reluctant to come to parent/teacher meetings are now present in larger numbers. The staff of the school feel that these strategies, which have enabled them to work in partnership with parents and local associations, have also contributed to a decrease in violence at the school.

A collège *in Lille*

The *Collège Chasse Royale* is a lower secondary school in a priority zone of Lille. The area is a traditional working class suburb with high unemployment, but relatively low levels of immigration. The principal is a local leader in a series of pilot experiments across the country on how to improve parental participation in schools. He is convinced that "if parents participate, the school is transformed". Parents, he believes, are generally intimidated by school because of their own negative experiences and often only come to their child's school when he or she is having problems.

The strategy at *Collège Chasse Royale* is to make parent-school contacts a positive experience. The first step, according to the principal, is to start on neutral ground before students have attended the school (and experienced difficulties). Therefore a meeting is held every June with parents of pupils coming up from primary grades, to inform them about the school. All the school staff are present – including the secretary, the nurse, and the social worker. The principal introduces the different classes, explains the school organisation and the curriculum and asks parents what they think of their child's most recent report card. A second meeting is held before school starts again after the summer vacation. The parents meet the teachers, discuss the programme, the timetable, and have a drink and an informal chat. Parents are made to feel welcome, and normally more than 90 per cent attend.

Another meeting the following Saturday morning is organised to answer any questions regarding school organisation, and the homeroom teacher is there to talk with parents individually over coffee. About two weeks later parents are invited to have breakfast at the school and identify any problems they have encountered since school started. Homework is discussed and the student's "agenda" is explained. (This is a notebook/diary used for written communication between teacher and parents.) About half the parents usually come to these meetings. The next parent-teacher meeting is in December, when the pupils' first report cards are talked over, in individual encounters between teacher and parents – as well as a collective meeting for more general information. The turnout is generally between 70 to 90 per cent.

The result of this strategy, according to the principal, is that parents feel more at ease and are generally less aggressive towards the school – which helps children feel more positive too. The fact that parents attend meetings affects how children view the school and diminishes truancy.

A mainstream approach to parental involvement

The *Collège Rouge Barres* is situated in a middle class neighbourhood in Lille. There are a number of prestigious catholic private schools in the area and the public *collège* feels the competition. In order to upgrade the school's performance, a support class was set up for low-achieving student, with the idea being that parents could come to school to improve their understanding of the curriculum, and discuss any problems the students might have.

Since the school had been informed via a newsletter (*La lettre des collèges*) that the Lille *académie* was encouraging schools to set up parent-school partnerships, the support class was welcomed by the principal. Parents were informed by letter and telephone that there would be a parents' meeting to explain the French programme for the year.

Work was presented in a positive light so as not to alarm the parents, but rather to make them feel involved with their children's work. Parents were informed as to the course content throughout the year, how the work would be organised, how they could help their children, and what kind of methods they could use to assist their child with certain tasks. Parents felt better informed after these meetings, but most of those attending were those who already belonged to parents' associations. Parents of children with serious problems tended not to come. As a way of addressing this difficulty (which is common to many schools) the parents themselves have been active in trying to mobilise other parents, and the numbers have increased.

A local authority in partnership with schools: *Département des Hauts de Seine*

The *Conseil général des Hauts de Seine* has been in partnership with schools in the *département* for the last seven years in their "fight against school failure". Beyond the *département's* budget for school building, a significant sum of money (26 million francs per year) was set aside for educational purposes. It was decided that these funds should be used to help children with difficulties by creating innovative strategies in school (but outside the regular hours) and in partnership with families where possible. Although linking up with the family is still at an early stage, it is considered to be a very important aspect of success in school. The following projects are now in place:

PAL – *Programme d'aide à la lecture* (programme for help in reading)

PAL was established in 1989 and now includes 86 schools, both primary and kindergarten. The objectives of the programme are to reinforce and support school activities by motivating children to read. The "modules" last about one and a half hour per session throughout the year and take place in the evening after school or on Wednesday afternoons. The personnel are about 70 per cent teachers and 30 per cent mothers and the activities include reading stories, writing poetry, creating a newspaper and working on the computer. The idea is to motivate children with difficulties to want to read, but not to provide yet another "remedial" class. Sometimes reading sessions take place at one of the children's homes (12 to 13 children in a group) and parents become involved in the reading activity.

APRES – *Ateliers pédagogiques pour la réussite scolaire* (pedagogical workshops for success in schools)

These workshops are intended for lower secondary school students aged 11 to 15 years who are having difficulties at school. During 1996, nearly 50 000 students registered in 532 different workshops, run by the *département*. The purpose is to help students acquire skills in the workshops which they can use in their school work. The workshops are of three types:

- Study skills, where students learn how to organise themselves.
- "Challenge of the text", a workshop open to all students (not just those experiencing difficulties) for developing reading skills and pleasure in reading; some workshops have been run in partnership with journalists (sometimes a parent) and students have created a local radio programme.
- "Science and technology workshop" is an occasion for students to work on concrete problems, construct useful household objects (such as a lamp) and develop their curiosity and interest in scientific experimentation.

PREMIS – *Plan pour la réussite à l'école et une meilleure insertion sociale* (plan for school success and improved social integration)

This strategy addresses students with very serious difficulties regarding their performance in school and their social integration. Some are involved in delinquent activities and known for their violent behaviour. Some 300 students are involved in this focused activity which is based on two complementary strategies: workshops of six to eight students structured around areas of interest to the students, chosen in collaboration with the school; individualised attention whereby a "tutor" is assigned to work with the individual in school and in the family. Tutors are local resource persons; they can be a teacher, a janitor or secretary in the school, a parent, or a university student. The important qualification is having good contact with the student, and being able to make links with the family and social environment in order to help create a situation that will improve the student's integration in school.

Since March 1996 when the Ministry launched a programme to curtail violence in schools, the *Conseil général des Hauts de Seine* has created the role of "mediator" in schools – two young persons in each *collège* (lower secondary school) who are either university level students or young people who have completed their schooling (*baccalauréat* level is necessary). Their role is a full time one wherein 39 hours of presence are required; they must be familiar with the local community and capable of dialogue with students, ready to step in when there is a problem and help resolve it without violence. The *Conseil général*'s education department meets all the mediators once a month for a de-briefing and training session.

GERMANY

OVERVIEW

Germany is a large and complex country with a long federalist tradition, which is still significant today and assigns exclusive responsibility for the school system to the 16 states (*Länder*). This structure offers scope for the various historical, political, cultural and religious traditions of different regions. All of these have influenced relations between schools and families, and the diversity which results makes for a rich variety of interests and associations. The German education system is well-established and not subject to the sometimes short-lived innovations which some other OECD education systems have experienced. It offers a coherent and well-tried model of parent-school co-operation which deserves study.

Co-operation between the school and family in Germany follows a similar pattern nationwide, and is based on Article 6.2 of the Federal Constitution, which states that "the care and education of children are the natural right of parents and first and foremost their duty". A Federal Constitutional Court judgement in 1972 ruled that parents and schools have a duty to co-operate, and this is incorporated in the law on education of most states. For example, the education law of Baden-Württemberg states that "parents have the right and duty to take part in education at school. The responsibility shared by parents and schools for the education and upbringing of the young calls for close co-operation between them" (Article 55.1). After the re-unification of Germany in 1989, the former East German states were "twinned" with West German partners and they adopted similar regulations.

The great strength of the German system is that parental participation is well-entrenched in federal and state law, and is based on a coherent representational structure above all at class and school level. Parents have real powers to call teachers to account for the education of their children, individually and, collectively, at school level. Teachers involve parents in a co-operative approach to the education of their children. However, the schools themselves have limited autonomy within the centralised state educational system and this places limits on the ability of parents to participate in defining the ethos and objectives of schools.

SOCIAL BACKGROUND

Germany is noted for several features of its educational organisation and traditions which mark it out from other countries. One is the "dual system": the strongly developed system of company-based vocational courses and qualifications, which runs parallel to the more academic and general educational courses leading – as in other countries – to school-leaving certificates and university entrance. Indeed, compared with most other OECD countries, the German education system is highly differentiated throughout. Selection begins at an early age when pupils are allocated to one of three routes through lower secondary education. Even though much more flexible forms of transition are now common – including the teacher's recommendation, a two-year orientation stage to confirm the appropriateness of this recommendation or, in some cases, a jointly-organised orientation stage – this transition can still cause tensions between parents and the school system.

A second feature which distinguishes education in Germany is the length of the school day which is very short – often morning-only. This reflects the power of social traditions over German education – in this case the role of mothers and housewives who did not pursue careers outside the home – as well as another feature: the substantial autonomy enjoyed by German teachers who, even at primary level, are not obliged to attend school when they are not teaching, but can prepare for their classes at home.

These features have significance for the relations between families – as well as the wider community of employers and society – and the school. Currently, this is becoming an acute political issue because schools increasingly need the overt backing of the family, as a result of the social changes which are transforming German society. The growing plurality of values which has resulted from the immigration into Germany of many millions of people of different faiths and languages makes the traditional, often unconscious, understanding between teachers and parents about the values and norms which underpin education more problematical than in the past. Parents generally, and single parents in particular, are increasingly deprived of the old safety nets of extended families and close neighbourhood ties, and look to schools to play a more active social role than in the past. Teachers are in many cases overwhelmed by new social and educational duties. As a result, both sides feel, with increasing urgency, the need to cooperate. The emergence of unpredictable situations and special demands is particularly marked in the new states of East Germany, since the discontinuation of detailed government regulation and the control over the school system which was characteristic of the former German Democratic Republic. The range of possibilities involved in developing freedom of opinion, the freedom of movement and the competitive society have been experienced by many as a shock.

There is a strong tradition of independent schooling in Germany, with both religious schools and foundations more specifically based on educational ideals – such as the Steiner (*Waldorf*) schools – contributing to an educational culture in which parents actively choose the ethos in which they wish their children to be educated. This culture has produced or at least influenced the activists among the parents and teachers, even in public schools, and helps to explain the rich variety of parental organisations that are trying to influence German schooling.

POLICY CONTEXT

Germany is a federal country, in which the provision and control of education are vested in the individual states, but it used to be a state, in which country-wide practices and norms were well-established. These traditions still underlie the more recent forms of organisation, and make for a strong sense of belonging to a national system – despite the regional structure.

For example, provision for the creation of parents' associations has existed since compulsory education was first introduced in the German Republic in 1919. The Federal Constitution, and federal institutions such as the Standing Conference of Ministers of Education (*Ständige Konferenz der Kulturminister der Länder*), also limit the actual variations between the constituent states. There is at present a widespread movement to give schools greater autonomy from the state authorities, so that they can adapt better to parents' and pupils' needs. This may not, however, be entirely to the liking of the teachers' associations – if it turns out that individual teachers' autonomy is decreased in order to give school principals and parents more flexibility of organisation. "Parent power" is certainly seen by some teachers as a threat.

In a federal system, educational policy changes tend to move horizontally from state to state; but national associations also play a role in spreading innovation. The most significant parents' associations mostly operate at national level, although their influence is stronger in some states than others. The Catholic Parents' Association is more influential in the southern states of Baden-Württemberg and Bavaria and the Protestant Forum (*Bad Boll*) in the north, for example.

WHY INVOLVE PARENTS?

As in Denmark, legislation in most German *Länder* reflects a desire to train pupils and parents for democracy in a formal sense, as well as outlining parents' rights and duties with regard to education. Despite the limited degree to which parents in Germany are formally involved in decision-making, they can genuinely influence important matters such as the appointment of the headteacher, when a school is having difficulties and the teaching staff are divided. The parental organisation also acts as a useful channel for dissatisfaction with poor teachers, and can exert considerable pressure on individuals in these circumstances.

THE LEGISLATION

The legal rights and duties of German parents all derive from the Basic Law of 1949 (*Grundgesetz*), which established that education is a natural right of parents who "have the right to freely provide for the support and education of their children according to their own beliefs and to refuse state intervention in this area". Article 7.1 established education as a state matter. States are required by the constitution to structure their school system according to a liberal, social and participative model, but detailed regulations are left to them. Each state therefore has its own education law, and this includes legislation on the rights and duties of parents.

However, since they do not differ greatly apart from Bavaria in respect of parents' rights, the model of Baden-Württemberg is here offered as an exemplar. The education law of 1983 and 1993 lays down a formal framework of representation at different levels – from the individual school class up to the state government level:

The *class parents' meeting* is made up of the parents of the children in a particular class, and their teachers. It must meet at least twice a year, and the meeting is chaired by an elected representative of the parents, with the class teacher acting as deputy. The parents' meeting functions as a forum for advice, suggestions and the exchange of information and experience as well as for planning social events.

The *parents' council* in each school is made up of the elected parents' representatives for each of the classes. Overall, it is responsible for co-operation between parents and the school, and is the first recourse for parents who have concerns that they do not wish to discuss directly with the teacher or school head. The work of the parents' council is to promote the school's ethos as a whole and its educational atmosphere in particular.

Each school also has a *school council* made up of three pupils' representatives, two parents' representatives and six teachers' representatives. It is chaired by the school principal, with the chair of the parents' council acting as deputy. (To give an example of the variations between states: in North Rhine-Westphalia the school councils are made up of equal numbers of parents and teachers.) The council has decision-taking powers – although only with regard to such matters as school rules, a five- or six-day week, the suspension or expulsion of pupils and the creation of voluntary associations and clubs. (Article 47 of Baden-Württemberg's education law.)

The *state parents' council*, made up of the elected parents' representatives, advises the Ministry of Culture on general educational issues, especially with regard to drawing up curricula and authorising textbooks (Article 60 of the education law).

KEY ELEMENTS OF CO-OPERATION BETWEEN SCHOOL AND FAMILY

Parental involvement in school governance

The idea of school governance which is common in less centralised systems is inappropriate in the German context. Each school is governed (in curricular and assessment terms, as well as in matters such as the appointment and payment of teachers) by the state Ministry of Education. The construction and maintenance of buildings is normally a matter for the local municipality. So the scope left for decision-making by the head and the school council is relatively limited.

Experiments with a greater degree of autonomy are being carried out in many states, but few yet allow the head – even in experimental schools – to choose his or her teaching staff. Sometimes, for example in Kiel, comprehensive schools have been set up which give the head and teaching staff greater autonomy in appointments, organisation of the school day and even curricular matters. Such innovations at these and other schools have helped to make schools today more sensitive to parents' opinions and preferences.

A national voice for parents

The voice of parents in Germany is heard at state level rather than at national level, and states are very reluctant to have decisions made – or even opinions voiced – about education at national level. Nevertheless, there is a federal Ministry of Education which has competence in some important areas like vocational and higher education which impact on schooling. The Standing Conference of Ministers of Education is a federal body. It has an important role in co-ordinating education across the states in matters such as mutual recognition of qualifications and university entrance requirements.

Parents are represented by the Federal Parents' Association (FPA). It receives a grant from the federal Ministry but is not recognised formally by the Standing Conference – although it is often asked for its opinion. The association plays an important role in bringing together the state parents' associations and the other national organisations. Fourteen of the 16 states have official parents' associations and these send delegates to the twice-yearly meetings of the FPA. All delegates have to be current parents of school children and they retire from the FPA when their children leave school. This, together with the lack of official recognition and minuscule secretarial resources, make continuity of organisation or campaigning difficult and means that the association is a very fragile vehicle for a national parental voice.

Since most of the states have state school councils, in which parents have a voice alongside employers, trade unionists, churches and others, the state is probably the best category for comparison with the united political systems of other countries. In many states there are official newsletters for parents, quarterly in Baden-Württemberg for example, aimed at stimulating parental participation and at informing them of educational developments in the state.

Some of the most active nationwide parents' organisations are religious, such as the Catholic Parents' Association (*Katholische Elternschaft Deutschlands*).[44] Others, such as the *Aktion Humane Schule* (AHS) which, as its name suggests, is concerned with transforming schools into more flexible and child-friendly institutions, were formed for specific purposes.

The school and the community

In a centralised educational system as exists in each of the German states, the school is seen not primarily as an element of the local community but as part of a state function. Moves to grant greater autonomy to schools are intended to develop better community relations, but there is no equivalent of community representation on governing boards as in England and Wales.

Although there is no community role in school governance, co-operation with the local community – mainly through the parents – is strong in many schools, especially in cultural and social matters. School parties are often open to the public and plays, concerts and exhibitions are frequent occurrences. In urban areas where the schools have pupils of different cultures, particular efforts are made to create links with the religious and linguistic groups from which their pupils are drawn. Co-operation in local environmental matters is especially well developed in German schools.

Hauptschulen and *Realschulen*[45] have always had closer ties with local employers because of the nature of their curriculum, which involves training for apprenticeships and technician posts. Feedback from employers is seen as particularly valuable by teachers in the *Hauptschule* which have in many ways the closest relationship with employers because these schools are the most "local", especially in rural areas. As unemployment has grown as a problem for *Gymnasien* students, attempts are being made to develop stronger links there with local industries and firms, in work experience schemes or in sponsorship.

Parental influence on the curriculum, its delivery and the life of the school

The curriculum is centralised in the German *Länder* so it is mainly at state level that parents can influence what is taught. The state parents' council is the body through which parental advice on curricular matters is channelled to the Ministry of Education. Most states also have a state school council (SSC) in which parents' representatives are in some states joined by representatives of employers and trades unions, churches and other associations. In Schleswig-Holstein and Baden-Württemberg, this body has to be consulted on all new educational regulations and laws and the Minister of Education is obliged to listen to its opinion. This may concern basic issues of school organisation and the management of teaching, the provision and training of teachers, or design of the curriculum. Such a structure implies substantial participation, but no formal right of co-decision.

Traditionally, parents were expected to provide support at home for school activities by supervising homework, for example, and also helping to organise extra-curricular activities. They were not expected to get involved either in defining what was taught or how their children learned in school. In some innovative schools this has began to change and parents are invited to participate more closely in curricular and pedagogical matters. At the same time, pupils' social and behavioural problems both in the family and at school are bringing teachers and parents closer together. The traditional separation between the school and the home is beginning to shift towards greater co-ordination and co-operation, not only in educational but also in curricular matters.

The class parents' meeting is a significant forum for discussions between teachers and parents on issues such as educational standards, children's behaviour and learning problems, and assessment. Parents also have the right to hold teachers accountable when they are not satisfied with the teaching of their children's class which is potentially an important constraint on teachers' autonomy. Those who sit on individual school councils can also have some influence on the extra-curricular content of the school's provision and on issues such as the choice of textbooks – but not on the state curriculum.

Communication between parents and schools

The statutory parents' meetings are the main avenue of communication between schools and parents, and form teachers have considerable latitude to develop further lines of contact and information. There are usually parents' evenings before the beginning of the school year when pupils are beginning new schools (first and fifth grades). It is also common for schools to organise occasional newsletters for parents. In some schools, parent-teacher associations exist to promote discussions of a more social or wider educational nature – for example they might invite speakers to address meetings of parents and teachers about the problems of drugs. Numerous possibilities for developing co-operation are open to both parents and teachers, including conferences, training seminars and weekend courses (Köhler, 1994).

However, stronger than the parents' interest in such events is their commitment to the welfare and progress of their own children. Attendance at meetings organised by the school is highest when parents have the opportunity to meet teachers to discuss these matters individually. In some schools, the few parents who do not attend these meetings are visited in their homes by teachers.

Parents receive a written report, termly or twice a year depending on the state, which comments on pupils' attainment in subjects and in general behaviour. After the first two grades, pupils receive a mark out of six for each subject, and the report contains a formal record that the pupil has reached (or not, as the case may be) the level required to progress to the next grade. In practice, parents will have been summoned to the school to discuss their child's progress if there is any question of repeating the grade. Meetings between form teachers and parents often become very tense in the final year of primary school when the teacher's recommendation is the decisive factor in the selection of a secondary school.

Psycho-social support

This is an area of growing concern to both teachers and parents, partly as a result of the increasing heterogeneity of the school population – especially in urban areas where very large proportions of students come from immigrant or non-German families. This is associated with greater strains on the schools and an increase in social tensions. A range of federal state and voluntary agencies offer training to parents and teachers, and co-operate with schools in tackling problems among their students. Drug problems among young people are a particular cause of concern. An alliance of many different groups and associations – including parents' associations and education authorities – offers help in the form of information packs, individual advice, parents' evenings and day courses, and discussion forums.

Special needs

So far as special educational needs are concerned, schools have resources to provide a first level of targeted remedial measures. Each school has an educational adviser who liaises with an education advice centre at local level. Between them, they offer a wide range of responses to pupils and their parents concerning pupils' social and psychological development. Parents are consulted at every stage of the process and there is now a period of observation in some *Länder* if a child is placed in a secondary school with which the parents disagree.

There are a number of influential parental pressure groups – in which a leading role is sometimes taken by educational psychologists who are also parents. The parents of dyslexic children are particularly well-organised, and in some areas they now have rights to extra tuition, and can be considered as a special category.

CONCLUSION

The German system of parental rights has many strengths, of which its entrenchment in federal and state law is probably the greatest; but it also has some weaknesses, especially in comparison with those countries where the local community exercises real control over relatively autonomous schools. Parents have a strong place in the decision-making process at school and state levels and individually they are well informed about their children's progress and have ample means of expressing concern or seeking information.

The system of electing two or more parental representatives for each school class, upon which the whole structure of school, state, and national representation rests, ensures good two-way communication and is genuinely representative, especially as at all levels only parents with school-age children are eligible to stand. Parents are drawn into participation at the point which most interests them – the welfare and progress of the class in which they have their own children. Not surprisingly, therefore, the communication and participation works best when it concerns academic and social matters directly affecting pupils. Indeed, when there are problems affecting pupils' academic progress or behavioural difficulties parents can exercise real direct influence at both form and school levels. When there are no major problems and it is a question of participating in the general running of the school, German parents are, in comparison with parents in other countries, less willing to give their time; but this reluctance is less widespread than it used to be, as a result of significant and influential experience gained at innovative schools.

Communication between individual parents and teachers about children's progress or problems is guaranteed in law and applied in practice. In some states, *e.g.* Schleswig-Holstein, parents have the right to attend the class meetings (*Klassenkonferenz*) when all the teachers who take a form discuss pupils' marks and curricular matters. Variations are evident, which result from different levels of commitment by schools and teachers in terms of following up those parents who do not attend meetings. Many schools in Germany currently find themselves in the middle of a learning process, in the course of which they are increasingly changing their practice to meet the needs of different groups of parents (ethnic minorities, single parents, or working mothers, for example).

The limits of parents' influence are set by the centralised nature of the educational system in German states and the power of the teachers' associations. The first means that some of the key decisions concerning a school are taken centrally, and the role of the school council is correspondingly limited. The second means that although parents have formal means to air their grievances and desires, the teaching staff can block changes when they feel that their working conditions will be too strongly affected. The federal system, under which education is a state responsibility, makes it more difficult for parties to articulate national campaigns about educational issues. For all their impressive system of formal representation, parents have not generally been able to achieve as much social support from schools as their equivalents in other European countries.

CASE STUDIES

A rural all-age school (*Grundschule* and *Hauptschule*)

The school is situated in a large village about 40 kilometres from Stuttgart, relatively prosperous and with low unemployment. It is a combined primary and secondary non-selective school, with a separate technical school (*Realschule*) on the same site. Set in a pleasant campus, the buildings are about 25 years old, decorated with good displays of pupils' work. The primary section (*Grundschule*) has 440 pupils and about 35 per cent of the primary pupils continue at the *Hauptschule*, which has only 202 pupils. Just under a third each go to the adjacent *Realschule* and to *Gymnasien* in other towns.

The school has a community scheme which is clearly focused on "problem pupils" in the *Hauptschule*, although it has spread down to the *Grundschule* as it has been seen to succeed. Both the principal and his senior colleagues refer to their Catholic faith as being the source of their concern for the social and family problems of their pupils. The starting point was the very poor attendance of parents at meetings. The principal, supported initially by only a few of the 40 teachers, began to visit parents in their homes. Parents often admit to problems in dealing with their children, particularly after they have "failed" the selection for *Realschule* or *Gymnasium* at tenth grade. The home visits are seen as useful in jolting the parents back into awareness of their responsibilities and in giving these pupils the proof that "someone cares". They also help teachers better understand the context of the pupils' behaviour.

The other aspect of the school's scheme is to remain open in the afternoon. From a modest, informal beginning when the principal and a few other teachers gave up their time voluntarily, this has grown to the point where it involves most of the teachers – who can see the benefits for themselves in improved class behaviour. Exploiting the greater autonomy now available to schools, the principal has managed to allocate his "teacher hours" flexibly to cover these extra sessions – which also now cover early morning pre-school attendance. (Legislation permits more flexible organisation for work with pupils who do not speak German at home, but the school extends it to all who need help.) The early resistance from teachers' union representatives has dissipated. There are four categories of pupils involved: those who always attend because they lack parental support and have serious long-term problems in completing their work; those who temporarily come into this category; pupils who volunteer themselves; and those whose parents request it.

Attendance by parents at parents' meetings and school council meetings has improved as a result of the scheme – as have relations with the wider community. Local employers, who had been critical of standards at the *Hauptschule*, have been drawn into a closer co-operation, taking youngsters on pre-apprenticeship visits, and have now begun to use the same methods as the school with their apprentices. Bigger firms have "mentors" who try to establish relationships with the families and to follow up on problems. Other indicators of the success of the scheme are improved attendance and examination results. There are no exclusions of pupils at this school and all pupils take the leaving examination.

A *Gymnasium* in Leipzig

Built on the outskirts of the city in the 1960s in a large public housing complex, this is a "special" *Gymnasium* with 400 pupils and 35 teachers, which has survived re-unification. It has a science/mathematics orientation and is selective by special examination, priding itself on catering for gifted children. The school is beginning to attract sponsorship; cratefuls of computers donated by a West German firm were being unpacked in a newly created computer science room. However, for a specialist science school it is still very badly equipped, with only one modern laboratory (for chemistry) and no technicians. The teachers complain about the lack of job security, and say that growing violence and bad behaviour are making their work harder.

The structure of parental representation at the school was modified to bring it into line with West German norms. There are two elected representatives per class, one of whom sits on the school parents' council. The school council has three elected parent representatives, one of whom is the chair of the parents' council, plus three pupils and six teachers; it must meet at least twice a year (but in practice normally meets three times). The principal chairs its meetings but cannot vote. The council discusses all important issues other than pedagogical – though even here parents can and do raise questions about discipline, curriculum coverage and text books.

These arrangements do not represent a big change from those which operated under the old system. The main difference is that the balance of power has shifted from teachers to parents. In the past, class parent-teacher meetings were called and chaired by the class teacher rather than parents as now. Teachers used to read out pupils' marks and brought collective pressure to bear on individuals; they were also encouraged to promote working class children and to steer children towards careers in the army or police force. The existence of Communist Youth organisations was a factor in promoting better discipline and closer relations between teachers, pupils and parents.

One seventh-grade class (described as gifted) in which there is a particularly supportive parents' group, had put on a display of musical, foreign languages, science and investigative projects of extremely high quality. The investigative project in particular was very professional. (They wrote to members of Parliament, the Minister of Education and text book publishers with their findings, and have since been consulted by the publishers.) The principal is quite sure that the quality of the pupils' work is related to the school's co-operation with families and the wider community, and it is clear that she and her staff give this high priority. The parents are described as being more "intellectual" than the average, and have contacts which have led to sponsorships or to special tutoring for the school's science project. As well as the statutory bodies described already, this school has a parents' association which has a social and fund-raising focus. Parents help with clubs and transport, give talks, and last year were active in saving the school from closure.

School council meeting

All twelve representatives were present, and the three parents, three students and six teachers were clearly on good terms. The principal ran the meeting at a brisk pace, speaking for most of the time but also responding freely to questions. The main subject was declining birth-rates and the resulting school closures. The principal read out a statement from the city council and commented on it. This school may need to move to another building if other schools close. There was some resentment generally at the way the closures are being conducted: some schools were told at the last minute that they would not have an intake this year, and the heads had to inform the parents of pupils who had already enrolled. At the principal's suggestion, all agreed to sign that they had read the city council 's paper but did not agree with it. Other subjects covered were school meals, trips, the Abitur and entry to higher education, and the school's new computer room.

A teacher-training institute, Schleswig-Holstein

This institute is contracted by the Land government to provide support for school-family co-operation. One of the heads of departments has the responsibility – admittedly a relatively low priority among many others – for the training of parents for their representative roles, and of teachers and teacher training students to co-operate with parents. The leaflets produced by the institute are aimed at new parents and are distributed via school principals. Subjects covered include: *What is your task?*; *What can you do?*; *What can you read?*; *Legal References*; *The Structure of Parental Representation*; *How to set up a Meeting*; and *Model Letters of Invitation*.

The institute also sets up courses for parents, including a Parents' Day once a year which is attended by about 150 parents from the whole *Land*. The agenda covers communication, the mass media and group training in a variety of subjects – including how to handle conflicts with teachers. Local groups of parents can ask for speakers on subjects they choose, and the institute contacts and pays the speaker, and meets all the expenses. In the past, the institute has organised "cascade training" whereby a central group of parents and teachers meet four or five times a year to organise a programme, which is then delivered to parents and teachers throughout the *Land*.

In general, in-service courses for teachers are also open to parents to attend. When the subject is of particular interest to parents (such as increased autonomy for schools), the *Land* parents' council is informed, and invites attendance from its members. Parents in Schleswig-Holstein produce a parents' journal drawing on a budget provided by the Ministry of Education. They express their opinions freely in its pages, sometimes upsetting the Ministry and the teachers.

IRELAND

OVERVIEW

The education system in Ireland is in the throes of substantial structural reform – later than in many other OECD countries, which is giving Irish policy-makers an opportunity to observe the strengths and weaknesses of other national reform programmes. The nation is currently at an educational crossroads, as the White Paper (1995), which was drawn up following the Green Paper (1992) and the Education Convention (1993) is, piece by piece, translated into legislation.

Efforts to develop strong relationships between home and school have been a significant feature of recent policy and practice in Ireland, and current thinking emphasises the complementary roles which parents and teachers play in children's education. A key feature of the new structures will be the involvement of parents at all levels at the system – but they are not yet all in place. When the reforms have been achieved, however, Ireland will have one of the most parent-participative systems in the world.

Under the new legislation, parents will be involved at all levels – in school, in school governance, and at national level. Although education in Ireland has hitherto been mainly managed from the centre, the White Paper proposes ten new regional education boards,[46] on which parents will have a statutory right of representation – although the plan to set up the boards is somewhat controversial and the subject of lively political debate.

In most countries, policies aimed at involving parents more closely must proceed sensitively in order to foster a productive partnership among a number of different interest groups. But Ireland is unusual, in that not only must the interests of the teacher unions be considered, but – even more so – those of the churches, which for centuries have made a crucial contribution to Irish education. Although parental involvement in the education of their children is seen by the churches as a valuable emphasis in counter-balancing changes which have weakened the influence of the family, parental participation in school governance is viewed with a more cautious eye. Many clerics of various denominations are reluctant to give up their traditional influence – and are anxious that the traditional ethos of Irish schools should be preserved.

One of the first moves made by the government in recent years in relation to increasing the amount of parental influence was to create a National Parents' Council (NPC) in 1985. This body – especially the primary school sector – has markedly increased the level and quality of parental input into policy-making, both at national level and in terms of individual schools.

Perhaps the most focused policy to date is the Home-School-Community Liaison Scheme, through which 180 schools identified as serving those areas of most severe socio-economic disadvantage[47] have been allocated liaison workers, funded by the Ministry of Education, to work full-time on improving the relationship between home and school. In most schools, this initiative has resulted in a marked increase in parent involvement. School-based courses aimed at helping parents to support their children at home have also led to personal and educational development among parents themselves. In some cases they have moved into adult education, gaining the qualifications they missed at school. Such developments are resulting, in some areas, in an increasingly articulate and empowered local community.

SOCIAL BACKGROUND

In Ireland, the family is acknowledged as having a central role in children's education. The Irish Constitution identifies it as the "primary and natural educator of the child", and guarantees "to respect the inalienable right and duty of parents to provide, according to their means, for the religious and moral, intellectual, physical and social education of their children".[48]

But, like other industrialised countries, Ireland is undergoing major social and demographic changes which are tending to undermine traditional family networks. Perhaps the most obvious effect has been the weakening of the traditional nuclear family through a decline in the marriage rate, an increase in the rate of marital breakdown, and a rise in births outside marriage. All these trends have contributed to an increase in the number of single-parent families, which now stands at over 10 per cent of the total.

Although the Irish economy is growing at a faster rate than most OECD countries, unemployment is still high – especially among the young and unqualified. In 1992, the unemployment rate for those with only a primary school education was five times that of workers with a third level (non-degree) qualification; and half that year's school leavers were without a job one year later – compared with a quarter of those who had finished upper secondary school. Kellaghan et al. (1995), focusing on the incidence of poverty and underachievement at school, estimate that, using a sliding scale, up to 16 per cent of Ireland's population could be regarded as educationally disadvantaged.

At the same time, other changes in Irish society are leading to a realignment of the power structure in the educational system. The traditional power of the churches is decreasing, the population is more educated, and structures are evolving to enable them to achieve more of their aspirations than in the past. So, while both the state and some religious bodies are now promoting more active involvement of parents in their children's education, there is a strong interest too from families and communities.

POLICY CONTEXT

In spite of the Irish family's central role in education as expressed in the Constitution, in practice families have traditionally played little part in their children's formal schooling. Education in Ireland has always been a political affair – the main participating institutions being the churches and the state. At the local level, most schools were (and still are) managed by the church authorities through boards of management, according to regulations issued by the Minister of Education.[49] The curriculum is prescribed from the centre, and the Department of Education also runs the examination system and carries out school inspections.

Of course, many Irish parents did, in the past, involve themselves in their children's education – particularly by providing a home environment which supported their development, and by fund-raising for the school and helping with extra-curricular activities. But now parents are generally more educated than in the past, and see a greater role for themselves in their children's education, and their aspirations are encouraged by the government and (to a lesser extent) the churches. The recent White Paper, which sets out detailed reforms for almost every aspect of the education system, places parents at the centre of policy on schooling.

In recent years, in advance of these root-and-branch reforms, the Department of Education in Dublin has instituted a number of initiatives aimed at increasing co-operation between schools and families, and recognising parents as legitimate partners in education. These include:

- introducing boards of management to govern primary schools, two members of which must be elected by the parents of pupils currently enrolled in the school (1975);
- setting up an elected National Parents' Council which is grant-aided by the state (1985);
- establishing a Home-School-Community Liaison Scheme in areas of disadvantage (1990);

- introducing a pre-school education and enrichment programme in disadvantaged areas (Early Start), which includes a high degree of parental involvement (1994);

- launching "Breaking the Cycle", an initiative which targets schools in Ireland's most disadvantaged areas (1996). The programme focuses on 25 large urban schools, and 25 clusters of small rural schools. They receive extra support, which includes: smaller classes; special grants; and targeted in-service training for the teachers. This last is aimed at improving teachers' skills in working with families, and in collaborating with parents to raise the school performance of their children.

WHY INVOLVE PARENTS?

The underlying rationale for the new policies towards parents in Ireland is threefold. Parental involvement is seen as a democratic issue – both in terms of individual rights, and as a way of making the educational system more democratic and devolving more power to the local level. The whole country needs to raise its level of educational attainment, and this cannot be achieved without the co-operation of parents (especially those who are deprived or disadvantaged) in supporting their child's learning at home. Active, committed parents who understand the education process are an important resource for the education system. Indeed, some view parental involvement in school as one way of addressing some of Ireland's social problems, which are seen as resulting from the weakening of the traditional family.

THE LEGISLATION

The last five years have seen an in-depth examination of the Irish education system, characterised by intense public debate. The publication of the Green Paper *Education for a Changing World* (1992) was followed by a ten-day National Education Convention which brought together representatives from 42 bodies, including the National Parents' Council in a "forum for mature reflection and focused debate". After the convention, a White Paper published in 1995 (*Charting Our Education Future*) set out the basis for new legislation.

The rights parents will have in the reformed system, set out in the White Paper, are:

- In accordance with their constitutional rights, parents will be central to the education process.

- Parents will have statutory rights of representation on all boards of management and education boards.

- A statutory duty will be placed on boards of management to promote the setting up of parents' associations in all schools in receipt of Exchequer funding.
- Parents will have statutory rights of access to their children's records in schools.
- School plans will set out a policy and specific procedures for the involvement of parents in the school.

The right of parents, through the National Parents' Council, to be consulted on important educational policy matters is affirmed, and will be given statutory confirmation.

KEY ELEMENTS OF CO-OPERATION BETWEEN SCHOOL AND FAMILY

Parental involvement in school governance

Parents are represented on the boards of management of all primary schools – although they form only a small proportion of board members. Two parents or guardians of children enrolled in the school (who must be one man and one woman) are elected by the rest of the parents. The board is responsible for the day-to-day running of the school, and the elected parents on the board participate jointly in the management of the school, while at the same time representing parents' views.

The governance of second level schools in Ireland is more complex. Strictly speaking, many of these schools are private. Although funded by the state, many belong to religious orders. Currently, not all second-level schools have boards of management. The composition of existing boards of management can vary from sector to sector, and from school to school. All, however, include two elected parents (one of each gender) and two elected teachers; the school principal acts as secretary. Discussions on the introduction of boards of management to all second-level schools are anticipated in the recent White Paper.

The White Paper outlines proposals for the future, under which the "core" board in primary schools will in future be made up of two nominees of the patron, two elected parents, one elected staff member, and the school principal. A possible future structure for boards of management at secondary level has not yet been published. The traditional interest of the churches in Ireland in what the government is doing opens up these issues to debate.

The boards of management in Ireland have no role in setting school budgets, or in paying teachers – both of which are carried out from the centre. However, the White Paper proposes the setting up of ten regional education boards, which will take over the planning and co-ordination of education in their area, and provide support services for the schools. The exact composition of these boards has not yet been agreed, but they will be representative of the school patrons, parents, teachers, public representatives, ministerial nominees and the wider community. This step is still under discussion and negotiation.

A national voice for parents

The setting up of a National Parents' Council has probably been the most important development so far in recognising the legitimate role of Irish parents in the educational process. In 1985, the Minister for Education asked the boards of management for primary schools to hold meetings in order to elect delegates to a National Parents' Council-Primary. The Minister also urged each board to set up a parents' association in the school – if one did not already exist. The council's role is to represent the views of parents, inform parents of developments in education, and foster co-operation between parents, teachers and school management. It has a three-tier structure which represents parents' associations in the schools, the county-level committees, and the national council or executive.

The National Parents' Council-Post-Primary, also set up in 1985, represents the parents of students in second-level schools. Its structure is substantially more complicated – in that it has to co-ordinate parents' organisations which were already in existence. Currently it is made up of eight constituent associations, which makes it harder to produce a consensus.

The school and the community

Most schools in Ireland are denominational (*i.e.* of religious foundation) and therefore are based on parishes. To this extent, they are naturally rooted in the community – but the extent of real partnership varies a great deal, being much stronger in rural areas and in settled urban communities. In newly-developed urban areas, schools may lack contact with the community, although a number has become the focus of community development in the area through being the first public building in the new community.

At secondary level, there is a wide variety of types of school. Community and comprehensive schools, and vocational schools and community colleges (which are run under the auspices of local education authorities and encouraged to form links with the community) are often open for longer hours than most secondary schools, offering facilities for adult and community education programmes, and sport and leisure facilities for members of the public. Those secondary schools which are private institutions may form links with the local community as a matter of individual practice.

Community spirit and local networks are currently rather strong in Ireland, and over the last decade or so there has been a proliferation of community groups mushrooming in both urban and rural areas. However, since most community involvement is a matter for the individual institution, it is hard to estimate how widespread links between school and communities are in reality.[50] Certainly, local people with particular interests are sometimes invited into the classroom to talk to students or run workshops. Musicians, artists, theatre groups, poets and writers may visit, as well as representatives of different careers or companies as part of a career education programme. Some schools encourage educational visits from local Garda (police) and health education personnel.

Parental influence on the curriculum, its delivery and the life of the school

Ireland has a national curriculum at primary level. This curriculum is currently being reviewed by the Department of Education's Advisory Body (the National Council for Curriculum and Assessment – NCCA) which will make recommendations to the Minister of Education. The National Parents' Council can influence the curriculum at the national level – through its members who sit on the council and on its individual subject committees.[51]

Normally, parents do not have any influence on the approach taken by individual schools or teachers to the teaching of the curriculum. However, the White Paper proposes that in the future a school's board of management – on which parents sit – will have a statutory right to examine, amend and approve the School Plan[52] developed by the school in consultation with parents and other interested parties.

As is true in many countries, Irish primary school parents work as "partners in pedagogy" by supporting their children educationally at home. What is less usual, however, is that much of this support involves supervising their homework from an unusually early age. Although the Department of Education has not issued any guidelines on this issue, research shows that Irish 9-year-olds are much more likely to be given homework than children of similar age in other countries, and about half regularly receive help. The National Parents' Council-Primary has published guidance for parents which discusses the aims of homework and its use as an educational tool, concluding that it offers a good opportunity for the development of a practical partnership between parents, child and teacher.

In many schools, parents support teachers in delivering the curriculum by helping out in sports and cultural activities, and on educational tours and outings. Some schools organise parents' meetings at the beginning of the school year. These focus on such topics as the curriculum to be covered during the year, homework and the amount of supervision expected, and future projects or educational visits. This practice is not widespread, however. Even less common is to find parents assisting in the classroom in mainstream schools.

However, the Home-School-Community Liaison Scheme, an initiative aimed at schools in socially and economically disadvantaged areas, involves parents more intimately as partners in pedagogy. Some teachers working within the scheme accept parents as helpers in the classroom, mainly so that the parents come to understand the educational process better.

Education and training for parental involvement

Development and education for parents is a strong theme in Ireland, although it is still in the process of being developed. There are two main sources of training:

- The National Parents' Council-Primary has developed a parent education and training programme, designed by the parents themselves. This programme has three aims: to find ways of enabling parents and teachers to work more closely together; to provide support to parents in setting up and running their own associations, so that they can become more effective parent leaders at both local and national levels; and to undertake innovative projects, through which new ways of meeting children's needs through partnership and parental involvement can be explored. Several projects designed to achieve these objectives have already been developed and implemented, and the NPC's post-primary section is currently setting up a similar programme. The NPC also promotes leisure activities among parents.

- Adult education organisers in some areas have been in the forefront of developing community education programmes for parents within their children's schools. These programmes typically focus on literacy, personal development skills, general education (especially for parents who left school with no qualifications), and training parents to train other parents and act as link workers in their schools and communities.

The Department of Education offers in-service courses for teachers, to enable them to develop new ways of working in partnership with parents. However, little attention is normally paid to the issue in pre-service education – although occasionally, for example, a Home-School-Community liaison teacher may be invited to give a one-off session to student teachers.

Communication between parents and schools

Most of the communication between schools and families in Ireland flows from the school to the family. For example, schools normally contact parents before the child enrols, sometimes through a brochure which outlines the aims of the school and gives information on its curriculum, extra-curricular activities, school rules, and the role of the parents' association.

Schools at all levels generally provide written reports on pupils' progress. The usual accepted frequency is once a year in primary schools, and twice a year in second-level schools. Teachers also meet parents on a formal basis at least once a year to discuss their children's progress. Even primary schools often issue their pupils a homework notebook, and parents are asked to sign the book when the work has been done. This book can become an important avenue of two-way communication between home and school, with teachers and parents communicating regularly through notes, comments and messages. In secondary schools this practice is almost universal.

As well as individual meetings, most schools also hold group meetings for parents, normally in the evening. These may be for the parents of new pupils, for example, or for those who are making key curriculum or career decisions in secondary schools. Some schools run discussion programmes with guest speakers or invited experts; parents attend to gain information and discuss topics such as drug or alcohol abuse, or the parenting of adolescents.

It is hard to estimate how widespread such initiatives are. However, plenty of information on good practice is disseminated by school boards of management, parents' associations and the National Parents' Council. Organisations which represent minority groups, such as Educate Together (multi-denominational schools) and *Gaelscoileanna* (schools which teach through the medium of Irish) are also active in this field.

Most schools handle complaints from parents in relation to their children at the level of the class teacher or class tutor. The parents or teacher may then refer the problem to the school principal. If the problem is not resolved at this level, it is then referred in writing to the board of management; if the board is unable to resolve the issue, the matter will be referred to the Department of Education.

Psycho-social support

Many elements in the Home-School-Community Liaison Scheme fulfil the function of supporting parents with various types of need – and enabling them to support their children more effectively. If families experience difficulties in mainstream primary schools which are not part of the scheme, the first phase of support is offered by the class teacher, the principal teacher, and the remedial teacher (where there is one). The type and degree of available support varies from school to school – especially in relation to the size of the school. Ireland has a great many small primary schools, and if the problem – for whatever reason – cannot be dealt with by the school, the principal will refer the pupil for assessment to the Director of Community Care in the local health board.

The Department of Education in Dublin runs a psychological service for both primary and second-level schools, but its scope is limited. The primary school service employs 14 psychologists who focus on about 400 schools, mostly in disadvantaged urban areas.[53] Post-primary psychologists act as a back-up for guidance counsellors in second-level schools, and also assess individual students.

A pilot scheme to address the problem of disruptive and disturbed pupils in primary schools was launched in September 1995; 27 special teaching counsellors were appointed to specific schools already participating in the Home-School-Community Liaison Scheme. The teaching counsellor's role is: to co-ordinate a whole-school approach to devising effective strategies (including liaison with parents) and putting them into action; and to teach and counsel small groups and individual pupils who persistently disrupt lessons.

Most second-level schools offer a guidance counselling service, which focuses on personal and social guidance, educational guidance and career guidance; recent research suggests that about one-fifth of counsellors' time is spent on personal and social guidance, some of which includes contact with parents. There is currently a growing emphasis in Ireland on preventing psycho-social problems among young people through health education and personal development programmes, such as the Health Promoting Schools Project. Parental involvement is central to this international scheme – which in Ireland has involved five primary and five second-level schools during a three-year pilot study. "Health" is taken as a broad concept, including personal development, parenting skills, family relationships and the building of healthy communities as well as diet and exercise.

CONCLUSION

Apart from general improvements in the degree of parental involvement, and the quality of the communication between school and home, Ireland's most marked strengths in this field are two-fold. The first is the development of the National Parents' Council, which in a relatively short time has made its mark on the education scene, is widely respected, and genuinely consulted by government.

The second key strength is the emphasis on reaching out to parents in disadvantaged areas. Some of the most intensive efforts to increase the involvement of Irish parents in their children's schooling have been directed towards schools in socially and economically disadvantaged areas where the overall level of education in adults is relatively low, and in which parents' support for their children's education is seen as being rather weak. Both the Home-School-Community Liaison Scheme (see case study below) and the new initiative "Breaking the Cycle" aim to involve these parents, with the intention of raising the achievement levels of their children. Although many of these intiatives have yet to be officially evaluated, early findings and anecdotal evidence suggest a measure of real success.

Government and parents alike are looking for more parental involvement in the system. The relationship which is being promoted is one of partnership – in which teachers and parents are seen as having essential and complementary roles in children's education. The consensus is strongest in relation to this type of parental involvement – and teachers too seem in favour of it. But there is some resistance, especially in some church circles, to giving parents a more powerful voice in managing schools. Complex negotiations concerning the precise structure of the new boards of management are likely to continue for some time.

So, although there has already been much progress (more than in most other countries), and partnership in schools is imbued with a sense of excitement and optimism, conservatism and tradition mean that there is a long way to go before the new ideas are taken up enthusiastically and effectively in the majority of schools. And without mainstream schools adopting a specific outreach strategy, many parents and their children, particularly those from disadvantaged areas, will remain on the margins.

CASE STUDIES

Examples of innovation in schools serving pupils in areas of socio-economic disadvantage

Corpus Christi Primary School, Moyross, Limerick

A large primary school with 668 pupils, Corpus Christi School serves a local authority housing estate on the northern outskirts of Limerick City which suffers from a high level of unemployment (over 80 per cent). Resources and amenities are very limited, and crime levels are high. The population of 5 500 people is mostly young families: 20 per cent of these are headed by single parents, and over one third of the population is under the age of 12. In spite of those difficult circumstances, the school is free of vandalism.

The school is participating in the Home-School-Community Liaison Scheme (HSCL) and has a very active HSCL co-ordinator, who for a number of years has been visiting families and persuading parents – especially young mothers – to become involved in the school. A strong community has grown up around the school, and the two are closely intertwined. A large number of parents are now actually employed by the school in Community Employment Projects. Extra-curricular activities are run in the community centre, also supervised study sessions for older children with homework to do. Parents are represented on a large number of local committees, including the HSCL committee, and the Adult Education Committee. The school's community education programme is supported by the very active Adult Education Organiser for the City of Limerick – who is a key mover in local policies to educate and empower disadvantaged parents.

Since 1991, the school has had a key experimental project running with one cohort of pupils – the Moyross Intervention Education Pilot Project, which has been funded as part of the EU Poverty 3 Programme. All 75 children who entered the school in 1991 have been part of a special programme with four key elements: close involvement of parents; smaller classes; a specially adapted curriculum; extra support materials. The three classes were given extra teacher-time – and assistance from parents working as teachers' aides. After school, each child attended a weekly session with a parent or other family member, and they worked together on enrichment activities using a wide variety of materials. Parents are involved in managing the project at every level, and have been offered relevant adult education courses such as nutrition, literacy, parenting skills and training as teachers' aides.

Our Lady Immaculate Primary School, Darndale, Dublin

This school for pupils aged between 4 and 12 is situated in a suburb in north Dublin. Because Darndale is disadvantaged,[54] with a great many problems – poverty, unemployment (70-80 per cent), alcoholism, drug addiction and a high proportion of single-parent families – this school is also taking part in the Home-School-Community Liaison Scheme.

Part of this scheme is an Early Start programme for pre-school children, in which 60 pupils take part. They are divided into four groups of 15, and each group receives five half-days per week of intensive pre-school education: educational games and toys, language development, early literacy and numeracy, and art activities. The programme involves parents in the education of their young children, and is a powerful educative mechanism for them too. Parents, teachers and children take part in numerous activities, outings, and parties.

During the past year, the Early Start teachers have had lengthy individual meetings with parents to discuss the importance of co-operation between home and school in early learning, to give parents ideas as to what they can do at home, and to explain what the classes are designed to achieve. They have found these meetings very fruitful. Parents have turned out to be intensely interested, and most have asked for copies of the checklists used by the teachers to assess the progress of the children – so that they can work through them at home. They are more independent and better socialised than those who have not had Early Start.

The programme includes an implicit adult education element in its approach, but it also offers parents classes on topics such as parenting, childcare and personal development. Some of the parents involved have been stimulated into carrying on with further college courses, and a few have gained recognised qualifications. When new parents join the scheme, previous participants act as links and explain the programme. In June 1995, for example, they ran sessions on helping in the classroom, the toy library, and the parents' association.

St Lelia's Primary School, Kileely, Limerick

This small three-teacher junior school for pupils aged 4 to 7 is situated in a disadvantaged housing estate on the edge of the city of Limerick. There are 55 pupils in three classes. The very energetic and committed principal was herself brought up in this area and attended the school. She is very aware of how much wasted talent exists in pockets of disadvantage like Kileely. She launched the community project 11 years ago, and has run it ever since together with the women in the area.

With the support of the City of Limerick Adult Education organiser, St. Lelia's offers a wide range of classes to local women – many of whom gained little from their schooling but have blossomed with the chance to learn subjects such as hairdressing, cookery, keep-fit, yoga, assertiveness, stress control, swimming, literacy, maths, carpentry and how to support children's educational development. Some of the teachers are volunteers; others are paid. The school itself, which includes a crèche and a pre-school class, is run with the help of eight local people who work as classroom assistants, maintenance workers and night-watchmen[55] on a Community Employment Project.

After school is over, "3 o'clock school" begins. Children of all ages and their parents work together on reading, writing and art activities, and go on group visits, walking trips and holidays. In this way they both learn and enrich their family relationships, and experience aspects of the world outside their own area which otherwise would have been impossible.

Examples of innovation in mainstream schools

Scoil na nAingeal (Guardian Angels), Blackrock, Co. Dublin

This primary school serves a suburban area of Co. Dublin. The 370 pupils come from a wide range of backgrounds and the principal and his teaching colleagues encourages parents to feel involved. They are welcome in the school at all times, and are consulted on all the broad educational issues in the curriculum and circulars from the Department of Education. The school has an active parent-teacher association which organises a wide range of sporting, artistic and social fund-raising activities. The two elected parents (one man and one woman) who sit on the school's management board have taken part in training programmes organised by the National Parents' Council-Primary.

Firhouse Community College, Firhouse, Dublin

This 950-pupil community school, which has a flourishing parents' council, is notable for having a student council – very unusual in Ireland. Every class nominates members to the council, and elections run by the students take place every September. In October, the 36 members of the council (one from each class) undergo a brief training programme, and also spend a full day organising an agenda for the year. The student council raises money for charity and for the school, and campaigns on student welfare issues. The students bring requests to the board of management, who consider them and may agree to them (for example, the wash rooms are now fitted with hot air hand driers; girls can now wear trousers as part of their school uniform). Students are not, however, represented on the board.

Last year, the students' council, the parents' council and the teachers all took part in a joint seminar entitled: "Partnership in education in Firhouse Community College: Valuing respective roles". The principal believes that this type of involvement gives all parties more of a stake in the school, and creates a more lively and committed ethos – but most secondary principals, he says, are unnerved by the idea.

Christ King Secondary School, Turner's Cross, Cork

Christ King is a girls' secondary school, run by a religious order (the Presentation Sisters) but with a lay principal. Situated in a fast-growing part of Cork City, it is a very popular school, having grown from 600 to nearly 900 pupils in the last five years. The principal is committed to building partnerships with parents and on her office wall is pinned a key definition of partnership: "Partnership is a working relationship that is characterised by a shared sense of purpose, mutual respect, and willingness to negotiate. This implies a sharing of information, responsibility, skills, decision-making and accountability".[56]

The school's parents' council is enthusiastic and effective. Members are elected annually by the parent body, and are accountable to the school's board of management (on which parents are also represented), which evaluates their activities. The council organises a wide range of meetings for parents, sometimes to explain new curricula or examinations. One recent series of evening workshops on issues such as drug awareness and family relationships attracted 150 parents to each session. The council identifies key activities for each year – and one year organised a draw for a car, which raised 100 000 (pounds). They intend to set up a scheme whereby each new pupil will be "befriended" by an older girl until she has found her feet, and there is also a plan to visit prospective pupils at home before they start at the school.

The council is outward looking, and sends representatives to meetings of the Regional Parents' Council. At one meeting the Minister of Education was present, and the parents who attended felt that she genuinely listened to what parents had to say. The school is part of the Health Promoting Schools Network, and the parents are involved in developing the new curriculum associated with it (although one said they would have to educate themselves first).

There seemed to be rather a gap between these well-educated, energetic parents, and the more disadvantaged families (estimated at about one in ten), most of whom take little direct interest in the school. Since the school itself is not a school with designated disadvantaged status, no extra resources are available for this group; but a retired Presentation Sister acts as a home-school co-ordinator. She visits the parents of first year students – and has found that some are isolated and lonely. As a result, she has formed a support group which meets once a week to chat over a cup of tea, and has now developed into an informal self-education group. She now runs short courses on topics such as parenting and self-esteem, and has found that these parents have gained in confidence with regard to the school and that she is giving and receiving important relevant feedback – but they do need a "comfortable warm parents' room".

JAPAN

OVERVIEW

Japan is planning a wide-ranging series of reforms of its education system, based on a set of reports from the National Council of Educational Reform which recommend the main direction for Japanese education during the next century. No aspect of the system will be left untouched, including educational administration and finance, higher education, and lifelong learning. Elementary and secondary education, too, will be brought up-to-date, and the need to rethink the respective roles of family, school and community and to develop a new partnership is explicitly identified.

Like other countries, Japan's education system has grown out of its national values and culture, and nowhere are these values more evident than in the relationship between schools and parents. Parents – particularly mothers – are seen as having a crucial role to play in their children's personal development, but the pressures of social change means that they need more and more help in doing so. The school is responsible for the academic achievement of young people, but, increasingly, has also been called upon to play a major role in socialising them. At the same time, parents are putting a great deal of effort into pushing their children to achieve academic success, often paying for extra private lessons in the evening.

The wish to link schools and families more closely in Japan seems to be a problem-oriented policy. Although measured levels of attainment in Japan are among the highest in the world – and the envy of many Western nations – there is a great deal of anxiety among government policy-makers, who believe that the narrow lives of many young people mean that their development is distorted, and that parents should take their responsibilities more seriously, and take the time to broaden their children's experience. Partnership between schools and parents is also considered necessary in order to address phenomena such as bullying among schoolchildren (often because they are seen as being different in some minor way) and the refusal to go to school. These are seen as serious problems in Japanese society, and much effort is being spent in trying to solve them.

Compared with staff in many other countries, Japanese teachers are called upon to perform a very wide range of duties – particularly since until recently Japan had a six-day school week. Due to concerns that children were not developing in a balanced way, and were losing touch with their peer group and local community, the Japanese government has officially reduced the school week – but very gradually and in the face of some resistance from parents. Currently, every other Saturday is spent at school, and by the beginning of the 21st century Japanese children should have all their Saturdays free. Whereas in other countries, governments are encouraging parents to work harder in supporting their children's academic performance, in Japan the Ministry of Education is trying to persuade parents to place less emphasis on high marks at school, and more on all-round social and emotional development.

In spite of the key role played by Japanese parents in supporting and motivating their children, there is no legislation which identifies the rights or duties of parents in relation to their children's schooling – except for the simple stipulation that parents must ensure that their children receive nine years of general education.[57] Parents play no part in the governance of schools in Japan's highly centralised system. Neither do they have a role in establishing the curriculum, which is also centralised, and taught mainly through a limited number of compulsory text books.

SOCIAL BACKGROUND

As in many countries, the respective roles of Japanese families and schools is changing. Over the last decade or so, the schools have had to take on more and more tasks, as the family, under the pressure of socio-economic change, has become less capable of socialising young people into society's norms and values – or perhaps less willing to. These developments are causing policy-makers much concern.

Japanese families are much smaller than they used to be; they usually contain only one or two children, and houses are very small – so children do not get so much opportunity to play with others, and often live a long way away from grandparents and other relations which reduces their experience of interacting with adults other than their parents. There are more single parent families, more women work, and rapid advances in technology and automation have raised the stress levels of many employees. Long working hours are the norm, and many parents are exhausted.

Japan's extremely fast industrialisation and urbanisation have meant the break-up of traditional communities, and also mean that many children have less freedom than in the past. There is anxiety that they have lost touch with the natural environment, and the physical skills which came naturally when they led a more rural existence. At the same time, both schools and families are preoccupied with the necessity for high academic achievement. Japan has few natural resources, so its economy is dependent on human resources. This results in an unremitting emphasis on educational performance, which exerts a heavy pressure on young people in their teenage years. Their studies do not leave them much time or space for personal development, and this can lead to frustration and violent outbursts – especially among those who cannot keep up at school.

POLICY CONTEXT

Education policy in Japan is currently in the process of change, and a new partnership between family, school and community is to be at the heart of the new approach. The National Council of Educational Reform, which met during the mid-1980s and submitted four reports to the Prime Minister between 1985 and 1987, recommended in its second report that such a partnership would be essential if the system were to meet its aims for lifelong learning among the population of Japan.

The main thrust of the council's conclusions was that the respective roles of school and family in Japan needed to be analysed afresh, and that families should be encouraged to take back responsibilities which over the years had been handed over to the school, increasing teachers' burdens. Parents and local communities, concluded the report, should become more involved in educating the young, particularly with regard to out-of-school activities. It called for the expansion and improvement of facilities for young people to enable them to develop in a balanced way, to learn in a more active and creative manner than they usually do in school, and to relate more directly to the natural environment.

Policy-makers and employers are concerned that if education does not swiftly take account of recent changes in the industrial and employment structure, globalisation, and advances in science and (especially) information technology, and adopt a more problem-solving approach to learning, the Japanese worker of the future will not be flexible and adaptable enough to cope with change and uncertainty.

Although education in Japan is highly centralised, the local prefectures do have a key role to play in increasing the involvement of local communities. However, many are rather passive and content themselves with carrying out instructions from above, and there has been some criticism of the fact that membership of school boards is an honorary post which does not attract activists or creative thinkers. Indeed, the average age of local school board members tends to be higher than that of other local institutions.

One of the key ideas put forward by the National Council of Educational Reform, and by the 15th Central Council as well, is that of community schools. The first report of the 15th Central Council, which was published in July 1996, stresses the importance of the co-operation between the school, the family and the community. This would necessitate a real shift from school-centred education (which is currently the norm) to community-based education.

This shift will be hard to achieve, though, using Japan's usual approach to educational change – from the top down, by means of Ministry circulars. In order to elicit positive responses from the parents, teachers, members of the community and local politicians who will have to develop the new policy and put it into action, some form of bottom-up movement will have to be stimulated. But, given traditional ways of working, this could be hard to achieve.

WHY INVOLVE PARENTS?

Policies to involve parents in Japan do not seem to be, as in most other countries, primarily related to a wish to increase political democracy or local autonomy – although these will have to be invoked if the reforms are to become a reality. Whereas in many OECD Member countries the support of parents is solicited in order to improve children's academic performance, the aim in Japan is to increase family and community input in terms of social and personal development, and to discourage parents from emphasising "cramming" at the expense of other forms of learning.

THE LEGISLATION

The Japanese constitution does not specifically mention parents' roles or rights with regard to the education of their children, but Article 26 does state that: "All people shall have the right to receive an equal education corresponding to their ability, as provided by law. The people shall be obligated to have all boys and girls under their protection receive ordinary education as provided for by law".

The Fundamental Law of Education (enacted in 1947) further elaborated the aims, methods and principles of the Japanese system, and the second report of the National Council of Educational Reform (1986) identifies the need to analyse and define the respective roles of parents and schools in the overall education and development of young people.

KEY ELEMENTS OF CO-OPERATION BETWEEN SCHOOL AND FAMILY

Parental involvement in school governance

In Japan, schools do not have individual governing bodies, but are administered by local boards of education. The members of these boards are not elected, but are appointed by governors and mayors with the consent of local elected assemblies. The prefectural boards of education consist of five members, appointed for four years. The superintendent of education for the prefecture[58] is appointed by the prefectural board of education, and must be approved by the Ministry of Education, Science and Culture.

Cities, towns and villages have municipal boards of education consisting of three or five members, appointed by local mayors with the consent of the municipal assemblies. They also hold office for four years. The superintendent of a municipal board of education is appointed from among the members of the board, and must be approved by the prefectural board of education. Parents are sometimes appointed as member of boards, and members appointed in other capacities may be parents as well.

School principals are appointed by the relevant division of the prefecture – and are moved to other schools every two or three years. The education budget comes direct from Monbusho to the prefecture and the municipality; it is distributed by the board to individual institutions according to their needs. Hence, the role that parents (and members of the local community) can officially play in influencing school policy is virtually non-existent – although the parent-teacher association (PTA) in some areas is relatively powerful and may co-operate with the headteacher in order to raise money for a particular project or initiate change in some other way.

A national voice for parents

The most important parents' organisation is the National Council of the PTA in Japan. This association has a long and complex history, and goes back to a pre-war government-controlled body. In 1946, however, the United States Education Mission to Japan introduced the American-style PTA. Local schools were encouraged to organise PTAs, which were integrated into a national federation in 1952.

In Japan, the PTA is primarily a lobbying organisation, and is not normally consulted about government policy – but, for the first time, its President has a seat on the 15th Central Council for Education organised in 1995. There are nearly 34 000 members, mostly parents, and it is dominated at the national level by men – although the grassroots activities are almost entirely run by women. A highly active organisation, it has been the springboard for many to a local political career. The National Council has 60 members[59] (one from each prefecture and designated city with more than 500 000 population), who belong to a series of standing committees. One of these is the Mothers' Committee – set up to take into account the views of Japanese mothers.

The council focuses on issues of concern to parents, and has found that in the last five years its preoccupations have changed considerably as a result of changes in lifestyle. Bullying and violence in school, and school refusal are now high on the agenda, as is advice to parents on how to use free Saturdays constructively. It also lobbies government on behalf of children – on issues such as gambling, the sale of alcohol, and the quality of television programmes – and is trying to persuade employers to give their (mostly male) workers paid leave for spending time with their offspring. It also found a new role after the Kobe earthquake; more people became interested in volunteering, fostering initiatives such as cleaning up the environment, or donating money and goods to children in poverty-stricken countries. Partnership with Monbusho is increasing, partly because the country's social and education problems cannot be solved without co-operation, but also because volunteering and concern for others is seen as an important element in the social education of young people.

In spite of the fact that the chairman of a PTA in an elementary school or a junior high school must be a parent, they are frequently controlled by teachers and school principals (although those principals who are in favour of more parental involvement give them a freer hand). Their most common role for school-based PTAs is fund-raising, but since the advent of the five-day week, they have been more involved in extra-curricular activities and forming links between the school and the community.

The school and the community

A number of schools in Japan are beginning to open their doors to the local community, and many open their gymnasiums, libraries and other facilities during the school holidays. But, in general, schools are reluctant to welcome members of the community into the classroom – except for the parents of pupils under strictly limited conditions. There are a few, however, who are willing to let parents and members of the public observe classes outside the official class observation days.

In a new initiative, the government has designated 17 towns and villages as "model communities", in which schools, welfare agencies, the police and the public co-operate in an attempt to solve local problems such as bullying and delinquency. The experiment, which is funded by Monbusho, is still in the research phase; but if it is successful, all prefectures and municipalities will be asked to set up something similar.

Although the Japanese feel strongly that their communities are becoming weaker and fragmented, they still take for granted traditions which, to an outsider, seem to represent a high degree of social cohesion and joint responsibility. For example, parents do not individually take their children to school (except perhaps for the first few days of the first grade). At the elementary level, the older children of a local area are responsible for marshalling the younger ones, and they all walk to school together. And in the evening, after school, the musical chimes of a municipal vehicle can be heard in the streets at seven o'clock, warning the little ones that it is time to go home.

Parental influence on the curriculum, its delivery and the life of the school

The tight control which the Japanese Ministry of Education and local school boards exercise over the school curriculum does not normally allow parents any say in the curriculum-making process.

Japan has a well-established national curriculum (known as the Course of Study), which is revised about every tenth year.[60] The curriculum is largely contained in an official list of textbooks authorised by the Minister of Education which is sent out to the schools through the prefectural boards of education. Some of the books actually used in the classroom – upon which all teachers base their lessons – are written and published by the Ministry itself.

Each school organises its own curriculum, based on the Course of Study, taking into account the characteristics of the local community, the individual school, and the pupils. The curriculum consists of three areas: academic subjects, moral education, and special activities. These last include class projects, the student council, clubs and school events such as ceremonies, presentations, promotional events related to health or safety, school excursions and community service activities. Any of these would seem to benefit from parental involvement, but although parents often help out, schools do not seem to see them as partners in the process of constructing this aspect of the curriculum.

Neither do they perceive them as potential classroom helpers, with or without a teaching role. In elementary schools and lower secondary schools, teachers normally divide the class of 40 or so into six or seven fixed groups, and combine whole-class instruction and activities with work in these groups.

Homework is particularly important for Japanese students. Research published in 1991 showed that the Japanese were given more homework than students in England, Finland, Sweden, and a number of other countries. In Japan's highly competitive system, teachers often have to resort to setting lengthy homework assignments in order to cover the curriculum (especially since the basic textbooks assume a six-day school week).

Japan is famous as an achievement-oriented society, and parents, in particular, believe that effort is more important than innate ability. Parents are keen that their children should be given plenty of homework, and in the early years they often tutor them at home. (Japanese mothers, most of whom do not go out to work, are probably the most highly educated in the world.) As their children grow older, and school work becomes more complex, many parents pay for their children to attend extra lessons or private "cram schools" (*juku*) in the evening – usually between two and three times a week for sessions lasting between 1.5 and two hours. In 1993, over 23 per cent of elementary school pupils, and almost 60 per cent of students in junior high school were attending *juku*.[61]

Children attend these private schools and classes for a number of reasons; high-achieving students want to pass the entrance examinations for good high schools, which will then make it easier to get into a prestigious university – passport to a good job. Those who are getting left behind in class will be sent to *juku* to improve their grades. These supplementary schools not only help children to keep up – they also offer child-care after school, and somewhere for children to socialise in small groups. Indeed, many parents complain about the large classes in Japanese public schools, and feel that many children, especially those who are struggling, do not receive enough attention. The fees paid to cram schools represent a sizeable private investment, which is underpinning the success of the public system.

Parents who can afford it often choose to send their children to private schools, which enables them to bypass the university entrance examination. Manipulating the system in order to give their children an advantage is a key activity for concerned Japanese parents – and one in which they have a real effect. However, as in other countries, this is an avenue of influence which is only available to parents who understand how the system works, and can afford the school fees.

Communication between parents and schools

The key link between schools and families in Japan is the class teacher – generally known as the homeroom teacher – who is responsible for every aspect of the daily living of his or her class, not just their academic achievement. Japanese pupils up until the end of lower secondary school (the age of 14 or 15) are grouped in mixed-ability classes. Elementary school children have all their lessons with the same homeroom teacher. In lower secondary school, students are taught by different subject specialists.

There is a great deal of communication between school and family in Japan, but it tends to be one-way. Teachers tend to set the agenda, and are very keen to let families know what is required of them – but it is often hard for parents to voice concerns or complaints, especially in public meetings. Without a real effort by a member of staff (usually the vice-principal) to open up private channels of communication, parents' feelings concerning school policies often go unrecognised.

The government is encouraging local schools to set up positive relationships with their local community, and to move towards an accessible, "open door" style of management. But in a country where it is common to see notices in the playground warning that no one (including parents) is allowed on school premises without the express permission of the principal, such policy changes are hard to realise. The fact that parents do not take their children to school means that the casual encounters with the teacher in the school yard or at the classroom door, which are familiar to parents in other countries, do not often happen in Japan.

There is a wide range of communication channels available to Japanese teachers, including:

- *School and class newsletters*: Each grade publishes a regular newsletter, which contains announcements, advice from teachers to parents, and requests for parental support in relation to school management and discipline. Many teachers publish newsletters for their own classes, giving notice of future events and advice on good study habits, and exhorting parents to make sure that students do not forget books or stationery.

- *Daily communications notebook*: In the elementary school, many class teachers make use of communication notebooks (*renraku-cho*) to inform parents on the day's timetable, and homework assignments. Every child takes notes in his or her book, which parents are expected to read and reply to, and so a regular communication system is built up.

- *Daily diaries*: In most junior high schools, students keep diaries, recording how many hours they have studied for, special things they have done, and their feelings, attitudes and problems. Their homeroom teachers check them, either daily or weekly, and return them with comments. This system helps each homeroom teacher to communicate with his or her 40 students on a confidential basis, and the diary is seen as an essential tool in building personal relationships between students and teachers – and in enabling teachers to control students' behaviour. These diaries are not, however, seen as an appropriate medium for communicating with parents.

- *Home visits*: In Japan, the new school year begins in April, and homeroom teachers visit the homes of every one of their new students during April or May during Home Visit Week. The visit is a rather routine, 10-15 minute event, during which teachers and parents meet each other, and exchange information on school and classroom policy, and the individual characteristics of the pupil concerned.

- PTA *and class meetings*: Many schools have parent-teacher associations on the American model, which meet regularly. These do not always represent an equal partnership however, since teachers often use such meetings to assert themselves as authorities in relation to both academic matters and discipline. In lower secondary school, three-part meetings between student, teacher and parents are held once a year to discuss the student's future education and possible career. Most of these meetings are attended by mothers rather than fathers; they are held during the day, which makes it hard for working parents to attend. Evening meetings are the exception, rather than the rule.

- *Classroom Observation Day*: Unique to Japan is the system whereby most schools offer demonstration classes for parents once a year or, in some schools, up to four or five times a year. These classes are not, however, seen primarily as opportunities for observing the teacher in action, and making judgement on the quality of his or her teaching. Rather, parents focus on the behaviour and responses of their own child. After the demonstration, teachers and parents discuss the strengths and weaknesses – both academic and disciplinary – of the class as a whole, and of individual children.

- *Report card*: State schools have three terms a year, and parents are sent report cards at the end of each term, informing them about their children's progress. These are seen as an important means of communication between school and parent. Although the format varies among different school districts, most contain a modest space in which parents can add a short written comment. However, each student also has a personal cumulative record. This is confidential and kept in school, and is not shared with his or her parents.

Psycho-social support

Both elementary and secondary school teachers in Japan are expected to instruct and also counsel and advise their pupils. Apart from school nurses, specialist personnel have not traditionally been employed in Japanese schools. But the increase in problems such as bullying and school refusal – both of which have been very disturbing to Japanese parents and the government – has forced the government to look at the effectiveness of part-time school counsellors working on campus. A two-year experimental project began at the start of the 1995 school year in order to assess the effectiveness of this approach in reducing such behaviour problems (see case study).

Special education programmes for children with disabilities are well-developed in Japan; parents have access to guidance at a number of different agencies – public health centres and child guidance clinics. Young children receive compulsory health checks at 18 months and 3 years, and if they show signs of developmental delay, or other problems, they will be regularly monitored. Sometimes early intervention programmes are available, and kindergarten education may be offered to children with mild disabilities.

Most families with children who have special educational needs want them to go to mainstream schools, but the schools can decide whether or not to accept such children. Parental rights to have their child educated in accordance with their wishes are not as strong in Japan as in some other OECD countries. A number of pressure groups campaign for improved education for children with disabilities and for parents to be more involved in decision-making, including the Parents' League for the Mentally Retarded, and the Japanese Association for Autistic Citizens.

CONCLUSION

The involvement of Japanese parents in their schools is strictly limited, and the basis on which it takes place tends to be controlled by the teachers. Parental involvement is only really welcome if it is in support of the status quo, and most of the communication between school and home is to this end. The school structures the parents' role, and identifies the sort of behaviour it requires. Parental involvement is normally limited to home tutoring, paying for private lessons if their children are falling behind or need to pass a particularly difficult exam, and school choice.

The lack of parental involvement in governance is dictated by the traditions of Japanese political life. Until recently, direction from the centre has served Japanese education well – but now that the system needs to change in response to new pressures, the traditional lack of local involvement makes it hard to mobilise schools and communities alike.

The government is currently looking to change the emphasis of the education system, but the parents remain committed to the highly academic, competitive system which is in place. Ironically, in spite of the high degree of centralisation, there is a real limit to the effect that Monbusho can have if parents are not prepared to change. However, the problems now manifesting themselves among young people, and the efforts of schools and parents to co-operate in solving them, may stimulate a change of heart. Parents, being mostly young, energetic and heavily committed to the education process, represent an important resource, somewhat neglected by teachers. However, Japanese teachers are accustomed to a certain power, which they will have learn to share if they want to work in partnership with families and communities.

CASE STUDIES

Tamagawa Junior High School, Kusatsu City, Shiga Prefecture

This junior high school of 519 pupils has a very active PTA with 459 members. The principal is very much in favour of parental involvement which, he says, helps both the children and the school. As well as events – such as sports festivals – which enable parents to see how their children are progressing, teachers hold class conferences to discuss particular issues (such as, for example, the entrance examination for high school). Parents come to the school at least once a month for some sort of event or for a class observation session. Events are publicised through a parents' telephone network.

The PTA itself is organised into sections, each with a different responsibility: local activities, health, publicity, research (on how education might be improved) and human rights education. Each class has a parental representative, and they meet regularly as a group. There is general concern that junior high school students do not participate enough in community activities – in sports clubs, for example, or going to the library – because they are under too much pressure at school, and then do not want to do anything active or constructive when they get home. The main aim of the "local activities" section is to encourage the young people to join in healthy pursuits. During the summer vacation and in the evening, PTA members patrol the local area to keep an eye on what is going on.

The research section organises lectures on topics such as better parenting or family relationships, which are normally attended by over 100 people. They carry out informal research among the parents beforehand, and select the theme and expert speaker accordingly. A "home education" class takes place about once a month – for example, a librarian may come and discuss suitable books for teenagers. In the summer term, home education classes visit the local high school, to find out about the curriculum there, and what their children are being prepared for. The research section has been on a day trip to a local tourist spot, in order to get to know each other better and create more solidarity and understanding between them. PTA members find it hard to get fathers to participate, partly because they have demanding jobs, and partly because they see education as part of the women's sphere of influence. Usually, fathers only get involved when there are problems. The steering committee of the PTA has 15 members, of which only three are men.

Koganekita Junior High School, Matsudo City

The parents of this junior high school first became involved in 1994, in response to a bullying crisis (in another school) in which the victim committed suicide. This made the school face up to the fact that many problems, according to the principal, can no longer be handled by schools on their own; they have to ask for help from the family and the community.

The response has been to set up an advisory committee on Healthy Life for Students; its members include parents, the principal, the vice-principal, the head of curriculum matters, the head of guidance, the principal of the local elementary school, the school nurse, and an official from the school board. Setting up the committee took a great deal of time and energy because such initiatives are unusual in Japan, but it is now well established – although not yet integrated into the rest of the school. However, parents from the committee frequently visit the school board to discuss problems, so this level of influence has also been opened up to parents. The head of the school board is now advocating this pattern to other schools, and the ex-principal is setting up a similar committee in his new school.

Before these steps were taken, there had been serious bullying and a protection racket in the school for nearly a year. But within six weeks of the committee's being established, the problem had been dealt with. There was a strong message conveyed to the students that they all belonged to the school, and were responsible for what went on in it. The bully received "strong guidance", and two parents supported the family of the victim. Members of the committee discussed the problem with both sets of parents, and discovered that they both felt isolated and suffered from a lack of support in the local neighbourhood.

The committee has now developed a conscious strategy for making sure that such a situation will not develop again. The key is social skills training, particularly through a volunteer programme. For example, some ninth graders (aged 13 and 14) help in a community home for disabled people, some are involved with a sheltered workshop for people with cerebral palsy, and others help out in a local nursery school.

Hachioji-Daiichi Junior High School, Tokyo

Every year, ten schools in the Tokyo City school board area are chosen to be Healthy Student Development Schools. The aim is to reduce bullying and school refusal, by improving the atmosphere of the school, and encouraging links between the school and the parents, and each of the project schools receives 700 000 yen for this purpose.

In this junior high school of 518 pupils, a special counsellor assigned and paid for by Monbusho (as part of a two-year experimental project) is available for between one and two days a week, and advises students and their parents in individual sessions. Parents are also invited to meetings and lectures on such topics as bringing up children, and the psychology of adolescence.

Teachers, too, are part of the strategy, and have been encouraged to develop a "counselling frame of mind". Normally, they are responsible for the social and emotional well-being of their students, and at first they felt apprehensive and suspicious in relation to the new counsellor. But they then began to co-operate with her in order to deal with behaviour problems, and now they trust each other and have a good working relationship.

One result of the counsellor's intervention is that the teachers are now more aware of the way in which they approach parents, and the importance of their communicative style when dealing with sensitive issues. Accustomed to seeing themselves as the senior, more knowledgeable partner in the relationship, they are now realising that they need to recognise the parents' own expertise with regard to their children and co-operate with them in solving problems – rather than telling them what to do.

New efforts are now being made to welcome parents into the school; three school observation days are held each year, as well as other opportunities (for both parents and local citizens) to visit classrooms. Whereas teachers used to run school events and activities single-handed, they now make a point of enlisting the help of the PTA – and a special group has been formed to promote the idea of "Children Healthy in Body and Mind". Many school events are now held on Saturdays, to make it easier for parents and others to attend, and members of the PTA help with sports day, swimming lessons and visits to workplaces and factories – indeed, they have recently researched and compiled a list of companies who would welcome school visits.

SPAIN

OVERVIEW

The Spanish education system has undergone a series of radical reforms since Spain's return to democratic government, and the establishment of a new constitution in 1978. Some are still being implemented. During this period there has been also a progressive decentralisation,[62] which has transformed the country from a unitary state to a quasi-federal one.

So the revival of democracy has been marked by a reaffirmation of regional, linguistic and economic distinctiveness. These differences – once ignored but now celebrated – profoundly affect the context within which educational reform is being carried out. Leaving space within the national core curriculum for regional and school-level additions and interpretations is an important element in such diversity.

The reforms give an important role to parents and their representatives – both in shaping the national framework and in the management of individual schools. Parents have influenced developments at both levels. They have a voice in the consultative organs of state, particularly the State School Council, which gives them access to information and also the opportunity to influence policy as it develops. Their influence within the school councils governing individual schools can be decisive in establishing the school plan and making key appointments – although in practice the teachers' voice is normally the more influential. Parents have a legal right to information about their children's progress at school and to consultation with teachers which compare well with good practice in other countries.

However, the low and declining rates of participation by Spanish parents in elections to school councils – especially at secondary level – threaten to undermine the strong position which parents have gained. The government and the national parents' confederations are aware of the problem and have initiated measures aimed at stimulating parental interest. To some extent, this apathy may reflect the comparative lack of involvement in local associations which is traditional in most regions of Spain. It may also be explained to some extent by the culture of the school, and the long established autonomy of teachers in Spanish upper secondary schools.

The development of a wider range of extra-curricular and complementary activities – of which there are encouraging signs of good practice – may be the best way of stimulating family involvement in schools. The participation of local communities in the work of schools is a still more recent phenomenon, set in motion by the 1995 law which offered financial support and a legal basis for local authorities to open schools to a wider public.

SOCIAL BACKGROUND

Political transformation has been accompanied by profound social, economic and cultural changes. There has been rapid urbanisation during this period, the number of working women has risen sharply and the birth rate has fallen to one of the lowest levels in the developed world. While the population remains, by and large, Catholic, divorce has been legalised and abortion decriminalised in certain circumstances, and the freedom that young people enjoy within the family has increased greatly. The standard of living of most people has risen, but unemployment is higher than in most countries of the European Union. All these changes have influenced the nature and quality of education and the roles of parents and students in schools.

One feature which marked Spain out until recently from many of its neighbours was the important role played by the Catholic Church in society generally, and in education in particular. Despite strong initial opposition from the Church, the 1985 educational reform confirmed the incorporation of the confessional schools into the national educational system.

About one in three pupils attend private or state-aided schools, 90 per cent of which are Catholic. Most of these pupils attend state-aided Catholic schools, where the national curriculum is taught and teaching costs are paid by the state. However, the ethos and teaching conditions are very different from in the state schools. The law concerning the participation of parents and students in the governance of schools applies in outline to these schools too, but its application differs in practice. In choosing a school with a religious character, parents are implicitly confirming the educational ethos of the school – so their participation is of a different nature from that of parents in state schools, who can to some extent shape the ethos of the individual school.

POLICY CONTEXT

The democratic process has led to profound changes in the Spanish educational system. These have been guided by key principles: equal opportunity; a guaranteed right to education; improvement in the quality of education; and the involvement of society in general and teachers and families in particular in educational decision-making (at national and regional levels, and in educational establishments themselves). Three laws passed between 1985-95 expanded on these constitutional principles.

WHY INVOLVE PARENTS?

The main answer to this question, so far as the Spanish system is concerned, is that involving parents in the education of their children is seen as a fundamental element of a democratic education system and society. It is also considered to be an essential means of improving the quality of education and raising educational standards.

THE LEGISLATION

- The **Constitution of 1978** stipulates that the aim of education shall be the full development of the individual personality, respecting the democratic principles of co-existence and fundamental rights and liberties. The Spanish constitution recognises the right to education and the right of teachers, parents and pupils to participate in defining the scope and nature of educational services.
- The **1985 Law (LODE)** delegated the management of educational establishments to school councils, set out the roles of teachers, parents and pupils within the councils and recognised the right of assembly and association of parents and pupils. A decree of 1986 regulated the functioning of parents' associations.
- The **1990 Law (LOGSE)** set out the structure of the new education system. Parent participation is understood in the law to mean co-operation both in formulating the nationwide master plan for education and in particularising its intended objectives.
- The **1995 Law (LOPEG)** extended and consolidated the principles established by the LOGSE. In particular, it reinforced the functions of the school council, adapted school autonomy and organisation to the new structure of the educational system, and emphasised the role of school councils in determining the school plan and the school curriculum.

As a result, there are now three levels in the relationship between schools and families:

- through individual contacts between parents and schools, which enable parents to monitor their children's academic progress;
- through parent and student participation in school management;

– through parents' and pupils' associations which participate both in the management of schools and in the formation of national education policy (as a function of their membership of the State School Council).

KEY ELEMENTS OF CO-OPERATION BETWEEN SCHOOL AND FAMILY

Parental involvement in school governance

Legislation provides for the representation of parents on the school councils, which are executive decision-making bodies with the power – for example – to hire and fire the principal (who is elected to the post) and the head of studies. Broadly speaking, the law established a three-part representation: the teachers; the parents and/or pupils; and a heterogeneous group made up of the school principal, the head of studies, a representative of the clerical and administrative staff, and a local authority representative – plus the school secretary, who may speak but not vote.

In primary schools, parents have seven seats; but in secondary schools they share these seven seats with the students (three parents and four students). Parents are therefore in a minority at both levels, but their influence can still be substantial. When problems arise, and particularly in circumstances where the teachers do not speak with a single voice, parents' opinions and votes can be decisive. At least some of their members (two out of three in most secondary schools) speak on behalf of the parents' association. In some cases, the association holds a meeting before school council meetings, in order to determine parents' views on critical issues.

The degree of influence wielded by parents depends on how many get involved, and the quality of their participation. The decline of parental interest in school governance (as measured by the proportion who vote in the elections[63] and attend meetings) is therefore a serious issue. The problem has been recognised by the State School Council, which has urged the government to launch a nationwide media campaign and improve the funding for training for parents. A good deal of training already occurs, usually in local teachers' centres or teacher training institutions.

The school council elects the head, decides on admission procedures, approves the school budget and maintains the school's facilities. A parent member of the school council is normally delegated to serve on the school finance committee. The council also establishes the school rules, settles disputes and imposes disciplinary measures on students whose conduct is severely disruptive. It is responsible for the approval and evaluation of the yearly programme before the school inspectors see it, monitoring pupils' academic performance and implementing extra-curricular activities. It co-operates with the school inspectors in external evaluation of the school, and issues a report on the results of the inspection which must be made available to the families of pupils and the local community. In theory, no aspect of school life is outside the scrutiny of the parents – though in practice, unless there is a crisis of confidence in the quality of education the school is offering, they tend to leave curricular and pedagogical matters to the teachers.

In private schools, although the law applies in broadly the same way, in practice parental participation is more circumscribed. Catholic schools consider that parents who choose this type of school have implicitly accepted the ethos which the religious community provides; their role is seen as supportive rather than controlling. One example indicates this difference: when it comes to choosing a new principal, the role of the school council in the latter is to formally approve an individual nominated by the church authorities.

A national voice for parents

Involving parents at the national level is taken very seriously in Spain. There are two nationwide confederations: the CEAPA which represents parents in public schools, and the CONCAPA which represents Catholic parents – mainly in private schools. They nominate 12 parents to the State School Council, and three to the permanent committee. This means that three parents' representatives are consulted on every change to the law or regulations affecting education, and they are privy to the advice given to officials by other organisations. They can also raise issues of major interest to parents and families with senior officials and Ministers.

The main debate within the State School Council over recent months has been about the organisation of the school day – an issue on which parents have strong views. The basic alternatives are one long session finishing at around 3 p.m., or two shorter sessions with a lunch break. This has not yet been resolved but the committee is moving towards a consensus and parents have had a real influence on the debate. On some issues parents are divided, either on religious or political lines (CEAPA is secular and left wing; CONCAPA is Catholic and centre-right); on others they unite to support proposals. This was the case when the State School Council debated government proposals to strengthen school management by paying heads more and increasing their powers. Both parents' organisations supported the proposals as did the employers, against the teachers and trade unions – because most Spanish parents want better control and discipline in schools.

The biggest confederation of parents (CEAPA) is composed of 52 federal associations which elect a national committee of 11 parents every two years. The income of the confederation comes partly from government grants, but mainly from the membership subscriptions. CEAPA reckons that around 60 per cent of parents in public primary schools belong to affiliated parents' associations, but only 30 per cent in secondary. The confederation publishes a bulletin for its members and organises "training the trainer" sessions, so that courses can be offered to school parents' associations on matters of interest to parents.

The Ministry of Education provides grants to finance the activities of federations and confederations of parents at national, regional and local levels, amounting to over 100 000 000 pesetas (£500 000) in the last year. CEAPA and CONCAPA are the main beneficiaries, but any confederation made up of two or more province-wide federations is eligible for financial support and has a right to be represented in the state or regional councils.

The school and the community

Strengthening co-operation between school and local community is one of the objectives of the 1995 Law (LOPEG). This is a relatively new concept in Spain, where the involvement of outside communities in education has been largely confined to the Catholic Church – except in a few regions such as *Catalonia* where there is a tradition of local associations. Neither national nor regional political authorities are represented on school councils, though local authorities (which do not pay teachers' salaries or define schools' educational objectives) do have a seat. Local businesses are only represented if the school offers vocational courses.

However, the new law provides that local authorities may co-operate with schools to support extra-curricular and complementary activities and to encourage close relations between school planning and the local community. Some municipal authorities, for example, have agreed to provide health, traffic awareness or cultural programmes to which schools are invited. Such agreements often extend to the mutual use of facilities such as libraries, halls and sports facilities. In Madrid, the local authority finances the early opening of some schools where parents' work begins early; breakfast, social activities and supervision are all provided.

In 1994 the Ministry of Education launched a programme designed to encourage the use of schools in the early morning and evening for community purposes. The government provides complementary financing to support such activities and also offers paid volunteer support (by conscientious objectors to military service). The school council is free to initiate relations with community associations, but practice varies and this approach is not yet a major feature of Spanish schools. However, some examples of good practice are emerging.

Parental influence on the curriculum, its delivery and the life of the school

The 1990 Law (LOGSE) established a national core curriculum. Spain's seven autonomous regions (and eventually all the regions) are responsible for defining regional curricular objectives – concerning, for example, local languages – which round out the national core. Schools can then adapt the curriculum to their particular circumstances as part of their school plan (*proyecto educativo*).

Parents play a role at each of these levels. At national and regional levels, the law has established a State (and Regional) School Council on which the parents' and students' associations are both represented. The State School Council is consulted on all legislation or regulation concerning education, and its permanent committee is in continuous discussion with Ministry of Education officials. However, in practice the parents do not take a leading role at any level in discussions about curricular matters; this is seen as a matter for teachers. At school level, the formulation of the curriculum, assessment and pedagogical principles is discussed first by the teaching staff, before being presented to the school council for approval.

The school's curriculum project is included in the yearly project which is approved by the school council and sent to the inspectorate as the basis for evaluation of the school. It must include measures to ensure co-ordination with families, and this means opening up school visits and other educational activities to parents for their involvement and support. The law now makes provision for parents to play an active role in making sure that the school curriculum – within state and regional guidelines – is adapted to suit the particular area and the students. But tradition and perhaps also the resistance of teachers to any encroachment on their "territory" have so far limited parents in exercising their full rights. According to the president of the main confederation of parents, they still tend to feel insecure and lack knowledge of specific subjects.

Communication between parents and schools

Parents have the legal right to be informed of the academic performance of their children three times a year, via the individual school report written by the form teacher. This includes information on the how far the student has assimilated or achieved the knowledge and skills set out for the relevant stage of the national curriculum, and the grades he or she achieved during the period under review. If decisions are being made about whether the student should be promoted to the next grade – particularly if it is decided that promotion is not appropriate – then the parents must be given the opportunity to discuss the report before it is confirmed. The form teacher meets all his or her parents annually at least, to discuss that year's timetable and class activities, and his or her aims for the class. It is also common for head teachers to call a meeting of all parents at the beginning of the school year, to inform them of the school's objectives for that year.

The legislation establishes a specific weekly period for contacts between parents and form teachers, which is normally used for interviews with individual parents. This is usually at the invitation of the teacher when there is concern for the progress of a pupil, but the initiative can also be taken by the parents. Contacts of this kind are more frequent and varied in subject matter in primary than in secondary schools, and the parents of young children in the first two grades rate their relations with teachers very highly. The value which parents place on these meetings declines as pupils progress through the system.

Communication concerning more general issues is through the parents' associations, which usually have reserved places on the school council. Parents normally join the association when they first register their children at the school or attend their first meeting. Membership varies from 100 per cent of parents to very low proportions, and in most schools the active minority – which sometimes coincides with the executive committee – is small, often no more than a dozen parents. Often, they are also on the school council. This means that, though most heads treat them as representative of all the parents, they may not be. Most parents' associations send letters to all parents at least once a year and call a general meeting. They also play an active role in the elections to the school council. Communications between the parents' association committee members and with other parents is often informal, by telephone or by a committee presence at weekly activities.

There is a marked difference between state and private schools in their relations with families. In the latter, communication seems to be more one-way *i.e.* from school to parents, who are enlisted to support the school's extra-curricular activities. But while social events and extra-curricular activities also make up a substantial proportion of parental involvement in state schools, the parents' association also has a more representative role – in channelling parental requests or complaints, for example. As state schools begin to differentiate themselves, using their new autonomy, they are developing fresh forms of communication related to the particular characteristics of their parents.

Psycho-social support

Special needs

The educational authorities have created specialised educational psycho-pedagogical and occupational guidance services. At primary level, district teams made up of psychologists, educational specialist, social workers and sometimes hearing and speech therapists provide a referral service for schools. At secondary level, these teams also provide support and referral services and help co-ordinate curricular projects between primary and secondary schools. Secondary schools also have a counselling department which provides teachers with advice and helps students with behavioural and career guidance. In some schools the department is well established with a suite of rooms, including an interview room for meeting parents.

CONCLUSION

The reforms which are reshaping Spanish education place great emphasis on the participation of parents at all levels, from national consultative bodies such as the State School Council to the management of individual schools through the school councils. This is seen as a means of strengthening democracy, as well as ensuring that the interests of families are taken into consideration.

The education acts also attach great importance to participation as a factor for excellence, and school councils have a key role in evaluating the achievement of the school plan and in monitoring academic performance. There seems to be little doubt that parents have played a major role in shaping the new educational system at national level and their role in school councils is often decisive, especially when there are problems which lead to divisions among the teaching staff. Parents' right to information about the performance of their own children is entrenched in the law and this is the area in which parents' involvement with schools is greatest and most valued.

It is a matter of concern, though, that parental participation has declined over the period during which the reforms have been implemented. To some extent, the decline in parental influence in the secondary school may simply reflect the growing ability of children to look after their own interests – and this is recognised in the substitution of pupils for parents in four of the seven seats on the school councils of secondary schools. It may also reflect an attitude among teachers, particularly the more specialised secondary teachers, that parents should not encroach too far into educational management – an area where these teachers have traditionally enjoyed considerable autonomy. But all the same, it is not clear why parents at this level now seem less interested in playing their part than they were in the past.

Moves to involve families and the local community in the affairs of the school, and to open schools up to local associations for their activities, are relatively recent in Spain. There are encouraging signs that some schools and communities have eagerly embraced the new opportunities, but the picture is patchy and is likely to remain so for some time. The government and local authorities' efforts to raise awareness and to offer training and other assistance are moves in the right direction.

CASE STUDIES

A rural state secondary school

This is a new, well-equipped school, built two years ago in a historic village, roughly 150 kilometres from Madrid. The school has about 400 students and 34 teachers, and serves some 30 villages in a wide, sparsely populated area.

The president of the parents' association is also one of three parents on the school council. He is typical of the new breed of parent brought into the area by the recently installed nuclear power plant: a technician, articulate and well-educated, interested in education and the environment, and an organiser. Membership of the parents' association is 100 per cent, and it has an executive of 12 members drawn from different villages to facilitate communications. Parents were instrumental in getting the school built in the village by exercising political pressure, and the links between teachers and parents are strong.

The school council holds two general meetings per year. In the elections, 33 per cent of the parents voted for the school council representatives. They began work on their curriculum plan five months ago and it has been discussed by the heads of department and the pedagogical committee (which is made up exclusively of teachers). At the last meeting, the draft was given to the parents and the parents' association is planning a meeting to discuss it. The educational project was discussed over a three-year period, and parents were fully involved in it from the beginning. The theme (planning for diversity) was chosen with the parents' support.

The parents' association, rather than the school council, is seen as the main organ for consultation with parents. It has three committees: for End-of-year Activities, Examination Results, and Building. The second issue, in particular, is of great concern to parents; there is also a working group, made up of the principal and nominated parents, which deals with the school's educational standards. Parents' complaints are received and dealt with by telephone by the parents' association president. Letters are sometimes sent out to all association members when big meetings or elections are planned. For example, a meeting held at the school in November 1995 attracted 200 parents. The principal also sends a letter to parents at the beginning of the school year, setting out the timetable. A very successful innovation is the parents' room, which is part of a suite of rooms from which the school counsellor works.

Links with the community are strong in this school. Eleven local town halls have created a consortium to support transport to school, and there are also links with employers – including the nuclear plant which provides some work experience for older pupils in its laboratories. In 1995, the plant contributed 1 million pesetas (£5 000) to the parents' association.

A state school in an area of municipal housing in a suburb of Madrid

The school has about 500 pupils aged between 3 and 14 years, and 34 teachers. The pupils are from working-class backgrounds, many with social problems (broken homes, drugs, child abuse) and most families are poor. The lunch provided at the school is the only meal many children get. Between 10 and 15 per cent of the pupils come from a community of resettled gypsies. The buildings are modern and immaculate, with children's' work on display everywhere and evidence on every corridor of the wide range of activities which are encouraged.

This school is over-subscribed; its criteria for entrance (agreed by the school council) are: proximity to the school; low income; brothers or sisters attending; and handicap. The principal has been in post since the school was built 16 years ago, and is totally dedicated to it. In view of the problems facing so many pupils, he has asked for a permanent counsellor to be based in the school.

In this situation, parental support for the school has a different connotation from that in most schools in Spain. Parental involvement in the school council is of course important, but there is sometimes a problem of communication between the few activists and the mass of parents. Most parents are satisfied with the school and not inclined to get involved in school council-type activities. But they do participate in large numbers in extra-curricular activities – of which there are many. Parents help to organise an annual festival, making all the costumes for their own children and for others too. Pictures on display show huge participation and colourful floats. Sport (which gets the fathers involved), music, photography and cooking are also popular. The school runs money-raising campaigns for resources, and appears well-funded.

A unique feature is the *Escuela de Padres* (parents' school), organised by the teaching staff and attended by about 50 parents (mostly mothers, one father, and a few grandmothers). This initiative has developed over the last six years, since the school began running courses such as "How to help your child with learning", sex education and "How to save money". Teachers are unpaid volunteers, and bring in visiting speakers. The first course attracted 12 parents; this year over 80 have participated. These include several gypsy mothers, who led a highly successful session on the subject of xenophobia. The teachers believe there is a real educational benefit for the children of participating parents; they run a crèche to allow parents to attend if they have younger children.

A state school in Guadalajara

This school has 600 pupils aged between 3 and 14, and 29 teachers – plus one provided by the Church for voluntary religious instruction. The building is well cared-for and has a brilliant display related to its *semana cultural* (cultural week) which was attended by over 300 parents. There is a great deal of evidence of pupil activities.

The school's recent administrative history, however, has been troubled. It has a new principal, following a dispute between the former principal, some of his staff and the parents, concerning the circumstances surrounding the privatisation of the school meals service. An allegation that the parents previously had had no influence was contested by the school secretary – who maintained that in reality the parents' association tried to exceed its powers. The parents' association's complaints, it turned out, had not been recorded. In such cases, it seems, the regulations are not clear on the power of parents. The new principal was appointed by the Ministry, there being no volunteers from within the school. He is due to present his programme and stand for election in 1997.

The School's educational project (*i.e.* plan) has been studied by the school council and approved and sent to the Regional Council, which has approved a 1.5 million peseta grant for implementation. The parents' association has about 1 000 members (nearly all the parents) and an elected committee of ten. It holds at least one general meeting a year but only 50 parents came to the last one. The committee meets once a month and most members come to school every Thursday to monitor the extensive programme of extra-curricular activities.

All schools in Guadalajara have an agreement to be open to the community. There is a Ministry of Education initiative, backed by the region, to finance agreed projects for adult education and leisure activities. These are organised by the parents' association, which offers sports, computing, painting, gymnastics and karate for pupils, and environmental studies three days a week. Some of the activities are free for all, some require payment where parents can afford it. Local business sponsors these activities but the parents' association and teachers are wary of commercial exploitation. A chocolate factory had invited pupils to visit and had sponsored a large mural on the exterior walls of the school but wanted to add their name which was refused. A supermarket offered courses on consumerism. In Spain, young people can elect to work in schools instead of doing national military service. This school uses them to help administratively and with extra-curricular activities.

Teachers and parents agree that the school's academic results are not good enough, but differ regarding the reasons. The principal recently reported the results of a questionnaire sent to pupils, which showed that they were happy with the level of instruction at school but were not getting enough help at home with homework. As a result, a course on "How to learn" was arranged with the local training centre – initially for pupils and later for parents. The package includes booklets, worksheets and videos, and the course attracted 150 parents.

UNITED STATES

OVERVIEW

Although an overall vision of education policy and practice is virtually impossible in a federal country such as the United States, the GOALS 2000 framework for educational reform, adopted in 1990, can be considered as an attempt to make sense of the social, political, and educational objectives underlying the multitude of projects, research studies and experiments in the area of family-school co-operation in the United States.

In 1983, the report of the National Commission on Excellence in Education, A *Nation at Risk*, alerted Americans to the deficiencies of their education system within an ever more competitive international context. In 1990, the President and the governors of each state endorsed national goals intended to guide educational policy in the United States to the end of the 20th century. In 1993-94, Congress passed the GOALS 2000: Educate America Act, which includes the promotion of parental involvement as a critical aspect of successful schools. The aim of the legislation is not only to improve children's academic performance, but also to alleviate social problems such as crime, violence and drug abuse.

Federal policies and initiatives have not been the only motivating force that explains the increase in parental involvement in schooling. Research has consistently shown that parental partnerships with schools have multiple benefits regarding student achievement, social success, family support for teachers and schools and that the outcomes lead to considerable improvements for education.

A characteristic of developments in the United States is the great variety of innovative experiments, projects and school reform programmes in this area – encouraged through both private and state funding. These include: the Institute for Responsive Education's League of Schools Reaching Out; and its new Responsive Schools Project; Edwin Ziegler's Schools for the Twenty First Century; Robert Slavin's Success for All Programme; the James Comer's School Development Programme; Megaskills and so on. The plethora of such projects, even though they may be limited in terms of time and outreach, help to create a culture of parent and school partnerships. However, the fact remains that this type of activity is the exception rather than the rule in most of the United States.

SOCIAL BACKGROUND

As other countries, the United States has seen many changes in recent years in the structure and status of the family that affect the relationship between school and the community. Although the United States is one of the fastest growing economies in the world, and benefits from a high standard of living, large numbers of families live in poverty and difficult social conditions. More than one in five children lives in poverty; and although overall crime rates have declined over the past decade, youth crime has increased nationally. More children and youth are at risk from abuse and neglect: between 1981 and 1991 reports have doubled to 2.7 million. In 1995 a survey of the National League of Cities reported an increase in poverty rates for children, the number of families headed by single parents, the rate of babies born underweight, teenage pregnancies, juvenile violent crime rates and the number of children in foster care.

These worsening family and community conditions have stimulated much of the current interest by educators and policy-makers in family, community and school collaboration as one way of responding to what many see as a social and economic crisis. Despite the rising interest, however, practice tends to lag behind policies and research. Perhaps one in ten United States schools has moved beyond a few traditional ways of involving parents and families.

Historically, significant middle-class and affluent parental involvement increased in the 1950s when the school system was expanding, and national and state organisations were created to support the burgeoning system. Research shows, however, that schools are still resistant to parents taking on new roles; and although most parents would now like to get involved, many teachers are still untrained and even hostile to working with parents. Another major impediment to partnerships between parents and schools is the fact that parents – including two-thirds of mothers – are often at work during the day, and do not have time to link up with the school. Although this is an important factor, schools and parents could find new ways to ensure involvement if plans and schedules were adjusted to individual needs and interests.

POLICY CONTEXT

Parent and school partnerships in the United States are a high priority: in 1995, a higher percentage of American educators (95 per cent) said that it is "essential" or "very important" for schools to emphasise "keeping parents well informed and involved" than those in ten other OECD countries. The average in other developed countries was 82.3 per cent (OECD, 1995*b*).

The Department of Education in Washington has stated the importance of establishing legal frameworks, as well as actively supporting grassroots initiatives in the area of partnerships. In 1994 the Congress approved the addition of an eighth national goal to the goals for education: "Every school will promote partnerships that will increase involvement and participation in promoting the social, emotional and academic growth of children".

The eighth goal suggests a very ambitious agenda: every state will develop policies to assist local schools to establish partnerships that respond to the varying needs of parents and families, including the parents of children who are disadvantaged or bilingual, or parents of children with disabilities. All schools are to engage parents and the home in a partnership which includes supporting the academic work of children and sharing in educational decision-making; parents are also required to support the schools and hold them accountable to high standards. However, there is no legally binding way in which the states can be required to follow such policies.

Recent national laws, such as Title 1, support school-family-community partnerships, and target low-income children. The Department of Education has initiated a nationwide awareness-building programme that includes a network of 120 co-sponsoring organisations, reports and publications and televised conferences on the subject. A competitive grant programme from the Department of Educational Research and Improvement has also stimulated activities in research and development.

A number of states have passed laws to establish decision-making boards and councils at school level. These include parents and, in some cases, community representatives or students. Others have legislated on various aspects of the topic such as teacher preparation requirements, parent choice and charter schools, family education and support in the pre-school years. Some states have developed small grant programmes to encourage schools to develop new partnership projects such as family centres or home visiting.

WHY INVOLVE PARENTS?

The purpose of involving parents in their children's schooling in the United States is defined very broadly, and includes social, economic and educational benefits to the individual and the nation. The notion of "partnership" is interpreted literally and is seen as going beyond "parent involvement" or "home-school relations". It is understood as a formal alliance and contractual agreement to work actively towards shared goals, and to share the profits or benefits of mutual investments.

Parents as partners in education are seen in terms of business partners, wherein both sides need to clarify their mutual interests and common benefits. It is considered that schools can work more effectively when parents collaborate in the education process, and that parents will benefit from the school's input in their efforts to raise and educate their children.

At national level, the United States Department of Education is currently promoting the concept of "strong families, strong schools" as part of a national goal to improve education. It is believed that partnerships between schools and families can bring about safe schools and improved learning. Therefore, families need to be encouraged to provide a supportive environment for their children as well as to show interest in their schooling. It is estimated that family involvement could double the public investment in student learning. If every parent of a child aged between 1 and 9 spent one hour reading or working on schoolwork with his or her child five days per week, American parents would annually devote at least 8.7 billion hours to supporting their children's reading. If a teacher were spending this amount of time, it would cost taxpayers $230 billion. Family involvement can be couched in very concrete terms.

THE LEGISLATION

The national legislation gives each state the responsibility for developing its own plan and standards and then working with local districts to adapt and implement them. The role of the federal government has been essentially to monitor progress, finance innovative projects and administer the Title 1 of the Elementary and Secondary Education Act. (Title 1 gives financial support to activities in schools that encourage involvement of parents in school activities and in their children's schoolwork.) "The GOALS 2000 Act requires that parents be represented on state and local panels designing school improvement plans and be part of grassroots outreach efforts to improve schools and student learning" (United States Department of Education, 1994).

On a formal basis, legislation concerning parental participation varies significantly among states. There is no co-ordination among states or with federal laws. There is some state legislation, or implementation of Department of Education policies concerning various aspects of parent and community involvement, in nearly every state. Much of it is general and lacks any mandates or enforcement, and few states have comprehensive policies. As an example, an account of the key legislation for the State of Massachusetts follows – but it is by no means typical.

The Massachusetts School Reform Law requires that all public and elementary schools in the state shall have a school council consisting of: the principal (who shall co-chair the council); parents of students attending the school who are elected by parents in elections held by the recognised parent/teacher organisation; teachers (selected by teachers in the school). Other members who are not parents or teachers in the school are selected by the district's school committee (in practice names are usually recommended by the principal) from groups such as municipal government, business and labour organisations, institutions of higher education, or other human service agencies. At least one student must also be on the council if the school includes ninth and twelfth grades (roughly ages 15 to 18). There must be the same number of parents as there are teachers.

The councils are responsible for drawing up an annual school improvement plan which addresses such issues as: professional development for the school's teaching staff; the enhancement of parent involvement in the life of the school; safety and discipline; the establishment of a tolerant school environment; extra-curricular activities; meeting the diverse learning needs of as many children as possible, including children with special needs.

KEY ELEMENTS OF CO-OPERATION BETWEEN SCHOOL AND FAMILY

Parental involvement in school governance

Parents in the United States are increasingly taking part in school governance and decision-making particularly through parent leaders and representatives. Sample practices include: setting up active parent organisations, advisory councils, or committees (on, for example, curriculum, safety, or school problems such as drug abuse); setting up independent advocacy groups to lobby and work for school reform and improvements; establishing district level councils and committees for family and community involvement; making information on school or local elections for school representatives more freely available.

Parental partnership in school governance works especially well when both teachers and parents receive training in how to engage in collaborative decision-making. Some schools and a few community organisations have programmes to assist family members to be leaders and representatives, by training them in decision-making skills and by including parents as authentic contributors to school decisions. Information programmes, parent outreach and the provision of transportation are among the strategies that work in encouraging the participation of less affluent families in school decision-making.

The creation of charter schools[64] has provided a particularly important role for both parental choice and governance of schools; in most of these schools parents constitute a large part of the governing board, as well as playing other roles in the school. Most charter schools have their own board of directors, board of trustees, and policy council (the names vary with the schools). The board has legal responsibility for the school; it hires the principal, the teachers, and sets the school's rules.

In a few states, school councils which include parental representation are mandated or encouraged by law. Florida, for example, created local school or district advisory committees in the mid-1970s. South Carolina's law requires school councils in every school, with largely advisory roles. The University of South Carolina has set up a state-funded private agency to provide training and technical assistance for these councils.

Some funding may be allocated to the enforcement of legislation regarding parental involvement. For example, Minnesota's law provides for $5 per child enrolled to all local school districts, to be used "only to provide parental involvement programmes". The law calls on the state department of education to develop guidelines and model local plans for parent involvement including a mechanism for convening a "local advisory council composed primarily of parents or guardians to advise a district on implementing a parental involvement programme".

A number of private, non-profit organisations offer training for parents involved in school governance. Often the training is for low-income parents in urban schools: in Massachusetts there is an organisation called The Right Question Project, and Design for Change does the same in Chicago. Some state departments of education – California, Wisconsin, Massachusetts, for example – also provide some materials and encouragement for parent training.

A national voice for parents

The National Parent-Teacher Association (PTA), one of the country's largest private organisations, has affiliates in every state and in thousands of local school districts. After years of declining membership and influence, the organisation now reports increases in its membership and activities. Some local units are not affiliated with the state and national PTA; some use the term parents' association and do not include teachers as members. Massachusetts prefers a Parent-Teacher-Student Association, and includes students as members.

The national PTA convened a summit meeting in 1993 on parent-school collaboration and is currently developing "Parent and Family Involvement Programme Standards" to be launched in 1997 in the hopes of influencing policies and practices at both the state and local levels. The statement reflects a comprehensive view of family involvement, including participation as "full partners" in decision-making, which is a departure from the national PTA position in the past.

There is a considerable difference in the activities of PTAs at national, state and local levels. At national level, for instance, the PTA in Washington is involved in educational politics, usually working closely with national administration and school board associations. They often get involved in mobilising more support for funding federal education programmes and measures aimed at protecting children's interests – such as protection against pornography on the Internet, or measures to encourage television networks to adopt "family programming" while children are still watching TV in the early evening.

Most state PTAs lobby on education matters, and are sometimes consulted by governors, education commissioners, or legislative leaders. At local level, PTAs usually limit their activities to raising money for the school, sponsoring fairs, and sometimes offering parent education programmes. Active local PTAs can be an important communication tool for the school, but this is seldom the case in urban schools.

To remedy this lack, several large cities (probably 15 to 20) have set up citizens' organisations (not just parents). Some of these groups, in New York for example, date back to the 1890s – others to the 1950s and 1960s. They work actively to support and/or serve as a pressure group for more efficiency and better results in the schools. The city-wide Education Coalition in Boston is one good example. These groups tend to be dominated by well-educated, middle-class people, including business leaders. They carry out research, sponsor conferences, issue newsletters for parents and others about school issues and lobby with the school board and legislature. These groups are normally independent of the schools and not as directly linked as the PTAs.

The school and the community

Increasingly community and business participate in providing such services as adult education after school hours, and in funding targeted programmes in many states and districts. School and community partnerships are found to be mutually beneficial particularly when they are well-designed, when they are supported by the good will of the community residents, when they go beyond the simple donation of money and equipment and when they contribute to raising the educational level of community members.

The trend to create school-business partnerships has been strong in the United States for about a decade now. Typically, local businesses provide schools with free or low-cost equipment or materials, small scale financial support, work experience for students and career opportunities in the work place, and summer jobs. A few businesses go beyond this, offering continuing technical assistance, mentors and tutors. Some businesses give employees time off with pay to spend time with their children. A few programmes, like the Boston Compact between schools and business, provide guarantees for training students and employing them afterwards if they fulfil their side of an agreement to reach a certain level of conduct and achievement.

Several hundred school districts across the United States have community education or community school programmes. These programmes include opening schools for extended hours and during vacations to hold courses for parents, as well as academic, vocational, self-improvement and recreation courses and activities for community children, youth and adults.

Some schools try to identify and integrate resources and services from the community to strengthen school programmes, family practices and student learning and development. Sample practices include: providing information for students and families on community health, cultural, recreational, social support and other services; distributing information on community activities that link to learning various skills, including summer programmes for students; schools, students and parents providing services to the community – such as recycling, art, music, drama, services for senior citizens; participation of adults in school programmes alongside students.

The Centre on Families, Communities, Schools and Children's Learning, a consortium of five universities,[65] and the Institute for Responsive Education with funding from the United States Department of Educational Research and Improvement were mandated to carry out research and developmental work towards building partnerships between families, schools and communities. The work was carried out between 1990 and 1996 at school, district and state levels with action teams and facilitators at all levels working with schools to ensure that school, family and community networks were set up.

The centre's role was to conduct studies on a wide variety of topics related to family and community partnership, covering all ages of children from birth through adolescence. The researchers in many of the projects worked directly with teachers, parents and community groups, often offering technical assistance and other support. Two large projects used action research methodology in which school teams usually included parents who were responsible for initiating and studying partnership activities. The Institute for Responsive Education worked with schools belonging to its 85-member League of Schools Reaching Out to do studies, offer training and disseminate ideas about good practices.

The results of the centre's research have been widely disseminated throughout the United States and abroad through numerous reports, publications and the organisation of policy forums. The centre has also acted as advocate of good practice by way of its network of policy-makers, giving testimony at congressional hearings and working with legislators and state departments of education. The main query concerning this type of research and development programme is to see how it can develop from "demonstration projects" to established and widespread practice.

Parental influence on the curriculum, its delivery and the life of the school

Parents have very little influence on the curriculum in most American schools and school districts. In most states, some of the curriculum is prescribed at state level, requiring for example that state history be taught or determining a certain number of hours of physical education, American history, maths or science. Sometimes these requirements are legislated, and sometimes they are actions of the state board of education, or the state education agency.

Most curriculum decisions are made at school district level. The recent trend towards "school site decision-making" gives the schools more flexibility than in the past in deciding curriculum; the constraints on this are exercised through standardised testing required by the district or state. Many states are developing new content standards and requirements for university admission. Textbooks have an important influence on local school curriculum throughout the country. In many states local school districts must buy textbooks from an approved list prepared by the state or the local district.

Parents are not required to be represented on local school boards; however about 98 per cent of local school boards are elected and therefore parents can run for election. They are also represented in school site councils, in states where they exist – although most studies indicate that most of these councils are controlled and dominated by school administrators. There are exceptions, however, and where the councils function as intended the parents (as well as teachers, students and other members of the community) have a real voice in discussing and contributing to making curriculum decisions.

Learning at home is increasingly considered an essential part of success in school. Therefore strong effort is made in some schools to provide information and ideas to families about how to help students at home with homework and other curriculum-related activities, decisions and planning. Some sample practices include informing families about the skills required for students in all subjects at each grade; informing parents about homework policies and how to monitor and discuss schoolwork at home; inform parents on how to assist students to improve skills on various class and school assessments; giving students homework that requires them to discuss and interact with families on what they are learning in class; getting families to participate in setting student goals each year and in planning for college or work.

A plethora of nationwide programmes have been set up to encourage parental involvement in the curriculum. These programmes may be funded by federal programmes such as Title I for poor children, or from local funds, or from funds set aside for reform projects, by grants from local foundations or businesses. The following are some examples :

- COMPACT is a programme wherein individual schools are asked to draw up "compacts", that is family-school agreements that define mutual responsibilities of home and school. Federal law (the 1995 version of Title 1) requires schools receiving the funds to devote at least 1 per cent of the fund specifically to various forms of parent involvement. In large districts annual Title 1 funding can range from two to ten million dollars.

- TIPS (Teachers Involving Parents in Schoolwork) encourages teachers to structure homework assignments in an interactive way so that parents become actively involved.

- HIPPY (Home Instruction for Pre-school Youngsters) is geared to mothers and 4- to 5-year-olds and has specially designed curriculum and materials to help mothers teach specific skills to their children to prepare them for kindergarten. Local parent aides visit families twice a month to explain the programme and review lessons.

- MEGASKILLS is a programme created by Dorothy Rich in 1988, and is designed to help parents help their children develop broad skills and values like confidence, effort and responsibility. Workshop leaders from schools, community organisations and businesses train parents and other caregivers, who then carry out learning activities at home with their children.

- In READ, WRITE NOW (a national programme of the Department of Education), parents agree to read to their children 30 minutes per day; businesses such as Pizza Hut, for example, produce tutoring videos, and libraries have become involved with parents, offering books and space for storytelling.

- The Buddy Project promotes the use of new technologies, and participating families can link up to the school with a computer. The "homework hotline" enables parents to keep track of their children's homework, and interact with the school readily in case of queries. The Buddy Project also provides children with computers to take home.

Parent volunteers are an important asset in helping some schools, which have worked out many different methods of recruiting and organising parent help and support. Programmes include finding innovative strategies to set up a school and classroom volunteer programme to help teachers, administrators, students and other parents; setting up a parent room or family centre for volunteer work, meetings, resources for families; an annual postcard survey to identify all available talents, times, and locations of volunteers; the creation of a class parent "telephone tree", or other structures to provide all families with needed information.

Communication between parents and schools

Schools are responsible for communicating with families about school pro-grammes and children's progress and for encouraging two-way communication between home and school which in the past has been very limited. The tradi-tional method for communicating with parents has been to send report cards two to four times per year. Nearly all schools require a parent to sign the report. A few schools, probably no more than 5 per cent, require the parents to pick up the cards and have a brief conversation with the teacher. In most schools, parents meet with teachers only when the teacher requests it, usually when the child is having difficulties. There are now increasing efforts to design more effective forms of school-to-home communications about school programmes and children's pro-gress. Programmes in this area include:

- the organisation of conferences with every parent at least once a year, with follow-up when needed;
- language translators to assist families when needed;
- weekly or monthly folders of student work sent home for review and comments;
- parent/student pick up of report card with conferences on improving grades;
- a regular schedule of useful notices, memos, phone calls, newsletters and other communications;
- clear information on choosing schools or courses, programmes and activi-ties within schools;
- clear information on all school policies, programmes, reforms and transitions.

The use of multiple means to reach different audiences is becoming more widespread, especially with hard-to-reach groups. Schools can use community organisations, institutions such as churches, health clinics, and Laundromats, and media such as cable TV, radio stations and local newspapers for communicating information to parents who normally avoid contact with the school. However, most schools use only the traditional methods.

Home visits by teachers are very rare in the United States; possibly one in 50 kindergarten teachers may visit homes once a year and fewer teachers in the rest of the grades visit homes. In some urban areas the concern for safety deters some teachers. More common are home visiting programmes where visits are carried out by paid or volunteer parents; these exist in about 10 per cent of schools in urban areas with low-income families.

Some programmes are specifically designed to overcome traditional barriers and even mutual distrust. The School Development Programme created by James

Comer in 1988 offers a good model encouraging parental participation. "Comer Schools" try to get parents involved in governance and management of the school, participating in curriculum planning and improving the school environment. Workshops are held for parents on how they can help their children to learn. Informal events, and dinners are organised to bring parents, teachers and school staff together to help improve mutual understanding and communication.

Psycho-social support

Parental involvement is seen by experts as a very important factor for combating disadvantage in "at risk" populations. One important example is ASPIRA, an association founded in 1961 by parents of Puerto Rican youth in New York to promote leadership and education. The movement has now spread to the Latino communities across the country, and includes programmes on building up cultural pride, counselling, job search, language teaching, extra-curricular activities and leadership training.

APEX (ASPIRA Parents for Educational Excellence) is a particular programme aimed at empowering Latino parents and helping them to develop the necessary skills to help their children in school. One of the main goals of APEX is to train parents to improve education in their communities, and to help them mobilise other parents by setting up community networks.

APEX runs a series of ten workshops which address such topics as self-esteem in parents and children, school structure, helping children improve their study habits, communication skills for the home, parent's rights in the schools, group dynamics and leadership skills. Funding for this programme comes from a private foundation.[66] A number of other business partners have been recruited – IBM has provided computers for a computer lab, local businesses have adopted schools and provided computers, Hyatt Hotels has set up a vocational training programme on hotel management in an inner-city high school to train youth for jobs.

A number of inner-city schools involved in the programme have set aside a parents' room, and parents help around the schools and in the classroom. Literacy training programmes for parents enable them to help their children with homework; some go on to continue their studies. Evaluation of the programme shows that as parents become involved in the programme their attitudes change, they have higher expectations for their children, become advocates and tend to volunteer for work in the schools. Motivation to attend the workshops is helped by the fact that parents can in turn become facilitators for other parents, and receive a stipend. This is a very promising programme, but reaches only a small percentage of urban schools.

Special needs

Policies for families who have children with special educational needs are separate from policies affecting families of other children. A strong federal special education law gives all parents of special needs children the right to participate in the development and approval of an individual education plan for their child (IEP). These plans function as a contract between the school, the child and the family, for services and programmes that will be provided for the child. IEPs give parents legally based authority on any decisions made about their child.

Nothing comparable exists for parents of other children. Many states have their own laws and policies within this national framework, extending the federal law but not contradicting it. These special education policies are usually observed more faithfully by schools, because parents can and do take schools to court if they are not satisfied. Special education parent groups, at national, state and local levels are significantly more powerful in the influence they exercise than other parents' associations.

CONCLUSION

Legislation, nationally funded programmes, state and district activities and school-parent-community initiatives all demonstrate what works in practice in the United States. Despite the richness of grassroots experiences, and the creative innovations which can be found all over the country, the findings of a number of research studies show that there are few comprehensive programmes in place, and that in most schools, current practices are episodic and highly dependent on the presence of funding. When the financial support stops, so do the activities.

Partnership activities tend to be concentrated on primary and pre-schools; as children get older, parental involvement in schooling diminishes. Parents, on the other hand, continue to report that they have a very strong interest and deep involvement in the education of their own children and in the schools. The National Goals Panel reported that in 1995, 77 per cent of parents of public school eighth graders attended parent-teacher conferences, according to teacher reports. In the same year, principals estimated that 62 per cent of the parents in their school participated in policy decisions. In 1993, 63 per cent of parents in third to twelfth grades said that they participated in two or more activities in their child's school; these activities included attending a general school meeting, attending a school or class event, acting as a volunteer, or serving on a school committee. Families reported reading or telling stories to their children regularly. Almost four out of five parents said that they check their children's homework and discuss school-related topics on a daily basis. Interest in and involvement with their children's education was consistently high across race, ethnic and income lines (United States Department of Education, 1995).

Teachers play a fundamental role in establishing partnerships with parents. In 1989, in a national Gallop Poll teachers were asked their opinion about the biggest problem facing their public school – and 35 per cent said that it was "lack of parent interest and support". This finding contrasts with many studies confirming the high level of interest and support that parents report, and would suggest a lack of communication between parents and teachers. Many parents still find schools unwelcoming or intimiding places.

For most families, the teacher is their only connection with the school, and teachers are asked to play important roles in partnership activities; yet they are rarely trained or prepared for these roles and have to squeeze them into an already busy schedule. They often have little say in developing the plans for collaborative activities that represent what may seem to them a dangerous break from traditional practices.

Despite these contradictions, limitations and paradoxes, however, the richness and variety of innovative practices in school-family partnerships in the United States do offer convincing examples of "what works".

CASE STUDIES

Project 2000, Washington, D.C.

Project 2000 is an inner-city programme that targets at-risk African-American boys. The United States Department of Justice reported in 1990 that 1 410 000 African-American men were paroled or on probation, 1 362 000 were in jail at some time during the year, and only 23 000 African-American men received bachelor's degrees. Spencer Holland began Project 2000 as a response to a need that black boys growing up in poor inner city have for male role models. Mr. Holland is convinced that the absence of responsible men to set an example for young blacks leads them to reject school.

Project 2000 Incorporated began in 1989 as a non-profit organisation to help support the academic achievement of students during their secondary school years from seventh to twelfth grades. The major strategies used are "academic support" through attendance at a Study Hall after school where adults and parents are present to help with homework; Saturday Academy where a variety of programmes are offered including recreational, educational and specialised workshops on the following topics: abuse prevention, conflict resolution, interpersonal skills development, leadership development and teenage pregnancy prevention.

"Mentoring" is an another important part of the programme. This involves providing each student with an "educational development mentor" every school year – that is, an African-American man whose primary duties are to take interest in the student during the school year, have personal contact at least twice a month, phone him every week, have some contact with parent or guardian, discuss the welfare of the student with the school and report monthly to the Programme Director. The mentors must attend a training session and two feedback meetings during the year.

The third main element of the programme is that students are required to participate in community service projects; these projects can be in their school or in the surrounding community where they live. Service projects may include peer-tutoring, junior teacher assistant programme and other community based programmes. The teacher assistant programme set up within the framework of Project 2000 involves the recruiting of adult male volunteers.

Spencer Holland believes that changes in the family have left young people vulnerable. Holland's project is, in effect, offering substitute fathers. He says: "We must assist schools and single parents to prepare these boys and girls to work in economic systems that do not lead to their incarceration or early death".[67] Statistically, the most at-risk segment of the school population today is the Black male child.

A community school, New York City

Intermediate School 218 Salomé Urena de Henriquez is a middle school located in the Washington Heights area of New York City, which has a reputation for high crime and violence. The population is made up mostly of recent immigrants from the Dominican Republic. The school, a modern, spotless building with large iron doors is a middle school serving sixth to eighth grades, with a full enrolment of 1 150 students.

The security guards at the entrance are friendly, and after a quick identity check, usher the visitor to a seat among numerous parents waiting to see the doctor, or the dentist with their child, or just having a leisurely chat over coffee in the school's tuck shop run by students. The school was opened on 3 March, 1992 as a "new entity" of the community, combining a broad range of services: formal education, parent education, health, dental, and counselling services, recreational facilities and summer camps, thus transforming the school into a community centre.

The school was planned from the beginning in partnership between the New York City School Construction Authority and the Children's Aid Society to serve as a focal point, uniting services ranging from education to health and recreation, for parents, children and other members of the community.

The building opens at 7.00 a.m. when children can come for breakfast and attend one of the school's "zero" period classes in dance, Latin band and sports. After the regular school day ends at 3.00 p.m., an extended day programme is offered to students in education enrichment classes, mentoring, sports, computer lab, music, arts, trips and entrepreneurial workshops. Educational enrichment activities include tutoring, homework help, English as a second language, advanced English and advanced maths.

In the evenings the school is open for the community to use for recreation, participate in arts and crafts activities, rap groups, career readiness workshops, leadership training and family life and human sexuality workshops. Parents can learn English, take aerobic classes, and attend parenting classes, family budgeting workshops and entrepreneurial skills training.

Parental involvement is a key aspect of this community school: as partners in planning activities, as volunteers or staff within the school, as members of the parents' association and partners in their children's education. Many immigrant parents come to learn English, and some end up working in one of the school's many services.

A "Title I" school: Comstock Elementary School, Dade County, Florida

All public schools in Florida receiving Title I funds are required to establish parent outreach programmes, including home visits from teachers. Dade County's public schools policy asks each Title I school to develop its own plan for parent involvement which must conform to federal amendments and the state Education Department's own Title I guidelines. A school's plan must include the following: information about the school's programme and instructional objectives and methods; support for parents to work with their own children in the home to help achieve the school's instructional objectives; training for teachers and staff about how to work effectively with parents; provision for participation by those with limited English language and/or literacy skills; home visits on Saturdays and during evening hours. Each school's yearly plan is reviewed by the district's regional office.

Comstock Elementary School has about 1 700 students from 800 families, many of whom are from African American, Mexican and Haitian Creole origin. The school is situated in Allapattah, a poverty-stricken, changing community that has all the problems of an inner-city, port-of-entry neighbourhood. Many students are recent immigrants to the United States and the high rate of turnover each year (48 per cent) is a major problem for the school's instructional objectives and its aim to reach, assist and involve a diverse group of parents. Of the various Title I programmes in the school, the principal identified four as being particularly important to increasing student success:

- *The parent co-operative programme*: Parents of students in four co-operative classes commit themselves to a minimum of three hours a week help in the classroom. The co-op programme provides workshops which orient parents in the instructional and social objectives in the classes, as well as developing their confidence and skills as classroom aides working with the teacher. Some outside help is also provided by the Florida International University and the county's adult education office, who are evaluating the effect of the programme on the social, affective and cognitive growth of the children, in relation to levels of parent involvement. The Cuban-American Planning Council provides English lessons for families who need them.

– PEARLS: Two volunteer teachers set up a project called Parents who Encourage Achievement in Reading, Learning and Self-Esteem. The purpose is to promote direct involvement of family members in their children's education at home and in school. About 450 parents agreed in writing to attend six evening workshops during the year on topics such as: helping the child improve test-taking skills; increasing academic achievement through the use of games; helping your children complete and set up a science fair project; child and parent self-esteem; communication between parent and child. Workshop sessions were offered in Spanish, Haitian Creole and English, and learning aids were developed for parents to take home.

– POP – *Parent Outreach Programme*: Six full-time Parent Outreach Workers were recruited, trained and put to work under the supervision of the school's full-time Title I Community Involvement Specialist. A parent resource room was created which provided office space for the outreach workers, for parents to meet in the school and the display of books, materials and community information. By the end of the first year the workers were expected to have visited about 600 families in their homes, in order to provide information about the school, make referrals to the school counsellors and to the Neighbourhood Social Service Centre, assist family members with forms and surveys for the school and give reassurance and encouragement concerning the importance of school, education and the family's role in the development of the child.

– *Partnership with Allapattah Neighbourhood Service Centre*: A continuing partnership was established between the school and the Allapattah Neighbourhood Service Centre, a branch of the Metropolitan Dade County Department of Human Resources. The centre is a source of information and "first aid" for children and their families in need of social services. Teachers, administrators, the two school counsellors and the Parent Outreach Workers refer children and families to the centre.

NOTES

1. The exact definition of "family" is somewhat contentious in many countries – and, in reality, most of the individuals involved in children's schooling are parents (normally mothers). In this study, the terms "family" and "parent" are used more-or-less interchangeably, in the recognition that there are many different forms of family, but (when children are involved) all of them must include someone who is primarily responsible for the raising of that child. The use of the word "parent", then, does not preclude grandparents, step-parents, older siblings, other relatives, carers, foster-parents, or anyone else who involves himself/herself with a school in order to support the education of a particular child. When it comes to electing parent representatives, different countries, local authorities and even schools have various regulations as to who "counts" as a parent, but such details are not the concern of this report.

2. In reality, it is not possible to give parents a real choice of schools without having large numbers of surplus places in the system – which is expensive and inefficient. In most countries, the most popular schools quickly become full up and usually end up choosing the pupils, rather than the other way round. The system in England and Wales is often cited as the key example of a system where parents have a free choice of school – and parents do indeed have more opportunity than in the past to send their child to the school of their choice. But in law they have no right to a free choice. Their only legal right is to "express a preference" and then appeal to an independent tribunal if they are dissatisfied with their allocation.

3. This is not to imply that all working class or ethnic minority families are excluded from quality education, or that they necessarily underachieve. There is growing evidence from Canada, the United Kingdom and the United States that ethnic minority children whose families support them in particular ways and whose value system is similar to that of the school, tend to do well – as indeed do many working class children in all countries. However, those who do experience failure at school, or are condemned to attend failing schools, are disproportionately from working class or ethnic minority families living in areas of socio-economic disadvantage.

4. Coleman (1988), an American sociologist, suggested that "social capital" was another important type of accumulated advantage passed down through families. This concept refers to the strength of the social relationships among members of a community, and, in particular, the social relationships which facilitate action.

5. This phrase is taken from the seminal American document on co-operation between school and family: *Strong Families, Strong Schools* (1994).

6. In fact, as indicated above, no system can genuinely offer all parents the school that they want. According to Ball *et al.* (1996): "Choice [in England and Wales] emerges as a major new factor in maintaining and indeed reinforcing social-class divisions and inequalities". The reality in many countries is usually a limited amount of "managed" choice (OECD,1994b).

7. National Parents' Associations or PTAs perform a lively, but normally informal and *ad hoc*, lobbying function in virtually all the countries in this study.

8. Information for this indicator is based on estimates and judgement made by headteachers, or on information on national policies.

9. In England, Wales and Ireland, individual schools may set up student councils – and even have students represented informally on the school governing body – but this is the exception rather than the rule.

10. This is taken from "Two decades of school and community collaboration in the United Kingdom", an unpublished paper presented by Michael Hacker at a seminar organised by the OECD Programme on Educational Building (PEB) in Lyon in 1995. The seminar report is entitled *Making Better Use of School Buildings* (OECD, 1996c).

11. Some key feature of a *Zone d'éducation prioritaire* (ZEP) are: that regular interpretation facilities are provided free of charge; that certain charges for services and actitivies are reduced; that community facilities are made available to schoolchildren, and that formal links are established among school authorities, social services, parents and local politicians (OECD, 1996f).

12. Ireland's National Council for Curriculum Assessment is primarily an advisory body for the Minister of Education; it has a number of committees, on which sit representatives of all the stakeholders in Irish education, including parents.

13. This figure seems rather high, possibly because the information was gathered from headteachers – who might have an interest in presenting a positive picture.

14. Less frequent – although still common across the 12 countries involved – is information concerning the objectives and "pedagogical mission" of the school. In most of the countries, over 90 per cent of primary pupils are in schools where the parents receive such information "regularly" or "occasionally". Only in Ireland does the figure fall below 75 per cent (OECD, 1996a).

15. It is not possible in a relatively brief report to deal in detail with this important and specialist subject. The Centre for Educational Research and Innovation at the OECD has had a strong research programme operating in this area for some years, focusing in particular on the integration of children with special needs into mainstream schooling, and on services for children at risk (OECD, 1995c, 1995d, 1996f).

16. See discussion of the term "at risk" (OECD, 1995d).

17. France, interestingly, came out very much on top of the 12 countries when the public was asked if it thought that important subjects were well taught in French schools.

84 per cent of respondents thought they were – compared with only 40 per cent in Sweden and 46 per cent in Spain (the two countries with the lowest scores).

18. Although the United States does not have a national system of inspection, many of its secondary schools are reviewed and accredited by private regional accreditation associations (OECD, 1995e). Parents are not involved in the process.

19. The recent upsurge of support for, and interest in, this subject has enabled a sizeable body of evidence to be amassed – especially in the United States – which demonstrates the positive effect of well-planned, well-executed programmes of partnership. In particular, the work of the Centre for Families, Communities, Schools and Children's Learning based at the University of Boston has influenced federal, state and local policies in the United States.

20. The programme is funded by private donors and a variety of business and community agencies and is staffed mainly by volunteer teachers who work closely with other school staff and support agencies.

21. Charter schools may offer a special curriculum, or have a particular mission set out in a parents' charter. Many charter schools do not offer services for children with special educational needs, or may have other selective criteria which contribute to the increased segregation of students by school.

22. The upper secondary schools and vocational schools, which students move on to when they have finished their education at the *Folkeskole*, are the responsibility of the 14 counties.

23. Each *Folkeskole* has its own governing body – known as a school board. These should be distinguished from local school boards in some other countries (for example, Japan or the United States) which are responsible for all the schools within a particular district.

24. Apart from those who are being educated privately or at home.

25. The tenth grade in the *Folkeskole* is optional – and has been the subject of some discussion. It is seen as being both a final year of schooling for students who are leaving the system to start work, and a preparatory year for further education.

26. These were in 1903, 1937, 1958, 1975 and 1993.

27. Over 400 million Danish kroner were allocated to this programme, which consisted of 8 251 school-based "reform projects" chosen from 14 044 applications.

28. Pedagogical councils are elected from amongst the teachers in a school, and advise the headteacher on professional matters. They are less powerful than their predecessors – teachers' boards – which could dictate the school's policy on issues such as teaching methods and assessment. Principals sometimes have to carry out a delicate balancing act between their school board and their pedagogical council.

29. This survey looked at "extended class teacher duty" (which was part of the reform programme in 228 *Folkeskole*). Some 830 classes were represented in the responses.

30. Twice as many boys as girls receive special services. The population of children receiving special help in mainstream schools is made up (approximately) of the following five categories: 13 per cent with behavioural problems; 14 per cent with a low IQ; 6 per

cent with speech impairment; 7 per cent with sensory or physical impairments; and 60 per cent with "learning difficulties" – usually problems with learning to read.

31. General Household Survey, 1994.

32. Parents do not in fact have outright choice of school – they have a legal right only to "express a preference". But the Open Enrolment legislation means that a school cannot refuse to take a pupil so long as it has free places.

33. There are now over 1 000 GM schools as well as 15 City Technology Colleges, set up under a government initiative to increase choice and diversity.

34. *i.e.* a school not designated as a community school or college.

35. Two of the best known are IMPACT math (Involving Children, Parents and Teachers in Maths) and SHIPS (School-home Investigations in Primary Science).

36. In practice, many parents seek independent information, advice and support from voluntary organisations such as the Advisory Centre for Education or the Citizens' Advice Bureau, local newspapers, or political representatives (local councillors, or Members of Parliament).

37. These may be based in school or in local centres, and include: personnel handling special educational needs; bilingual support staff; health and welfare workers; specialists in behaviour problems; and education staff who support curriculum and professional development.

38. Grants for Educational Support and Training.

39. SHARE is coordinated by the CEDC, a national charity for community learning funded by the City of Coventry and two private foundations. It is also supported by the National Confederation of Parent-Teacher Associations.

40. For the purposes of education administration, France is divided into 28 *académies* with a rector as head of each one and the University Chancellor who is the direct representative of the state.

41. *Collèges* in the French system are junior high schools; all children using the public system attend them after leaving primary school at the age of 10 or 11. From there they move on to *lycées*, which are best described as senior high schools. They prepare pupils from the age of 15 or so for the *baccalauréat*, which is normally taken at the age of 18 or 19.

42. The government grants financial subsidies to the recognised parents' associations in order to help fund the training of parents who are representatives on the CSE or a CDEN.

43. The *Revue des parents* and *Famille et école*.

44. The *Bad Boll* Protestant Forum, although not a parents' organisation, is influential in educational and other matters.

45. German children start compulsory schooling at 6, in the *Grundschule*. After four or six years (according to the *Land*) they move on to secondary level, and may attend *Hauptschulen* (for general education), *Realschulen* (which have a vocational orientation) or *Gymnasien (grammar schools)*. Comprehensive schools *(Gesamtschulen)* also exist in some areas.

46. This step was recommended in the 1991 OECD review of Ireland's education system (OECD, 1995a).

47. About 10 per cent of the Irish primary schools (310) serve areas of disadvantage, and 180 of these are in the Home-School-Community Liaison Scheme, which is aimed at alleviating educational disadvantage.

48. Ireland, 1937, Art. 42.

49. Except for the vocational system, which was set up in 1930.

50. The parents of children in *Gaelscoileanna* (*i.e.* Irish speaking) and multi-denomination schools are particularly committed. There are currently 95 *Gaelscoileanna* and 13 multi-denominational primary schools, representing an exceptionally dynamic form of parental and community involvement.

51. It should be noted that the NCCA's role is advisory. Decisions about the curriculum ultimately rest with the Minister of Education.

52. See Chapter 12 of the White Paper (Department of Education, 1995).

53. In these areas, the ratio of psychologists to students is about 1 to 7 000.

54. The difficult nature of the area can be judged by the fact that the Early Start classrooms are regularly burgled or vandalised.

55. Most of these are paid by the central government through the FAS Scheme, a job creation scheme which, says the principal of St Lelia's, is "keeping the peripheral education system alive".

56. This definition was formulated by Pugh (1989).

57. This provision appears in Japan's Constitution Law and the Fundamental Law of Education (1947).

58. Japan has a two-tier system of local government. There are 47 prefectures, Tokyo being the biggest. These are run by directly elected governors, and representative councils. Every prefecture has a board of education which controls the prefectural public schools. Most upper secondary schools are controlled by prefectures.

59. Only one of these 60 members is a woman.

60. The most recent revision of the Course of Study took place in 1989.

61. Figures from the National Institute for Research Advancement, 1996.

62. Initially only to the autonomous regions, now seven in number, but eventually to cover all the regions of Spain.

63. The problem is particularly acute at upper secondary (*Bachillerato*) schools, where the proportion of parents voting fell from 21.8 per cent in 1986 to 6.67 per cent in 1992. The situation is much healthier in primary schools, especially in the first two grades where parental participation is high and co-operation between teachers and parents gives satisfaction to both.

64. Charter schools are publicly funded schools usually initiated by parents or parents and teachers; they operate outside the district structure – that is, they are freed from many of the state and district policies and regulations that govern all other public schools. The

term "charter" signifies that the school is operated under a contract or charter with the state or local government. The regulations may vary from state to state, but this autonomy is normally in return for a higher degree of accountability. Some 26 states have legislation authorising charter schools; Minnesota was the first state to pass legislation and has most of the schools. There are approximately 270 charter schools in the United States out of 75 000 schools throughout the country.

65. Boston University, The Johns Hopkins University, Michigan State University, Temple University and Yale University.

66. The DeWitt Wallace Reader's Digest Fund.

67. Interview in *Counselling Today*, March 1996.

BIBLIOGRAPHY

ANDREWS, K. and G. VERNON, with M. WALTON (1996), *Good Policy and Practice for the After-school Hours*, Pitman Publishing, London.

BALL, S.J., BOWE, R. and S. GEWITZ (1996), "School choice, social class and distinction: the realisation of social advantage in education", *Journal of Education Policy*, Vol. 11, No. 1.

BASTIANI, J. (1993), "Parents as partners: genuine progress or empty rhetoric?", in P. Munn (ed.), *Parents and Schools – Customers, Managers or Partners?*, Routledge, London.

BASTIANI, J. and S. WOLFENDALE (eds.) (1996), *Home-school Work in Britain: Review, Reflection and Development*, David Fulton Publishers, London.

BOURDIEU, P. (1977), "Cultural reproduction and social reproduction", in J. Karabel and A. Halsey (eds.), *Power and Ideology in Education*, Oxford University Press, New York.

BRIGHOUSE, T. and J. TOMLINSON (1991), *Successful Schools*, Education and Training Paper No. 4, Institute for Public Policy Research, London.

BROWN, P. (1990), "The 'Third Wave': education and the ideology of parentocracy", *British Journal of Sociology of Education*, Vol.11, No. 1.

CANADIAN SCHOOL BOARDS ASSOCIATION (1995), *Parent Involvement and School Boards: A Partnership*.

COLEMAN, J. (1988), "Social capital in the creation of human capital", in C. Winship and S. Rosen (eds.) (1994), *Organisations and Institutions: Sociological and Economic Approaches to the Analysis of Social Structure*, Supplement to *American Journal of Sociology*.

CORDINGLEY, P. and T. HARRINGTON (1996), *Communities, Schools and LEAs*, Association of Metropolitan Authorities, London.

DEPARTMENT OF EDUCATION (1992), *Education for a Changing world*, Green Paper, Dublin.

DEPARTMENT OF EDUCATION (1995), *Charting our Education Future*, White paper, Dublin.

DEPARTMENT OF EDUCATION AND EMPLOYMENT (1996), *Becoming a School Governor*, London.

DEPARTMENT OF EDUCATION AND SCIENCE (1991, 1994), *The Parent's Charter*, London.

EPSTEIN, J.L. (1992), "Schools and family partnerships", in M. Alkin (ed.), *Encyclopedia of Educational Research*, 6th edition, Macmillan, New York.

EPSTEIN, J.L. (1995), "School/family/community partnerships: caring for the children we share", *Phi Delta Kappan*, Vol. 76, No. 9, May.

EUROPEAN COMMISSION (1995), *The Role of Parents in the Education Systems of the Countries of the European Union*, EURYDICE Working Paper, Brussels.

EUROPEAN PARENTS' ASSOCIATION (1992), *Charter of the Rights and Responsibilities of Parents in Europe*, Brussels.

FULLAN, M. (1991), *The New Meaning of Educational Change*, 2nd edition, Teachers College Press New York.

GOLBY, M. (1993), "Parents as school governors", in P. Munn (ed.), *Parents and Schools: Customers, Managers or Partners?*, Routledge, London and New York.

HANNON, P. and A. JACKSON (1987), "The Belfield Reading Project: final report", National Children's Bureau, London.

HOGSBRO, K., JOCHUMSEN, H. and B. RAVN (1991), *Beyond Limits: Development of the School as a Local Cultural Centre in Denmark*, Danish Research and Development Centre for Adult Education, Copenhagen.

KELLAGHAN, T., WEIR, S., Ó HUALLACHÁIN, S. and M. MORGAN (1995), *Educational Disadvantage in Ireland*, Department of Education, Dublin.

KÖHLER, H. (ed.) (1994), *So kommen Eltern und Lehrer ins Gespräch*, Polygon, Buxheim.

LIKIERMAN, A. (1993), "Performance indicators: 20 early lessons from managerial use", *Public Money and Management*, October-December.

MACBETH, A. and B. RAVN (1994), "Expectations about parents in education", in *Expectations About Parents in Education: European Perspectives*, Computing Services Limited (University of Glasgow), Glasgow.

MACKAY, A.W. (1987), "The charter of rights and special education: blessing or curse", *Canadian Journal for Exceptional Children*, Vol. 3, No. 4.

MANSFIELD, M. (1995), *Home and School Links: Practice Makes Perfect*, The Campaign for State Education, London.

MERTTENS, R. and J. VASS (eds.) (1993), *Partnership in Maths, Parents and Schools: The IMPACT Project*, Falmer Press, London.

MORGAN, V., FRASER, G., DUNN, S. and E. CAIRNS (1992), "Parental involvement in education: how do parents want to become involved?", *Educational Studies*, Vol. 18, No. 1.

O'CONNOR, M. (1994), *Giving Parents a Voice: Parental Involvement in Policy-making*, Research and Information on State Education Trust, London.

OECD (1992), *Schools and Business: A New Partnership*, Paris.

OECD (1994a), *The Educational Infrastructure in Rural Areas*, PEB Papers, Paris.

OECD (1994b), *School: A Matter of Choice*, Paris.

OECD (1995a), *Economic Surveys – Ireland*, Paris.

OECD (1995b), *Education at a Glance – OECD Indicators*, Paris.

OECD (1995c), *Integrating Students with Special Needs into Mainstream Schools*, Paris.

OECD (1995d), *Our Children at Risk*, Paris.

OECD (1995e), *Schools under Scrutiny*, Paris.

OECD (1996a), *Education at a Glance – OECD Indicators*, Paris.

OECD (1996b), *Lifelong Learning for All*, Paris.

OECD (1996c), *Making Better Use of School Buildings*, PEB Papers, Paris.

OECD (1996d), *Mapping the Future: Young People and Career Guidance*, Paris.

OECD (1996e), *Schools for Today and Tomorrow*, Paris.

OECD (1996f), *Successful Services for our Children and Families at Risk*, Paris.

OECD and Statistics Canada (1995), *Literacy, Economy and Society – Results of the first International Adult Literacy Survey*, Paris and Ottawa.

POWER, S., HALPIN, D. and J. FITZ (1994), "Underpinning choice and diversity? The grant-maintained schools policy in context", in S. Tomlinson (ed.), *Educational Reform and its Consequences*, IPPR/Rivers Oram Press, London.

PUGH, G. (1989), "Parents and professionals in pre-school services: is partnership possible?", in S. Wolfendale (ed.), *Parental Involvement: Developing Networks between Home, School and Community*, Cassell, London.

RANSON, S. (1994), "Towards education for democracy: the learning society", in S. Tomlinson (ed.), *Educational Reform and its Consequences*, IPPR/Rivers Oram Press, London.

TIZARD, J., SCHOFIELD, W.N. and J. HEWISON (1982), "Collaboration between teachers and parents in assisting children's reading", *British Journal of Educational Psychology*, Vol. 52, pp. 1-15.

TOMLINSON, S. (1993), "Ethnic minorities: involved partners or problem parents?", in P. Munn (ed.), *Parents and Schools: Customers, Managers or Partners?*, Routledge, London.

UNITED STATES DEPARTMENT OF EDUCATION (1994), *Strong Families, Strong Schools*, Washington, DC.

UNITED STATES DEPARTMENT OF EDUCATION (1995), *National Educational Goals Report 1995*, Washington, DC.

VANIER INSTITUTE (1994), *Profiling Canada's families*, Ottawa, Ontario.

WILLIAMS, T.R. and H. MILLINOFF (1990), *Canada's Schools: Report Card for the 1990s – A CEA Opinion Poll*, Canadian Education Association, Toronto, Ontario.

WOLFENDALE, S. (1992), *Empowering Parents and Teachers – Working for Children*, Cassell, London.

WOLFENDALE, S. (1997), *Working with Parents of SEN Children after the Code of Practice*, David Fulton Publishers, London.

WOLFENDALE, S. and K. TOPPING (eds.) (1996), *Family Involvement in Literacy: Effective Partnerships in Education* Cassell, London.

MAIN SALES OUTLETS OF OECD PUBLICATIONS
PRINCIPAUX POINTS DE VENTE DES PUBLICATIONS DE L'OCDE

AUSTRALIA – AUSTRALIE
D.A. Information Services
648 Whitehorse Road, P.O.B 163
Mitcham, Victoria 3132   Tel. (03) 9210.7777
                          Fax: (03) 9210.7788

AUSTRIA – AUTRICHE
Gerold & Co.
Graben 31
Wien I   Tel. (0222) 533.50.14
                    Fax: (0222) 512.47.31.29

BELGIUM – BELGIQUE
Jean De Lannoy
Avenue du Roi, Koningslaan 202
B-1060 Bruxelles Tel. (02) 538.51.69/538.08.41
                    Fax: (02) 538.08.41

CANADA
Renouf Publishing Company Ltd.
5369 Canotek Road
Unit 1
Ottawa, Ont. K1J 9J3   Tel. (613) 745.2665
                        Fax: (613) 745.7660

Stores:
71 1/2 Sparks Street
Ottawa, Ont. K1P 5R1   Tel. (613) 238.8985
                        Fax: (613) 238.6041

12 Adelaide Street West
Toronto, QN M5H 1L6   Tel. (416) 363.3171
                       Fax: (416) 363.5963

Les Éditions La Liberté Inc.
3020 Chemin Sainte-Foy
Sainte-Foy, PQ G1X 3V6 Tel. (418) 658.3763
                        Fax: (418) 658.3763

Federal Publications Inc.
165 University Avenue, Suite 701
Toronto, ON M5H 3B8   Tel. (416) 860.1611
                       Fax: (416) 860.1608

Les Publications Fédérales
1185 Université
Montréal, QC H3B 3A7 Tel. (514) 954.1633
                       Fax: (514) 954.1635

CHINA – CHINE
Book Dept., China National Publications
Import and Export Corporation (CNPIEC)
16 Gongti E. Road, Chaoyang District
Beijing 100020 Tel. (10) 6506-6688 Ext. 8402
                       (10) 6506-3101

CHINESE TAIPEI – TAIPEI CHINOIS
Good Faith Worldwide Int'l. Co. Ltd.
9th Floor, No. 118, Sec. 2
Chung Hsiao E. Road
Taipei   Tel. (02) 391.7396/391.7397
                       Fax: (02) 394.9176

**CZECH REPUBLIC –
RÉPUBLIQUE TCHÈQUE**
National Information Centre
NIS – prodejna
Konviktská 5
Praha 1 – 113 57   Tel. (02) 24.23.09.07
                    Fax: (02) 24.22.94.33
E-mail: nkposp@dec.niz.cz
Internet: http://www.nis.cz

DENMARK – DANEMARK
Munksgaard Book and Subscription Service
35, Nørre Søgade, P.O. Box 2148
DK-1016 København K   Tel. (33) 12.85.70
                       Fax: (33) 12.93.87

J. H. Schultz Information A/S,
Herstedvang 12,
DK – 2620 Albertslung   Tel. 43 63 23 00
                         Fax: 43 63 19 69
Internet: s-info@inet.uni-c.dk

EGYPT – ÉGYPTE
The Middle East Observer
41 Sherif Street
Cairo   Tel. (2) 392.6919
                   Fax: (2) 360.6804

FINLAND – FINLANDE
Akateeminen Kirjakauppa
Keskuskatu 1, P.O. Box 128
00100 Helsinki

Subscription Services/Agence d'abonnements :
P.O. Box 23
00100 Helsinki   Tel. (358) 9.121.4403
                        Fax: (358) 9.121.4450

*FRANCE
OECD/OCDE
Mail Orders/Commandes par correspondance :
2, rue André-Pascal
75775 Paris Cedex 16 Tel. 33 (0)1.45.24.82.00
                     Fax: 33 (0)1.49.10.42.76
                     Telex: 640048 OCDE
Internet: Compte.PUBSINQ@oecd.org

Orders via Minitel, France only/
Commandes par Minitel, France
exclusivement : 36 15 OCDE

OECD Bookshop/Librairie de l'OCDE :
33, rue Octave-Feuillet
75016 Paris   Tel. 33 (0)1.45.24.81.81
                         33 (0)1.45.24.81.67

Dawson
B.P. 40
91121 Palaiseau Cedex   Tel. 01.89.10.47.00
                         Fax: 01.64.54.83.26

Documentation Française
29, quai Voltaire
75007 Paris   Tel. 01.40.15.70.00

Economica
49, rue Héricart
75015 Paris   Tel. 01.45.78.12.92
                     Fax: 01.45.75.05.67

Gibert Jeune (Droit-Économie)
6, place Saint-Michel
75006 Paris   Tel. 01.43.25.91.19

Librairie du Commerce International
10, avenue d'Iéna
75016 Paris   Tel. 01.40.73.34.60

Librairie Dunod
Université Paris-Dauphine
Place du Maréchal-de-Lattre-de-Tassigny
75016 Paris   Tel. 01.44.05.40.13

Librairie Lavoisier
11, rue Lavoisier
75008 Paris   Tel. 01.42.65.39.95

Librairie des Sciences Politiques
30, rue Saint-Guillaume
75007 Paris   Tel. 01.45.48.36.02

P.U.F.
49, boulevard Saint-Michel
75005 Paris   Tel. 01.43.25.83.40

Librairie de l'Université
12a, rue Nazareth
13100 Aix-en-Provence   Tel. 04.42.26.18.08

Documentation Française
165, rue Garibaldi
69003 Lyon   Tel. 04.78.63.32.23

Librairie Decitre
29, place Bellecour
69002 Lyon   Tel. 04.72.40.54.54

Librairie Sauramps
Le Triangle
34967 Montpellier Cedex 2 Tel. 04.67.58.85.15
                         Fax: 04.67.58.27.36

A la Sorbonne Actual
23, rue de l'Hôtel-des-Postes
06000 Nice   Tel. 04.93.13.77.75
                     Fax: 04.93.80.75.69

GERMANY – ALLEMAGNE
OECD Bonn Centre
August-Bebel-Allee 6
D-53175 Bonn   Tel. (0228) 959.120
                      Fax: (0228) 959.12.17

GREECE – GRÈCE
Librairie Kauffmann
Stadiou 28
10564 Athens   Tel. (01) 32.55.321
                      Fax: (01) 32.30.320

HONG-KONG
Swindon Book Co. Ltd.
Astoria Bldg. 3F
34 Ashley Road, Tsimshatsui
Kowloon, Hong Kong   Tel. 2376.2062
                      Fax: 2376.0685

HUNGARY – HONGRIE
Euro Info Service
Margitsziget, Európa Ház
1138 Budapest   Tel. (1) 111.60.61
                       Fax: (1) 302.50.35
E-mail: euroinfo@mail.matav.hu
Internet: http://www.euroinfo.hu//index.html

ICELAND – ISLANDE
Mál og Menning
Laugavegi 18, Pósthólf 392
121 Reykjavik   Tel. (1) 552.4240
                       Fax: (1) 562.3523

INDIA – INDE
Oxford Book and Stationery Co.
Scindia House
New Delhi 110001   Tel. (11) 331.5896/5308
                       Fax: (11) 332.2639
E-mail: oxford.publ@axcess.net.in

17 Park Street
Calcutta 700016   Tel. 240832

INDONESIA – INDONÉSIE
Pdii-Lipi
P.O. Box 4298
Jakarta 12042   Tel. (21) 573.34.67
                       Fax: (21) 573.34.67

IRELAND – IRLANDE
Government Supplies Agency
Publications Section
4/5 Harcourt Road
Dublin 2   Tel. 661.31.11
                       Fax: 475.27.60

ISRAEL – ISRAËL
Praedicta
5 Shatner Street
P.O. Box 34030
Jerusalem 91430   Tel. (2) 652.84.90/1/2
                       Fax: (2) 652.84.93

R.O.Y. International
P.O. Box 13056
Tel Aviv 61130   Tel. (3) 546 1423
                       Fax: (3) 546 1442
E-mail: royil@netvision.net.il

Palestinian Authority/Middle East:
INDEX Information Services
P.O.B. 19502
Jerusalem   Tel. (2) 627.16.34
                       Fax: (2) 627.12.19

ITALY – ITALIE
Libreria Commissionaria Sansoni
Via Duca di Calabria, 1/1
50125 Firenze   Tel. (055) 64.54.15
                       Fax: (055) 64.12.57
E-mail: licosa@ftbcc.it

Via Bartolini 29
20155 Milano   Tel. (02) 36.50.83

Editrice e Libreria Herder
Piazza Montecitorio 120
00186 Roma   Tel. 679.46.28
                       Fax: 678.47.51

Libreria Hoepli
Via Hoepli 5
20121 Milano   Tel. (02) 86.54.46
                      Fax: (02) 805.28.86
Libreria Scientifica
Dott. Lucio de Biasio 'Aeiou'
Via Coronelli, 6
20146 Milano   Tel. (02) 48.95.45.52
                      Fax: (02) 48.95.45.48

JAPAN – JAPON
OECD Tokyo Centre
Landic Akasaka Building
2-3-4 Akasaka, Minato-ku
Tokyo 107   Tel. (81.3) 3586.2016
                      Fax: (81.3) 3584.7929

KOREA – CORÉE
Kyobo Book Centre Co. Ltd.
P.O. Box 1658, Kwang Hwa Moon
Seoul   Tel. 730.78.91
                      Fax: 735.00.30

MALAYSIA – MALAISIE
University of Malaya Bookshop
University of Malaya
P.O. Box 1127, Jalan Pantai Baru
59700 Kuala Lumpur
Malaysia   Tel. 756.5000/756.5425
                      Fax: 756.3246

MEXICO – MEXIQUE
OECD Mexico Centre
Edificio INFOTEC
Av. San Fernando no. 37
Col. Toriello Guerra
Tlalpan C.P. 14050
Mexico D.F.   Tel. (525) 528.10.38
                      Fax: (525) 606.13.07
E-mail: ocde@rtn.net.mx

NETHERLANDS – PAYS-BAS
SDU Uitgeverij Plantijnstraat
Externe Fondsen
Postbus 20014
2500 EA's-Gravenhage Tel. (070) 37.89.880
Voor bestellingen: Fax: (070) 34.75.778

Subscription Agency/Agence d'abonnements :
SWETS & ZEITLINGER BV
Heereweg 347B
P.O. Box 830
2160 SZ Lisse   Tel. 252.435.111
                      Fax: 252.415.888

**NEW ZEALAND –
NOUVELLE-ZÉLANDE**
GPLegislation Services
P.O. Box 12418
Thorndon, Wellington Tel. (04) 496.5655
                      Fax: (04) 496.5698

NORWAY – NORVÈGE
NIC INFO A/S
Ostensjoveien 18
P.O. Box 6512 Etterstad
0606 Oslo   Tel. (22) 97.45.00
                      Fax: (22) 97.45.45

PAKISTAN
Mirza Book Agency
65 Shahrah Quaid-E-Azam
Lahore 54000   Tel. (42) 735.36.01
                      Fax: (42) 576.37.14

PHILIPPINE – PHILIPPINES
International Booksource Center Inc.
Rm 179/920 Cityland 10 Condo Tower 2
HV dela Costa Ext cor Valero St.
Makati Metro Manila   Tel. (632) 817 9676
                      Fax: (632) 817 1741

POLAND – POLOGNE
Ars Polona
00-950 Warszawa
Krakowskie Prezdmiescie 7 Tel. (22) 264760
                           Fax: (22) 265334

PORTUGAL
Livraria Portugal
Rua do Carmo 70-74
Apart. 2681
1200 Lisboa   Tel. (01) 347.49.82/5
                      Fax: (01) 347.02.64

SINGAPORE – SINGAPOUR
Ashgate Publishing
Asia Pacific Pte. Ltd
Golden Wheel Building, 04-03
41, Kallang Pudding Road
Singapore 349316   Tel. 741.5166
                      Fax: 742.9356

SPAIN – ESPAGNE
Mundi-Prensa Libros S.A.
Castelló 37, Apartado 1223
Madrid 28001   Tel. (91) 431.33.99
                      Fax: (91) 575.39.98
E-mail: mundiprensa@tsai.es
Internet: http://www.mundiprensa.es

Mundi-Prensa Barcelona
Consell de Cent No. 391
08009 – Barcelona   Tel. (93) 488.34.92
                      Fax: (93) 487.76.59

Libreria de la Generalitat
Palau Moja
Rambla dels Estudis, 118
08002 – Barcelona
          (Suscripciones) Tel. (93) 318.80.12
          (Publicaciones) Tel. (93) 302.67.23
                      Fax: (93) 412.18.54

SRI LANKA
Centre for Policy Research
c/o Colombo Agencies Ltd.
No. 300-304, Galle Road
Colombo 3   Tel. (1) 574240, 573551-2
                      Fax: (1) 575394, 510711

SWEDEN – SUÈDE
CE Fritzes AB
S–106 47 Stockholm   Tel. (08) 690.90.90
                      Fax: (08) 20.50.21

For electronic publications only/
Publications électroniques seulement
STATISTICS SWEDEN
Informationsservice
S-115 81 Stockholm   Tel. 8 783 5066
                      Fax: 8 783 4045

Subscription Agency/Agence d'abonnements :
Wennergren-Williams Info AB
P.O. Box 1305
171 25 Solna   Tel. (08) 705.97.50
                      Fax: (08) 27.00.71

Liber distribution
Internatinal organizations
Fagerstagatan 21
S-163 52 Spanga

SWITZERLAND – SUISSE
Maditec S.A. (Books and Periodicals/Livres
et périodiques)
Chemin des Palettes 4
Case postale 266
1020 Renens VD 1   Tel. (021) 635.08.65
                      Fax: (021) 635.07.80

Librairie Payot S.A.
4, place Pépinet
CP 3212
1002 Lausanne   Tel. (021) 320.25.11
                      Fax: (021) 320.25.14

Librairie Unilivres
6, rue de Candolle
1205 Genève   Tel. (022) 320.26.23
                      Fax: (022) 329.73.18

Subscription Agency/Agence d'abonnements :
Dynapresse Marketing S.A.
38, avenue Vibert
1227 Carouge   Tel. (022) 308.08.70
                      Fax: (022) 308.07.99
See also – Voir aussi :
OECD Bonn Centre
August-Bebel-Allee 6
D-53175 Bonn (Germany) Tel. (0228) 959.120
                      Fax: (0228) 959.12.17

THAILAND – THAÏLANDE
Suksit Siam Co. Ltd.
113, 115 Fuang Nakhon Rd.
Opp. Wat Rajbopith
Bangkok 10200   Tel. (662) 225.9531/2
                      Fax: (662) 222.5188

**TRINIDAD & TOBAGO, CARIBBEAN
TRINITÉ-ET-TOBAGO, CARAÏBES**
Systematics Studies Limited
9 Watts Street
Curepe
Trinidad & Tobago, W.I. Tel. (1809) 645.3475
                      Fax: (1809) 662.5654
E-mail: tobe@trinidad.net

TUNISIA – TUNISIE
Grande Librairie Spécialisée
Fendri Ali
Avenue Haffouz Imm El-Intilaka
Bloc B 1 Sfax 3000   Tel. (216-4) 296 855
                      Fax: (216-4) 298.270

TURKEY – TURQUIE
Kültür Yayinlari Is-Türk Ltd.
Atatürk Bulvari No. 191/Kat 13
06684 Kavaklidere/Ankara
                 Tel. (312) 428.11.40 Ext. 2458
                 Fax : (312) 417.24.90

Dolmabahce Cad. No. 29
Besiktas/Istanbul   Tel. (212) 260 7188

UNITED KINGDOM – ROYAUME-UNI
The Stationery Office Ltd.
Postal orders only:
P.O. Box 276, London SW8 5DT
Gen. enquiries   Tel. (171) 873 0011
                      Fax: (171) 873 8463

The Stationery Office Ltd.
Postal orders only:
49 High Holborn, London WC1V 6HB
Branches at: Belfast, Birmingham, Bristol,
Edinburgh, Manchester

UNITED STATES – ÉTATS-UNIS
OECD Washington Center
2001 L Street N.W., Suite 650
Washington, D.C. 20036-4922
                      Tel. (202) 785.6323
                      Fax: (202) 785.0350
Internet: washcont@oecd.org

Subscriptions to OECD periodicals may also
be placed through main subscription agencies.

Les abonnements aux publications périodiques
de l'OCDE peuvent être souscrits auprès des
principales agences d'abonnement.

Orders and inquiries from countries where Dis-
tributors have not yet been appointed should be
sent to: OECD Publications, 2, rue André-Pascal, 75775 Paris Cedex 16, France.

Les commandes provenant de pays où l'OCDE
n'a pas encore désigné de distributeur peuvent
être adressées aux Éditions de l'OCDE, 2, rue
André-Pascal, 75775 Paris Cedex 16, France.

12-1996